"A sweeping picture of the whole of Negro history from ancient Africa to the present.

Unlike many recently published books on Negro history whose authors are content to let a sentence like 'slavery was a cruel institution that hurt both the owner and the slave' stand alone, this provides extensive explanation—and therefore, depth, life and passion—to commonly known but ignored facts. Another of the book's strengths is that it takes a stand; it acknowledges and documents the brutality that Negroes have inherited in America . . . A readable synthesis of documented trends and patterns in Negro history, it's a necessity, written with an excellence that denies any potentially selectorial claims of holding enough material on the subject."

— *Library Journal*

D1274995

Other SIGNET and MENTOR Books
of Related Interest

☐ **THE TROUBLESOME PRESENCE by Eli Ginsberg and Alfred S. Eichner.** A comprehensive history of the Negro's struggle for equality from colonial days to the present time; a study of the background of "sit-ins," "kneel-downs," and "freedom rides."
(#MT667—75c)

☐ **THE SOULS OF BLACK FOLK by W. E. B. DuBois.** A brilliant socio-historical study of the Negro in America following the Civil War. (#CY458—$1.25)

☐ **BLACK LIKE ME by John Howard Griffin.** The startling, penetrating, first-hand account of a white man who learned what it is like to live as a Negro in the South. Winner of the *Saturday Review* Anisfield-Wolf Award. (#T3908—75c)

☐ **WHY WE CAN'T WAIT by Martin Luther King, Jr.** In this memorable book, the late Dr. King reveals the forces, pressures, and implications behind today's quest for civil rights. Included in this edition are the text of Dr. King's Memphis speech and of the President's remarks to the nation on the death of the civil rights leader. (#P2476—60c)

☐ **CHRONICLES OF BLACK PROTEST, ed. by Bradford Chambers.** A superlative documentary on Black Power from the pens of Booker T. Washington, Stokely Carmichael, Malcolm X, Martin Luther King, Nat Turner, etc. (#MQ907—95c)

THE

NEGRO

REVOLUTION

Robert Goldston

A SIGNET BOOK

Published by The New American Library

Library of Congress Catalog Card Number: 68-12088

ACKNOWLEDGMENTS

Permission to reprint the following copyright material is gratefully acknowledged:
To Harper & Row, Publishers, Inc., for "For a Lady I Know" from *On These I Stand* by Countee Cullen. Copyright 1925 by Harper and Brothers; renewed 1953 by Ida M. Cullen.
To Doubleday & Co., Inc., and to the Macmillan Company of Canada, Ltd., for selection from "The White Man's Burden" by Rudyard Kipling from First Definitive Edition, *Complete Works*: Reprinted by permission of Mrs. George Bambridge.
To The Macmillan Company for selection from "Simon Legree — A Negro Sermon" from *The Collected Poems* by Vachel Lindsay. Copyright 1917 by The Macmillan Company; renewed 1945 by Elizabeth C. Lindsay.
To Twayne Publishers, Inc., for selection from "America" from *The Selected Poems of Claude McKay*.

This is an authorized reprint of an edition published by The Macmillan Company.

For Josephine Conroy Goldston

CONTENTS

PROLOGUE: THE DARK CONTINENT 11

1 THE BIGHT OF BENIN   29

2 COLONIAL ECONOMICS VERSUS
  COLONIAL CONSCIENCE   43

3 THE PECULIAR INSTITUTION   59

4 THE FREEDOM ROAD—I   73

5 THE FREEDOM ROAD—II   87

6 TERRIBLE SWIFT SWORD   101

7 THE LIGHT THAT FAILED   113

8 DOMESTIC REACTION; FOREIGN
  ADVENTURE   129

9 FROM WHITE SUPREMACY TO
  "BLACK THURSDAY"   145

10 THE AGE OF ROOSEVELT   159

11 WE SHALL OVERCOME   177

EPILOGUE: THE FIRE NEXT TIME   195

BIBLIOGRAPHY   205

SUGGESTED READING   209

INDEX   213

THE
NEGRO
REVOLUTION

Prologue

The Dark Continent

Geographers, in Afric maps,
With savage-pictures fill their gaps,
And o'er unhabitable downs
Place elephants for want of towns.
                    —JONATHAN SWIFT

. . . BUT LISTEN TO THE TALES TOLD BY THE TRIBAL ELDERS, the wise, old men whose duty it is to remember the past from remotest antiquity and to tell the young. No, their ancestors were not savages squatting along the banks of the Congo, the Niger, the Blue Nile. They were heroic explorers, children not of darkness but of the sun: "And they wandered without let or hindrance to places where no man had ever been before. One could not look them in the eyes because their faces were so bright that it hurt one's own eyes to look at them. It was like looking at the sun."

The elders knew. And they tried to tell the European explorers who came to them in the eighteenth and nineteenth centuries. The fathers of the tribes were ". . . giants of prodigious force, and surprising feats [were] celebrated in their name. With one hand they dammed the rivers; their voices were so great that they could call from one town to another, and birds took flight in panic whenever one of them should cough. Their hunting expeditions drew them far from their dwellings; in a single day they would go hundreds of miles, and the animals they killed, hippopotamus and elephant, were carried easily on the shoulders of these fortunate hunters. . . . Their weapons were bows from the trunk of a palm tree . . . even the earth bore their weight with difficulty."

No Homeric bard could have better sung the mighty prowess or godlike majesty of the ancient Greeks before Troy. And the

11

old myths and legends of Africa are not unlike the epic poems of ancient Greece. They tell of times before the dawn of written history when heroes trod the trembling earth. But also like the Homeric epics, the tribal legends of Africa were dismissed as cunning fantasy by the first outsiders who heard them. They were not believed by white explorers, missionaries, or traders not simply because they were recited like myths—but also because it was necessary for the white conscience to believe that Africa had always been the "dark continent," Africans ignorant savages, that the benefits of "civilization" were now being introduced for the first time. But just as archaeological research was to establish the veracity of Homeric epic, so modern scientific investigation has begun to establish the amazing truth behind African legend.

About one hundred miles down the Nile from the modern city of Khartoum, capital of the Sudan, lie the sand-strewn, gigantic ruins of a city that flourished more than three thousand years ago. This is Meroë, capital of the ancient kingdom of Kush. Great pyramids mark the site, and within a few miles of the city's ruins stand tumbled-down temples, palaces, and monuments of a civilization which was famous throughout the ancient world. The Greek historian Herodotus knew of Kush and its famed Temple of the Sun—and so did the pharaohs of Egypt, who traded with the Kushites, conquered them from time to time, brought them the civilized techniques of smelting iron and learned in turn the art of working electrum (a natural alloy of silver and gold). The records of contact between Egypt and Kush are extensive. There are also records of contact between Kush and Carthage, Arabia, and even Rome. These "records" are not, of course, entirely written (in stone)—they are styles of sculpture, shards of pottery, and a great deal of informed speculation. But although the language of Meroë has yet to be deciphered, the archaeological evidence beneath the sands is definite—it tells of a mighty kingdom whose origins are lost in the mists of antiquity, and it tells of a people who, while they learned much from their northern and western neighbors, taught them much too.

By the time of Kush, of course, the history of man in Africa was a long one indeed. In the past it used to be fashionable to explain the growth of African civilization as being due to the migrations or incursions of anyone from the Hittites to the Portuguese—anyone at all, provided he was of white complexion. This was based on the major (if unspoken) premise that Negroes could not have developed a high civilization. Despite the major premise, however, it is now evident that man—Neanderthal man, Rhodesian man, and Homo sapiens, or modern

*The crumbling great pyramids at Meroë bear silent testimony to the splendor of
a vanished civilization.*

man—had been in existence in Africa from the dawn of time.
There is even evidence today to support the idea that mankind
itself first came into existence in Africa. Certainly there were
manlike apes, or apelike men living in South and East Africa
one million years ago. And the line of descent from these creatures, who in the words of archaeologist Raymond Dart
"trembled on the brink of humanity," to modern man is now
fairly clear. Of course, in discussing man as he existed a million
years ago, it is profitless to think in terms of Negro or white.
As far as outer appearances are concerned, the word "hairy"
would probably be much more useful. One thing is certain;
Homo sapiens has been defined as a "tool-using animal," and
the oldest tools in the world have been found in Uganda.

Migration from outside Africa did, of course, take place—so
did migration within the continent. While the interior lines of
migration in prehistoric times are only dimly suspected, it
remains generally true that African civilization spread from
north to south and from east to west. But in order to do so it
had to surmount the great barrier of the Sahara Desert. Not
that the Sahara had always been an arid waste. Once it was a
green and fertile land watered by mighty rivers which emptied
into the Nile and the Mediterranean Sea. But about five or six
thousand years ago, large-scale climatic changes began to dry
up the trans-Saharan rivers (their dry beds can still be seen)
and to transform the land into a sand-strewn waste. Travel
across this huge desert became increasingly difficult until, at

about 3000 B.C., it had become the all-but-impassable barrier we know today. North of the Sahara and east of it, civilization made great progress through trade and the mingling of many peoples; south and west of the desert progress was slower, development different.

Just at the time that the fertile Sahara began to dry up—about 5000 B.C.—new types of men began to flourish in the Sudan and the Negro, or Negroid type, was prominent among these. His ancestors may have been purely Stone Age people of African genesis, or, as seems more likely, a mixture of several types. The earliest specifically Negro skull fragments have been found near present-day Khartoum and as far west as the approaches to Timbuktu. Furthermore there is solid evidence to indicate that at least one-third of the population of pre-dynastic Egypt (before 3000 B.C.) was Negro. It has been said that Africa gave the gods to Egypt; it may one day be found that Egyptian civilization itself was fathered by the Negro ancestors of the Kushites and today's Africans.

Certainly the ancient world had no doubt about the power of Kush, nor the importance of its great capital at Meroë. Kushite armies troubled the peace of Roman-ruled Egypt during the first century A.D., and it was a Kushite official whom the Apostle Philip baptized on "the road which goeth down from Jerusalem to Gaza," shortly after the Crucifixion—a conversion recorded with great pride among the Acts of the Apostles.

Fully eight hundred years before the birth of Christ, Kush had won effective independence from Egypt. Not long thereafter (725 B.C.) the Kushites conquered Egypt and ruled all the land from the Mediterranean coast to the borders of present-day Ethiopia. But another dramatic upheaval came in 666 B.C. The Assyrians invaded lower Egypt, armed with weapons of iron. The stone-and-bronze-armed Kushites and their subject Egyptians were soundly defeated. The Kushites abandoned lower Egypt and retreated back into their home territories in the Sudan. There they successfully preserved their independence, made haste to learn the techniques of iron smelting, and (about 530 B.C.) established the city of Meroë as the capital of their kingdom. It is there that the ruins of temples, palaces, houses, and roads tell of a prosperous and royal civilization which flourished for centuries.

But during the first millennium B.C. new migrants had arrived on the African coast south of Kush. These were the highly sophisticated people of Southern Arabia who crossed the Red Sea to establish a powerful kingdom at Axum in what is now northern Ethiopia. The Axumites were the descendants of those same people who had sent the Queen of Sheba to visit

Solomon and who had for many centuries monopolized the seagoing trade along the African and Arabian coasts of the Indian Ocean. The rulers of Axum soon cut the Kushite caravan routes to the coastal ports. Wars followed and, not long after 330 A.D., Kush was defeated. Caught between a hostile Egypt to the north and the conquering Axumites to the south, the people of Kush lost their independence. Killed in battle, enslaved, dispersed to the west, the Kushites disappeared from the stage of history, and their great capital city of Meroë became a prey to the shifting desert sands.

Yet Kush left a great heritage to Africa. Within its former boundaries new Nubian kingdoms were to arise; Christian kingdoms for the most part, though surrounded by a sea of Mohammedanism. So enduring were to prove the fruits of that encounter between the Apostle Philip and the Kushite official on "the road which goeth down from Jerusalem to Gaza," that not until the sixteenth century A.D. were the armies of Islam finally to extinguish Christianity in the Sudan.

But long before then, even before its downfall, Kush had brought the Iron Age to sub-Saharan Africa. And along with iron, the gods of Meroë—the sun, the ram, the same divinities worshiped in ancient Egypt—had found new temples and new priests far, far to the west, even along the shores of the Atlantic Ocean.

In about 500 A.D. (within a century of the final downfall of Kush) a new civilization emerged in Western Africa, the kingdom of Ghana. It had legends of learned and mighty warriors coming from the east. Were these exiled Kushites? Possibly. In any event the Kingdom of Ghana owed its rise to Ghanian skill in iron working, an art most probably derived from Kush. Iron weapons and iron tools gave the Ghanians supremacy over neighboring peoples and over the land itself.

Inhabiting the rolling grasslands of the savannah between the jungles of the Congo and the arid wastes of the Sahara, the people of Ghana were able to control and tax the abundant gold trade as it moved from mines south of Ghana (the locations of which were a closely guarded secret even from the Ghanians) to the caravans which would carry it across the Sahara to gold-hungry Europe. After the Islamic conquest of North Africa (during the seventh and eighth centuries A.D.) these caravans were run by Moslems; one of them, El Fazari, writing soon after 800 A.D., called Ghana "the Land of Gold." Legends of the vast wealth of Ghana, filtering back to the Moslem caliphs and emirs of North Africa, soon whetted their appetite for more than mere trade. But it was to be more than two hundred years before the Moslem powers along Africa's Mediterranean coast

The Queen of Sheba makes a royal visit to the court of King Solomon in this ancient Ethiopian "comic strip" painting.

(COURTESY OF THE AMERICAN MUSEUM OF NATURAL HISTORY)

felt themselves strong enough to march their armies around and through the Sahara to conquer Ghana.

In the year 1054 A.D. (just twelve years before the Norman conquest of England), Ibn Yasin, the Almoravid ruler of North Africa, marched a great army southward to attack Ghana. The Almoravids were fanatical Moslem warriors who had already conquered most of North Africa and most of Spain. Yet they did not find Ghana an easy prize. Ibn Yasin himself did not live to see his conquest completed. Not until 1076 A.D. did the capital city of Ghana itself fall to Ibn Yasin's successor, Abu Bakr.

Part of the reason for the prolonged and hardy resistance of the Ghanians can be gleaned from the writings of one Abdallah ibn Abdel Aziz, known as El Bekri. A Moslem scholar writing in Córdoba in Southern Spain, El Bekri, although he did not himself visit Ghana, had at his disposal all the firsthand reports of officials and travelers. "Ghana," he observed, "is the title of the king of this people. . . . The king who governs them at the moment is called Tenkamenin [who] is master of a great empire and of a power which is formidable." Just how formidable?

"The king of Ghana," reported El Bekri, "can put two hundred thousand warriors in the field, more than forty thousand of them being armed with bow and arrow." Even allowing for exaggeration, this is an army many times the size of both the Norman and Saxon armies combined at Hastings Field.

The capital city of Ghana was really two cities about six miles apart—with many dwellings between them. Of the court of the pagan king of Ghana, El Bekri wrote: "When he [the king] gives audience to his people, to listen to their complaints and set them to rights, he sits in a pavilion around which stand his horses caparisoned in cloth of gold; behind him stand ten pages holding shields and gold-mounted swords; and on his right hand are the sons of the princes of his empire, splendidly clad and with gold plaited into their hair . . . The gate of the chamber is guarded by dogs of an excellent breed, who never leave the king's side, they wear collars of gold and silver."

Tribute from conquered peoples and the taxes exacted on trade between the gold-producing South and the salt-producing North were the bases of Ghanian prosperity. So badly did the Southern gold-producing people need salt from the North that they often traded equal amounts of gold for salt. Naturally, the ambition of the rulers of Ghana was to conquer both the gold regions of the South and the salt-producing areas of the North. While Ghana was eventually able to control the sources of gold (near the headwaters of the Senegal River), it was unable to capture the salt deposits of the northern desert.

The Almoravids, who completed their conquest of Ghana in 1076 A.D., came not only to convert its pagan people to Islam; they came also to loot. Although their rule was brief it was disastrous. Writing in the fourteenth century A.D., Ibn Khaldun, another Moslem scholar, reported that the Almoravids "spread their dominion over the Negroes, devastated their territory, and plundered their property. Having submitted them to a poll tax they imposed on them a tribute, and compelled a great number of them to become Moslems. The authority of the kings of Ghana being destroyed, their neighbors . . . took their country and reduced its inhabitants to slavery." By the thirteenth century, barely one hundred years after the Almoravid conquest, the kingdom of Ghana had sunk into decay and was but a vague memory.

But the economic basis of Ghanian power—the occupation of the savannah between the salt mines of the northern desert and the gold of the Senegal River—remained. On it other kingdoms, other empires grew. After Ghana's capital faded into insignificance, other great cities such as Timbuktu and Djenné grew into prosperity and international renown. Not that the empires of the savannah followed each other in mechanical order. Rather they represented the rise to power of different tribes, factions, interests, sometimes with different capital cities, usually with different borders, but all embracing generally the area between the Northern Sahara and the Senegal, between the Atlantic and the Sudan. Throughout that region, although invasions and wars disrupted the land, although empires rose, flourished, and then decayed, the process of civilization generally continued. The establishment of Islam by the Almoravids, however brutal, was permanent. The states which succeeded Ghana were Moslem states. And with their religion, the Moslems brought also the tradition of scholarship for which they were justly famous throughout the medieval world. The great cities of the savannah were to become renowned for their civilized ways as well as the richness of their commerce, under several succeeding empires.

The first of the savannah empires to succeed Ghana was the Empire of Mali. During the thirteenth century A.D. the Mali peoples won supremacy over their neighbors and established a state which was to control (as Ghana had not) those sources of salt and gold upon which the prosperity of the area depended. Rivalries between royal families, struggles for power between rival factions of the aristocracy, the rise of cities based on commerce, a continuing struggle between king and nobility (the one attempting to centralize, the others to fragment power in the state), all of this is curiously familiar. It is in fact the same pattern of development which prevailed in Europe during the Middle Ages. Basically the organization of central power supported by peasant agriculture and urban commerce was much the same in both areas. But these similarities should not be overstressed. Timbuktu, though a great and flourishing city, was not, after all, medieval Florence; nor were the great grasslands of the African savannah the small, subdivided, and intensively cultivated fields of medieval France. But in a very broad view, the same stages of economic development in Western Africa gave rise to much the same pattern of social and political organization as they did in Western Europe.

What did all this mean to contemporary observers? According to the writer El Omari, a city official of Cairo, when the Mali *Mansa* (emperor) Kankan Musa made his pilgrimage to Mecca in 1324 A.D., his camel trains stretched beyond the horizon; his splendidly equipped and arrogant bodyguard formed a formidable cavalry; his wives and gifts and trappings were so wonderfully impressive that the memory of their splendor lived in men's memories for many decades afterward. And it was estimated in Cairo that Kankan Musa's domains were as large as all of Western Europe.

Two hundred years after Kankan Musa's pilgrimage, Leo Africanus, whose knowledge of sub-Saharan Africa was profound, wrote: "In Timbuktu there are numerous judges, doctors, and clerics, all receiving good salaries from the king. He pays great respect to men of learning. There is a big demand for books in manuscript. . . . More profit is made from the book trade than from any other line of business." As for the city itself, it boasted large and delicately decorated mosques designed by architects imported all the way from Southern Spain, great palaces, broad boulevards, and untold thousands of flat-roofed houses. Peace reigned throughout the land; the caravan trails were free of bandits and, with few exceptions, the marauding peoples of the Northern Sahara were held at bay. In the year 1400, according to the Moslem writer Ibn Khaldun, the annual caravan from Mali across the Sahara by way of the Ahaggar Mountains consisted of no fewer than twelve thousand camels. And this was but one of many caravans; others followed different routes north. Still other caravans went to Egypt and some to the south, beyond the Niger River. For the gold and salt of

Mali they brought back articles of European manufacture such as silk and swords, swift horses from Arabia, cola nuts from Southern Nigeria, and many of the scholars and artisans for which Timbuktu was famed. Mali was a busy, enterprising, stable, and highly literate society; certainly comparable to many of the kingdoms of Europe at this time.

One of the subject peoples conquered by the great Kankan Musa were the Songhai. Their lands were centered around the middle of the Niger River. After Kankan Musa's death (in 1332) the Songhai began a remarkably swift rise to power. Within fifty years they had won freedom from the tribute they were supposed to pay to the Mali emperors; and by 1464 they had succeeded to the rule of the empire itself. The Songhai Emperor Mohammed Askia (known to awed Moslem writers of his day as Mohammed the Great) reigned from 1493 to 1528 and succeeded in establishing a government administrative system that went far toward subduing the old tribal powers of the peoples of Mali. Yet his empire lasted less than a century. In 1591 the Moroccan armies of El Mansur emerged from the Sahara, captured Timbuktu and the other principal Songhai cities, defeated the armies of Songhai, and destroyed the state. The Moroccan armies were led by a Spaniard named Judar. Although he had but four thousand men under his command, they were armed with guns (matchlocks or arquebuses) and were able to scatter the larger Songhai forces.

Judar looted Timbuktu, and what he had seized from the city was described by an English merchant who saw Judar return to Morocco after eight years of campaigning against Songhai. "He brought with him," wrote Jasper Tomson on July 4, 1599, "thirty camels loaded with *tibar*, which is unrefined gold . . ." valued, conservatively, at $3,500,000, "also great store of peppers, unicorns' horns, and a certain kind of wood for dyers, to some hundred and twenty camel-loads; all of which he presented unto the king."

Judar's invasion cost the Moroccans more than twenty thousand casualties, and their rule over Songhai lasted only until 1618. But brief as it was, the Moroccan invasion destroyed the Songhai civilization. The political cohesion of the state was lost, its cities declined, its trade vanished. By the middle of the seventeenth century all that remained was the legend of the wealth and scholarship of Timbuktu—a legend which would lure European explorers (mostly to their deaths) on quests for the "forbidden city" and its fabled civilization which had long since vanished.

What of the lands below the grassy savannah? Do they reveal the existence of civilization south of the Mali-Songhai empires?

And what of the East Coast of Africa below the ancient land of Kush? Modern archaeology has uncovered traces of so many kingdoms, empires, and civilizations in what was formerly known as "Darkest Africa" that there is room only to list some of their names. There were Sao, Kanem, and Darfur in the Old Sudan; the Southern Zanj and Kalambo on the Southern and Western coasts; Engaruka, Azania, Zimbabwe, and Mapungubwe on the Eastern coast as far south as the Transvaal, and many more. Their records are the ruins of cities and palaces and the words of legends. Much about them remains unknown or only guessed at; they inhabit a twilight of history into which the light of scholarship is only now beginning to penetrate. But two of these kingdoms—one vanished, the other still in existence—deserve attention here. They are the Kingdom of Benin in West Africa, south of what had been Mali-Songhai; and Ethiopia on the Eastern coast, south of the ancient land of Kush.

The thick forests below Mali-Songhai were as great a barrier to trade and communications as was the Sahara above the savannah. The Western Sudanese empires did send traders and Islamic missionaries south of the Niger River, but not even Kankan Musa or Mohammed the Great could effectively subdue the peoples of the forest or their emerging city-states. The broad area between the mouth of the Niger and the estuary of the Congo River, while it was certainly influenced by ideas filtering down from the North, developed its own unique civilization. The peoples there, with legends of forefathers coming from the East, with temples built to worship not only the earlier gods of Ghana but also the Egyptian deities, may well have been partly descended from exiled and venturesome Kushites.

The history of West Africa below the Niger suffers from a lack of written records and a corresponding lack of archaeological investigation. The learned men of Timbuktu or Djenné knew little or nothing of this southern region. It was only with the coming of European explorers, pirates, and traders in the middle of the fifteenth century that written descriptions of the land and its people began to appear. Unfortunately, the early Europeans who sailed down Africa's West Coast were more interested in pepper, gold, and slaves than in history. Nor could these hardened adventurers be described as learned—most could barely write their own names. And too, their business was with the coastal cities; they rarely penetrated into the interior.

As early as 1472 a Portuguese captain named Ruy de Siqueira had landed on the coast of the Bight of Benin; within a decade other captains of trading vessels (mostly Portuguese) had made themselves familiar with that huge indentation in the

African continent. What they found when they pushed up the delta rivers a few miles into the interior was the city-state of Benin, about one mile in circumference, surrounded by walls and a large moat. One of the early traders, a man named Pacheco, writing at the end of the fifteenth century, observed: "I was there four times. . . . Its [Benin's] houses are made of mud walls covered with palm leaves." The city-state had conquered the surrounding countryside to an extent "about eighty leagues long and forty wide. . . . [It] was usually at war with its neighbors."

In 1486 Affonso d'Aveiro, on a trading mission for the king of Portugal, was received by the *Oba* (king) of Benin. The king sent back with d'Aveiro an ambassador to the court of Portugal "because he desired to learn more about these lands, the arrival of people from them in his country being regarded as an unusual novelty." The ambassador, "a man of good speech and natural wisdom," returned to Benin with presents from the king of Portugal and a number of Portuguese trading agents and Catholic missionaries who were to remain in Benin. Reporting to the Portuguese king in 1516, Duarte Pires, Portuguese royal agent at Benin, wrote: "The favor which the king of Benin accords us is due to his love of your highness; and thus he pays us high honor and sets us at table to dine with his son, and no part of his court is hidden from us but all doors are open." Furthermore, the king of Benin ordered his son and several nobles of his court to study Christianity and had a Christian church built within the city. Certainly these early reports, if they do not describe a civilization to be compared with the mighty empires of Mali or Songhai to the north, do not describe a state of savagery. And the reports are supplemented by the surviving art of the region — the marvelous brass plaques of Benin.

The world-famed brass castings of Benin display not only the abstract form of art typical of primitive societies; they also include a high proportion of naturalistic masks and heads similar to the classical sculptures of ancient Greece. So fine is their workmanship, so advanced their technique, and so sophisticated their artistic conception, that these brasses were thought for many years to be of extra-African origin or at least based on European models and methods taught by the early Portuguese traders. Today archaeological discoveries have confirmed that they represent a natural growth of native abilities that go back at least to the thirteenth century. And these brasses speak of

The prosperous city of Timbuktu as it appeared to an early traveler. Note the "grid" street plan.   (HISTORICAL PICTURES SERVICE — CHICAGO)

The sophisticated art of Benin:
Left: *Large bronze plaque showing a chieftain and two of his warriors.*
Right: *A winged head in bronze, a bronze panther, and two carved elephant tusks.*
(RADIO TIMES HULTON PICTURE LIBRARY)

peoples who, however primitive their political organization, were highly skilled and deeply sensitive.

What the early European travelers found at Benin was a stable Iron-Age society, the influence of whose civilization spread far to the south, even beyond the Congo. And it displayed similarities—in its worship of the sun and the ram and in its conception of divine kingship—which spoke of much earlier Eastern influences. How this civilization might have developed if left in peace we shall never know. Its swift degeneration and destruction through the imposition of the slave trade will be described later. Here it may observed that the bloodshed and savagery which were to make the very name of Benin terrible to the European imagination of the nineteenth century were themselves European imports.

In about 400 A.D., long before the art of Benin had reached maturity, the great Kingdom of Ethiopia had risen far to the east. Unlike Benin, or for that matter all the rest of Africa, it was to maintain its independence (aside from the very brief rule of Benito Mussolini's Italy from 1936 to 1941) to the present day. The greatness of Ethiopia, its amazing continuity of civilization, impressed the ancient as well as the modern world.

In legend, Ethiopia was said to have been founded by the illegitimate son of King Solomon and the Queen of Sheba one thousand years before the birth of Christ. In the Middle Ages, Ethiopia, as an island of Christianity surrounded by a sea of Moslem and pagan peoples, was often mistaken by Europeans for the legendary kingdom of Prester John. The truth, while more prosaic, is hardly less interesting.

Ethiopia most probably inherited the lands and civilization of the ancient kingdom of Axum, of those immigrants from Arabia who had established themselves just south of Kush before the dawn of recorded history and who, by 400 A.D., had overthrown and destroyed the Kushite kingdom. But the sources of Ethiopian civilization were not Axumite alone. For centuries before Christ the Eastern shore of Africa had been a great trading center. Here came Arabian dhows, ships from India, and huge, seagoing junks from far-off China. All along the Indian Ocean coast of Africa are to be found the ruins of great trading cities and the debris of a vast international commerce that linked the region with the ancient civilizations of the Mid- and Far East.

The Axumite-Ethiopian king who finally defeated the Kushites some time after 300 A.D. was Aizanas. He celebrated his victory by striking medals and coins in gold. These coins were at first decorated with pagan symbols. But coins struck later in Aizanas' reign are marked with a cross. At some time during the intervening years priests from Byzantium, capital of the Eastern Roman Empire, had converted Aizanas to Christianity. And — isolated as the country was by hostile pagans and after the seventh century by people of the Islamic faith — Christianity was to be an important force in keeping Ethiopia united, in giving her people a feeling of uniqueness and a common bond against the outside world. The rise of Islam did, however, deprive Ethiopia of her Red Sea coast. The great Axumite-Ethiopian port of Adulis, where traders from all over the Orient had gathered, was taken by Islamic forces in the eighth century. But the Ethiopians, fighting among the hills and mountains of their homeland from strong fortifications (generally heavily walled palaces atop the hills), succeeded in preserving their independence. They were to continue to preserve that independence against all comers, including nineteenth century Europeans.

While Ethiopia, because of its religion and its geography, remained largely isolated from the rest of Africa, there are many indications that the interior civilization of East Africa, from Tanganyika to the borders of the Transvaal, drew its inspiration from Axumite sources as well as from the Oriental trade of the coast. Remains indicating the use of irrigation and the terracing of hill sides for agriculture, old Axumite skills, are to be found far to the south of the area of Axum, as are the still largely unexplored ruins of great walled cities.

The premodern culture of East Africa and of West Africa south of the Niger is still being explored. New discoveries are being made daily, and today's assumptions may be modified tomorrow. Only one fact emerges with definite clarity. Native cultures and highly developed civilizations existed in almost all of the continent. Some areas, such as Mali and Axum, were more advanced than others; but nowhere to be found was that state of savagery and barbarism so dear to the European imagination of the nineteenth century. When the European and American slave traders and invaders assaulted Africa during the centuries following the Portuguese landings at Benin in 1472, they were assaulting old and by no means primitive civilizations.

The coming of European power to the African continent had much the same impact on its developing culture as the invasions of the Huns had on ancient Rome and the incursions of the Magyars and the Norsemen had on feudal Europe. To the question, "Why did not African civilization progress after the coming of the Europeans as it had evidently progressed before?" an African might well reply, "How far would European civilization have progressed after the thirteenth century had the Mongol hordes of Genghis Khan conquered the entire continent?"

From 1472 to the middle of the nineteenth century, under the guns, the diseases, and the exploitive greed of Europeans and Americans, the various African cultures declined, decayed, and finally disappeared. When literate Europeans and Americans — missionaries, explorers, historians, and archaeologists — finally arrived on the African scene, they could find little to connect the semibarbarous African tribes they encountered with the magnificent ruins of forgotten cities over which they sometimes stumbled. Surely these ruins and the culture they bespoke must have been the work of other, non-African peoples who had come, built, and vanished in the mists of time. It was hard to believe they could have been produced by the direct ancestors of the tribes they knew. And so the legend of "Darkest Africa" — born in the troubled consciences of traders, conquerors, and slavers who would in any event have been indifferent to the cultures they were destroying — gained a pseudo-scientific respectability which it has only recently lost. There never was a "Darkest Africa" — there was only a darkness in the minds of those who came to enslave and exploit a continent.

1 The Bight of Benin

Beware and take care of the Bight of Benin,
Where few come out, though many go in.
—SEVENTEENTH CENTURY SEA SHANTEY

THEY CAME IN WOODEN SHIPS TOPPED BY CLOUDS OF SAIL:
the squat and high-decked caravelles and carracks of the
fifteenth and sixteenth centuries, the brigs and barkentines of
the seventeenth century, and, finally, the long, sleek Baltimore
clippers of the years before the American Civil War. Outward
bound from Lisbon, Cádiz, Liverpool, Marseilles, Hamburg,
Amsterdam, the West Indies, Boston, Baltimore, New York,
New Orleans, Charleston, and many a port in between, they
carried sailing orders to the Grain Coast, the Ivory Coast, the
Gold Coast, the Slave Coast, to Elmina Castle, Popo, Benin,
the Oil Rivers, Bonny, Biafra, and Old Calabar. They were
hard-handed men, but generally brave. They were of all nationalities, but especially Portuguese, Spanish, Dutch, English,
and American. They were respectable merchants taking on a
little extra cargo, derelicts who had been press-ganged onto a
slaver, adventurers eager to make a quick fortune, Bible-
pounding preachers who had gone money-mad, sedate clerks
representing respectable commercial companies, pirates, and
sometimes sadists seeking satisfaction.

The risks they ran were many and deadly. There were the
uncharted reefs and huge surf of the West African coast which
might dash their hulls to pieces; there were the fevers—malaria,
dengue, and yellow fever—which could burn through their
crews like fire through straw; there were crafty and fierce
native kings who might capture them on whim and put them to
death; there were the slaves who might revolt in mid-passage
and massacre crews and officers; there were pirates who considered a slaver a rich prize; and, toward the end of the slave-
trading days, there were the frigates and sloops of the Royal

Navy beneath whose guns they might be sunk or from whose yardarms they might be hanged. Yet the slavers came in their thousands and kept coming, more and more of them. Only the prospect of tremendous profits could have sustained their determination; and the profits were fabulous. Even allowing for the high mortality rate among slaves during the Atlantic crossing, profits of two or three hundred percent on a slaver's voyage were not uncommon.

For four hundred years the slavers plied their trade on the Africa coast. During that time it has been estimated that no less than fifteen million Africans were transported to the New World. From 1680 to 1688, for example, the English Royal African Company alone commanded a fleet of 249 slave ships and during those eight years transported more than sixty thousand slaves. During the sixteenth century about nine hundred thousand slaves were shipped from Africa to the Americas; during the seventeenth century almost three million were shipped. The four centuries of the slave trade brought about the greatest migration in human history—a migration which, for sheer misery and human suffering as well as for profits, was without equal.

The slave trade hardened and degraded almost everyone who engaged in it—from the stay-at-home merchants to the slave ship captains and crews to the African tribes themselves. Yet it would be well not to sentimentalize the trade, but to attempt to understand it.

Slavery itself, as a social and economic institution, was as old as the human race. All of the states of the ancient world, from Egypt to Cathay, from Greece to Babylon, from Judea to Rome, knew slavery. And the old African kingdoms—Kush, Ghana, Mali, Songhai, Benin, Ethiopia, Axum—and almost all the tribes and confederations throughout the history of Africa had practiced slavery. During the Middle Ages Moslems enslaved Christians and Christians enslaved Moslems; the Indian empires of Mexico and Central and South America practiced slavery. The earliest records of human history show slavery to exist, and there is excellent evidence that it is practiced clandestinely today in certain parts of Arabia. Nor has the institution been inflicted on a racial basis alone. Every race and description of man has suffered it at one time or another. And only in the last hundred years has it become a crime in the eyes of most of mankind—a crime which, like murder, extermination, and war, must be shouldered by all peoples in their history.

Originally, in the ancient world (including Africa), slaves were either enemies defeated in battle and captured or criminals. Slavery, as punishment for a crime or as the consequence of defeat, was preferable to death, which was the most probable alternative. But basically, slavery has always rested as an institution upon economic foundations. In a world without machines but with an expanding population to maintain, the human being was the machine—the means of production. And ownership of this human means of production brought wealth and power to individuals, classes, and nations. The vast numbers of slaves who worked the Iberian copper mines and the Greek sulphur mines for ancient Rome were as important to the Roman economy and to Roman power as the blast furnaces of Pittsburgh and the oil derricks of Texas are to the American economy; both are means of extracting natural wealth and transforming it into social wealth. Slaves were machines or tools in Egypt as in Louisiana, in Rome as in Haiti, and were looked upon as such. Nor did slaves themselves complain against the institution of slavery in the ancient world, but only against their personal enslavement. Early Christianity taught that slavery was an absolute moral evil, but Christian doctrine has seldom played a decisive part in the actions of Christian peoples. Only when the Industrial Revolution removed the economic foundations of slavery did the institution begin to disappear.

Negro slavery in Europe had begun as early as 1444 when a

Negro slaves in Egypt about 1350 B.C., *probably prisoners of war*
(PICTURE COLLECTION, NEW YORK PUBLIC LIBRARY)

Portuguese vessel landed a consignment of African slaves
(captured north of the Senegal River) at Lisbon. By the sixteenth century there were parts of Portugal where Negro slaves
outnumbered the native inhabitants. The demand for Negro
slaves in Portugal was based largely on the underpopulation
(due to wars, epidemics, and emigration) of Portugal's southern
agricultural districts. Elsewhere in Europe, aside from personal
household servants, the demand for Negro slaves never
reached great proportions. Negro slaves would have been in
direct competition with an already overcrowded peasant population and a jealously controlled (through guilds) artisan class.
Furthermore, the poorly paid and rigorously exploited labor of
European peasants and workers was actually cheaper than
Negro slave labor would have been due to the great cost of
importing and then maintaining a Negro slave labor force. The
great demand for Negro slaves was to come from the New
World. There were to be found the vast plantations, mines, and
fields which needed strong hands to exploit them—and in the
New World there was no supply of docile peasants, only the
native Indians, who in North America were too fierce to be
enslaved and in South America and the Indies too physically
weak to stand hard labor. Ironically, the importation of African
Negroes as slaves to the New World on a grand scale was
prompted, in part at least, by humanitarian motives.

In the year 1495, the Indians on the island of Hispaniola
(Haiti and the Dominican Republic) rose up against their Spanish masters. Columbus had discovered their land only three
years before—but already they had been reduced to abject
slavery by the greedy Spanish conquistadores who flocked to
the fabled El Dorado in the west in search of gold. About one
hundred thousand Indians marched on the Spanish capital, the
little town of Isabela, where Christopher Columbus was re-
fitting his ships for a return voyage to Spain. The Indians were
unused to slavery and especially to hard labor. They had sub-
sisted for generations untold by gathering wild fruits and
snaring small animals. When they were put to work panning
gold from mountain streams for fourteen hours a day, they
soon collapsed and died.

Columbus himself was not a cruel man. He had taken to
heart the admonitions of his royal patrons King Ferdinand and
Queen Isabella that the Indians should be treated "well and
lovingly." But if his voyages of discovery were to continue, if
Spain was to exploit the wealth of the Indies, and if the Indians
were to be converted to Christianity (an important point with
the authorities in Madrid), then this revolt had to be crushed.
And crushed it was.

Leading a force of two hundred armored infantry and twenty horsemen, as well as two dozen huge bloodhounds, Columbus marched out against the Indians. What followed was massacre. The Indians had neither weapons nor any idea of battle. They fell by the thousands. The Spaniards killed until their arms ached and their horses refused to trot. The remnants of the Indian force were hunted through the hills like beasts and either killed by the bloodhounds or captured and sent to the mines, where after a few days many of them simply died—unable to stand the labor or the captivity itself.

A witness to these terrible events was one Bartolomé de Las Casas, a priest who was later to become bishop of Chiapas in Mexico and earned the title "Apostle of the Indies." Horrified by what he had seen and by the conditions of slavery under which the Indians were dying wholesale, Las Casas returned to Spain to try to save them. In 1517 he pleaded with Charles I, successor of Ferdinand and Isabella, to save the last of the Indians. Instead of enslaving the Indians, the kindly priest suggested, why not import African Negro slaves for the colonies? A certain number of Negroes had already been brought to Hispaniola and they showed themselves to be hard workers who could stand the harsh conditions of tropical slavery. Charles I, moved no doubt by economic as well as humanitarian considerations, granted Las Casas' plea. The transatlantic slave trade expanded almost overnight into a huge and flourishing industry.

The Portuguese, as first explorers of the coast of Africa, had been granted exclusive rights to exploit the wealth of that continent by a Papal Bull issued in 1493. But Portugal, which had led the way in African exploration during the fifteenth century, was increasingly unable to defend her exclusive rights to that continent during the sixteenth. The French, English, Dutch, Prussians, and Danes all sent expeditions to the West African coast. Like the Portuguese, they established forts there, by agreement with the native kings. These forts, usually built right on the shore or on some commanding promontory, were intended both to protect the slave ships from pirates or competing nationalities and also to serve as supply dumps for the trade goods sent to purchase the slaves. The forts changed hands often due to the incessant wars of Europe. Cape Coast Castle, on the Guinea Coast, changed hands four times between 1652 and 1664. With the conquest of Portugal by Spain in 1580, Portuguese possessions in Africa passed into the hands of her conquerors—who, in turn, were unable to defend them against marauding Dutch and English fleets. Some of the more famous forts were Cape Coast Castle and Koromantine (English), Axim and Elmina (Dutch), and Accra, a native city near which stood the forts of three European nations—within gunshot range of each other.

The first well-known English slaver was Captain John Hawkins, one of Elizabeth's "sea dogs," part pirate, part trader, and part naval officer, who was to earn fame fighting against the Spanish Armada. His first slaving venture took place in 1562, when, in command of a small squadron of privately owned ships, he kidnaped and purchased Negroes on the Guinea Coast and sold them in Hispaniola in the West Indies. When Queen Elizabeth heard of this venture, she remarked that "It was detestable and would call down vengeance from heaven upon the undertakers." But when the queen saw Hawkins' profit sheet, her opinions changed sufficiently to enable her to become a shareholder in his subsequent slaving voyages.

So great were the profits to be made by slaving that in 1672, with the blessings (and investment) of King Charles, the

Sir John Hawkins
(RADIO TIMES HULTON
PICTURE LIBRARY)

English established the Royal African Company as a monopoly of English slaving. And, since British naval power came more and more to dominate the Atlantic and even the waters of the New World, the Royal African Company gradually came to exercise control over most transatlantic slaving, no matter what the nationality of the captains, crews, or ships involved.

How were a handful of Europeans, trading from their fragile wooden ships along the coast, able to establish a huge slave trade in the face of the by-no-means powerless native kingdoms with whom they dealt? They did not establish a slave trade per se. Slaving, as has been noted, was an old established custom in Africa (as in most of the rest of the world) long before the Europeans arrived. To the kings of the coastal nations, such as Benin, it made little difference whether slaves were sold to Europeans, or to other African tribes, or simply retained to work the local fields and mines. They were articles of commerce to be disposed of to the highest bidder. And the Europeans, with their cloth and beads and strange manufactured articles, but above all with their gunpowder and firearms to trade, were the highest bidders. And if the local supply of slaves ran out, a coastal king could always make war on some tribe in the interior to capture more. Armed with European weapons, and often aided by Europeans, the coastal kings were generally victorious in such wars.

As the demand for slaves increased over the years, those engaged in slaving, both Europeans and Africans, grew more and more callous. Native greed and demoralization kept pace with European cupidity. Small slave hunts, raids, and wars gradually grew into large-scale efforts penetrating deeper and deeper into the African interior until they brought ruin to much of African society. Yet the picture of Africans submitting docilely to slavery, painted even today, is false. Many tribes and nations simply could not be enslaved, and even among those that were, rebellions and uprisings against all but hopeless odds were frequent. The records overflow with accounts of how fiercely the enslaved Africans fought for their freedom. They rebelled as they were marched to the coast, chained neck to neck in long slave "coffles" (caravans); they rebelled in the "barracoons" (hutments in guarded compounds) as they awaited the arrival of the slave ships; they rebelled as they were transported from shore to ship in the long native canoes; they rebelled aboard ship during the lengthy Atlantic crossing; and, finally, if all previous efforts had failed, they rebelled again and again in the colonies to which they had been transported. If increasing greed and bloodshed corrupted the coastal kingdoms, until enslaving their neighbors became their prime industry, the majority of Africans, especially of the interior, resisted the slave trade to the end.

Why did not the Europeans simply conquer the nations and tribes outright, enslaving them all? First of all, because during the sixteenth and seventeenth centuries the European nations could not muster sufficient force to defeat even the local coastal kingdoms. Besides that, European nations during the centuries of the slave trade were generally busy fighting each other. But the greatest protection enjoyed by Africans during the slaving era was the barrier of fevers and contagious diseases that made their continent all but impenetrable to Europeans. The Africans had developed a certain amount of resistance to dengue fever and malaria and a host of other deadly diseases, a resistance that the Europeans did not share. In fact coastal Africa was known as "the white man's grave."

Africans fell into the clutches of slavers in any one of several ways. They might be criminals, sold by native chiefs as punishment; or they might be individuals sold by their own families during times of famine; or they might simply be kidnaped by Europeans or by native kings; or they might have been slaves in Africa and sold by their masters; or, most usually, they were prisoners of war. However they had been acquired, the slaves were marched to the coast and there lodged in barracoons. Then the bargaining started.

The local king who had slaves to sell might deal directly with the captain of a slave ship; but as the trade grew and became regularized, more and more the slaving companies were represented on the coast by permanent residents known as "factors." These men, of every nation and description, generally had a short but fierce life among the local tribes. If they did not succumb to rum or insanity or die violently at the hands of the local king, they were sure to perish of fever. Their establishments — supply warehouses, barracoons, and compounds — were known as "factories."

Payment for slaves was in trade goods — cloth, knives, cutlasses, rum, muskets, gunpowder, and the inevitable glass beads. After a bargain had been struck (and sometimes the bargaining went on for two or three weeks), the slaves were branded. Each of them was marked on the chest with a red-hot iron bearing the trademark of the company which had purchased him. Then they were marched down to the beach. And this was a critical moment. Many of the slaves had never even heard of the sea. Now suddenly they were confronted by the huge breaking surf, the vast expanse of ocean beyond, and the strange ship that looked like a castle riding on the water. The slaves would fling themselves onto the beach, clutching desperately at the sand, oblivious of the whips of Negro overseers or white traders; many tried to strangle themselves with their chains. But they were dragged or carried to the long canoes waiting at the water's edge and tossed aboard.

The canoes themselves were often seventy feet long, requiring as many as twenty paddlers, and able to transport up to eighty slaves through the mountainous surf. They were often manned by a tribe known as the Krumen—large and muscular coastal natives who had once been fishermen but who now made a profession of transporting slaves from beach to ship. The Krumen themselves were almost never enslaved. Many of them enlisted in the British Royal Navy, where they enjoyed an excellent reputation as seamen.

Paddling the long canoes through the surf was a dangerous business. The slightest slip and the canoe could turn broadside to the waves, overturn, and spill both slaves and crew into the shark-infested waters. The slaves aboard often leaped into the sea to drown rather than continue their journey to captivity.

Why did Negro slaves fight so desperately, even commit suicide when they could, to avoid slavery overseas when many of them had been slaves in Africa all their lives? African slavery was a comparatively (but only *comparatively*) bearable condition. Most African slaves were fed, clothed, and housed almost as well as their masters. Nor were they expected to do much more heavy physical labor than their owners. Many were partly house slaves and only went out into the field occasionally. They were generally well treated and, of course, they lived and worked among their own or related peoples. But the canoes and ships of the European and American slavers were going to carry them into the *unknown*—always a terrifying place.

Jean Barbot, a factor for the Royal African Company who made several voyages to the Guinea Coast between 1678 and 1682, emphasized another element in the terror with which African slaves approached their fate: "Many of those slaves we transport from Guinea to America are prepossessed with the opinion that they are carried like sheep to the slaughter and that the Europeans are fond of their flesh; which notion so far prevails with some as to make them fall into a deep melancholy and to refuse all sustenance, tho never so much compelled and even beaten to oblige them to take some nourishment; notwithstanding all which they will starve to death." For the slaves firmly believed that they were to be sold to a race of gigantic cannibals called *Koomi* whose nation was called *Jong sang doo*, "the land where the slaves are sold." And this belief was only partly wrong.

But before they reached the slave markets of Brazil, the West Indies, or North America the slaves had to survive the rigors of the Middle Passage—the weeks or, more probably, months it took a sailing vessel to cross the Atlantic from the Guinea Coast to landfall in the New World. And this was, in some ways, the worst part of their journey. As soon as the slaves had been put aboard a slaver from the native canoes, the male slaves were shackled two by two—the right wrist and ankle of one with the left wrist and ankle of another. Then they were sent down to the slave deck, in the hold of the ship. The women and children were allowed to roam the ship during the day but had to go down to their own slave decks at night. All the slaves were forced to sleep uncovered on the rough wooden deck floors; in a stormy passage the skin over their elbows and knees might be worn away to bare bones.

The hold of a slaver was generally about five feet high—but small as this space was it was further reduced by a shelf which was built all around the main slave deck, extending about six feet out from the side of the ship. The slaves below this shelf and the slaves packed onto it had about twenty-five inches of headroom—they could not sit up during the entire voyage. Every inch of space in a slaver was crammed with human flesh. So tightly were the slaves wedged together, that often they could sleep only on their sides, packed like spoons in a drawer.

The sanitary accommodations for four or five hundred slaves might consist of two or three buckets, so that for most of the voyage, the slave deck was a reeking mass of excrement. Slavers could often be told from a distance by their indescribably foul odor—noticeable five miles downwind. Added to this was the fact that the only ventilation allowed for the slave deck was the heavy gratings above it—and these were often sealed during a storm.

The daily routine aboard ship was generally as follows: If the weather was fine, the male slaves were brought up on deck at eight in the morning. Their leg irons were attached to a great chain that ran the length of the ship along the bulwarks on both sides. At nine they were served a meal which might consist of boiled rice or corn meal or stewed yams and a half-pint of water. When this gruel had been consumed, the ceremony known as "dancing the slaves" began. This forced exercise was meant to combat melancholy. It consisted of making the slaves jump around as best they could in their chains—under the watchful eye of crew men armed with whips—to the joyless music of a drum or a banjo. The slaves were also supposed to sing. These proceedings, which resulted in nothing more than bleeding ankles (from chafing against the irons), lasted about an hour. At about three in the afternoon the slaves were given a meal that was a repetition of boiled rice or yams or sometimes horse bean pulp. This was the end of their day. After the "meal" they were sent below and stowed in their spoonlike fashion by whip-bearing sailors.

Not surprisingly, some slaves went mad under these conditions. Then they were flogged to make certain they were not pretending and eventually knocked on the head and thrown overboard to feed the schools of sharks which always followed a slaver. Yet this fate was so far preferable to life aboard a slave ship that whenever they could slaves would jump overboard to certain death, and a close watch had to be kept against suicide. Another favorite method of suicide was refusing to eat. But against this the slavers were armed with an instrument known as the *speculum oris*, or mouth opener. It was a wedge-

A nineteenth century dhow from Zanzibar, with cutaway section showing how slaves were stowed in the vessel's holds

(HISTORICAL PICTURES SERVICE — CHICAGO)

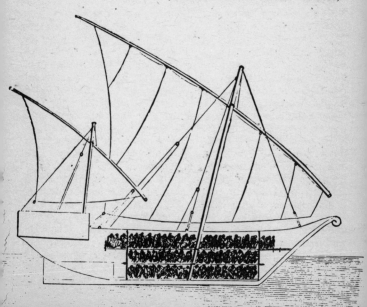

shaped device, notched, and with a screw in the middle—like a
pair of dividers. The small end of this instrument was ham-
mered between the recalcitrant slave's teeth, then the screw
was turned, thereby forcing open his mouth so that gruel could
be poured into it.

But the deadliest scourge of the slave trade was disease. In
their intolerably crowded and filthy conditions, the slaves were
prey to various fevers and epidemics. Yellow fever, smallpox,
measles, malaria, dysentery, hookworm, elephantiasis, and
leprosy all flourished aboard ship. And as they infected the
slaves, so, too, they infected the crews. And since science had
as yet no cures for these diseases and one man could infect an
entire ship with any one of them, as soon as the telltale pox or
the "bloody flux" or any other sign of disease appeared, the
unfortunate victim was thrown overboard. The mortality rate
from all causes (but especially from disease) during the Middle
Passage depended upon the vessel and luck. Many ships lost
more than fifty percent of their human cargo during their crossing of the Atlantic—some lost as few as four or five percent.
The average seems to have been about thirteen percent.

But even those slaves who did not fall ill would often be
thrown overboard if water and rations ran low. This was because the slave ships were insured against, among other things,
"jettisoning" their cargo. Thus, if a slave was not likely to survive the voyage, he might never bring money at an auction in
the Indies; but if he were jettisoned, he was not a total loss,
since the insurance company would pay something to the
owners for him.

For those slaves who survived the Middle Passage, the most
terrifying part of their voyage was often its end—when, upon
arrival at the Indies or North America, they were sold. Sometimes the entire cargo had been ordered in advance by some
large plantation owner, but more often the slaves were sold
either by a West Indian factor or by the captain of the slave
ship. In such cases the slaves (barely more than walking skele-
tons now) were paraded through the streets of the port city,
preceded by bagpipes or drums to arouse local interest. Then
they might be auctioned or, more likely, they would be sold at
"scramble." In this procedure a set price was agreed upon for
men, women, boys, and girls between prospective purchasers
and the factor or ship's captain. The slaves were assembled in
the port's public square, or in barracoons, or sometimes aboard
ship, and at a set signal the buyers would race each other to
the slaves to tag the strongest and healthiest among them. To
the terrified slaves, who still believed they were to be eaten,

the sight of a mass of whites swarming down on them was often the final straw—many went mad with fright.

But the horrors of the auction block or "scramble" were as nothing compared to the rigors to which the slaves were exposed after their purchase. Then came the period of three or four months known as "seasoning." During that time the slaves were broken to labor discipline and trained for work in the fields and mines or, if they were among the lucky few, as

An abolitionist cartoon of 1833 showed slaves being jettisoned in mid-Atlantic.
(RADIO TIMES HULTON PICTURE LIBRARY)

domestic servants. It has been estimated that as many as five percent of the slaves captured in Africa died on their march to the coastal barracoons and that a further thirteen percent died during the Middle Passage. But fully thirty percent died during the process of "seasoning." Thus for every two Negroes condemned to slavery on the Guinea Coast, only one would ever survive to labor in the New World.

Along some points on the Guinea Coast, while the slaves were being whipped into the Krumen's long canoes, European bishops seated on thrones upon the sandy beaches would baptize the struggling, terrified horde of natives wholesale. It is unlikely that any of the slaves realized that this ceremony was meant to insure their eventual entrance into paradise; it is certain, however, that what they found on the other side of the Atlantic was a hell on earth.

2 Colonial Economics Versus Colonial Conscience

> . . . *if a slave can have a country in this world, it must be any other in preference to that in which he is born to live and labor for another.*
>   — THOMAS JEFFERSON

IN 1619, ONE YEAR BEFORE THE *Mayflower* UNLOADED HER Puritan passengers onto the stern and rock-bound coast of Massachusetts, a Dutch privateer put into the newly established English colony at Jamestown, Virginia. There she discharged and sold a group of twenty Negro slaves whom she had probably pirated from a Spanish merchantman. As far as is known, these were the first African slaves to arrive in British America. But they were not to be slaves for long. Most probably they were bought by the colonial government. Since according to the Dutch sailors, they had been baptized, they were Christians — and under British law they could not be enslaved upon British territory. Instead, they were no doubt indentured — bound for a specific number of years to serve the masters who had purchased their labor. But any children born to them would be free, as they would be when their terms of service expired. Thus, at the very beginning of Negro slavery in America, economics (in this case the usefulness of slave labor in developing the raw colonial wilderness) was at war with conscience (in this case represented by British law). But the struggle was always one-sided; indeed it is something of a grim credit to human ingenuity to see how rapidly, convolutedly, and brazenly conscience was made to accommodate economics over the ensuing years.

The Negroes landed at Jamestown were not the first to reach continental America. Balboa had thirty Negroes among his followers when he gazed out over the Pacific, and Cortés im-

43

ported three hundred Negroes to help him subdue the Aztec Empire of Mexico. Negro slaves were brought to Brazil in 1538 and by 1700 they formed almost two-thirds of the population of that Portuguese colony. The first slaves to reach what would later be the United States were probably those brought in 1526 by Lucas Vásquez de Ayllon, who attempted to found a colony near where Jamestown, Virginia, was later situated. But after fever had struck down Ayllon and some of the other leaders of the expedition, the slaves revolted and the colony was abandoned. Certainly there had been slaves at Spanish-owned Saint Augustine, Florida, since its founding in 1565.

One of the first Negro slaves being sold in Jamestown, Virginia, as imagined by a nineteenth century artist   (HISTORICAL PICTURES SERVICE — CHICAGO)

The arrival of Negro slaves at Jamestown did not signal the beginning of a wholesale importation; that was to commence toward the end of the seventeenth century. The reasons for delay are fairly clear. First of all, unlike the West Indies, the North American colonies had not, as yet, developed large plantations. There were no vast fields of sugar or cotton or tobacco which required huge gangs of labor. And in the Northern colonies, with their hills, rocky soil, mountainous districts, and colder climate, such plantations were never to develop. Besides that, until the middle of the eighteenth century, the British North American colonies had an abundant source of labor in indentured servants shipped out from the home country. These were unfortunates who had been convicted of any one of hundreds of petty crimes, or kidnaped, or, if they were Irish or Scots, taken during rebellions and wars.

White indentured servants had, from their masters' viewpoint, certain advantages over Negro slaves: they spoke English and required no lengthy period of "seasoning"; their contracts were usually cheaper than the purchase of a Negro slave; and, when those contracts expired (usually after five or ten years), the master was free of all responsibility for their support. Their treatment during their voyages from Liverpool or Bristol to Boston or Charlestown or New York was (because they were less valuable) possibly even worse than that accorded Negro slaves during the Middle Passage—certainly a higher percentage of them succumbed to the rigors of the trip. Ships carrying indentured servants sailed with hatches closed. When they reached the New World, the hatches were opened, the living sent ashore and the dead tossed into the bay. Between 1750 and 1755 more than two thousand bodies were tossed into New York harbor alone. Their fate did not seem to trouble colonial consciences.

The standard justification among colonial Americans for practicing slavery was that verse from The Book which reads "Both thy bondmen and thy bondmaids, which thou shalt have, shall be of the heathen that are around about you; of them shall ye buy bondmen and bondmaids" (Leviticus 25:44). But as for "the heathen that are around about you," the Indians (many of whom were captured during King Philip's War in 1675) were either too fierce and skillful to be held in captivity or, like their brethren in the West Indies, simply languished and died of melancholy under slavery. And when that verse about "the heathen" was applied to Irish Catholic and Scotch Presbyterian indentured servants it made North American colonists distinctly uneasy. The obvious solution to these vexing problems of conscience was the introduction of Negro slavery.

By the end of the seventeenth century the plantation system in the Southern colonies, especially in South Carolina and Virginia, had gotten a good start. The great agricultural staples of the American colonial economy, rice and tobacco, were already being planted on a large scale. And Negroes (primarily from the West Indies) were being imported as slaves at the rate of about one thousand per year. It was also during the latter part of the seventeenth century that the English Royal African Company came into effective control of the slave trade. So as the demand for Negro slaves increased with the rise of the great plantations, the possibilities of supplying them also widened. But what of conscience?

A new Biblical verse was found, and coupled with an anthropological error. The error was in supposing that Negroes were descendants of Ham (or Canaan), a rebellious son of Noah; the Biblical justification, Noah's curse: "And he said, Cursed be Canaan; a servant of servants shall he be to his brethren" (Genesis 9:25). And for those who still doubted, English Bishop Berkeley advised that Negroes were "creatures of another species who had no right to be included or admitted to the sacraments."

The period during which Negroes were regarded as being on the same legal level as white indentured servants lasted only a few decades—just until the economic need for chattel slavery became pressing. Virginia, in a series of official acts from 1640 to 1667, gradually transformed the status of Negroes within the colony from that of indentured servants to that of perpetual chattel slaves whose children to the last generation were to be considered slaves. The same transformation was accomplished more speedily in other colonies. The Carolinas in 1663, Maryland in 1664, New York in 1664, Pennsylvania and Delaware in 1682: all recognized Negro slavery as legal. In the New England colonies, a comfortable obscurity of official status was preferred. Negro slaves who had been imported to Massachusetts and Connecticut since 1638 were sometimes referred to as "servants." But to the Negroes there was no question as to their status.

In the Southern colonies Negro slaves were largely employed as field hands in the rice and tobacco (and later the sugar cane) fields. In the Northern colonies Negroes were employed in small numbers as farm hands and very often as artisans: carpenters, blacksmiths, shipwrights, clerks, sailors, et cetera. In both areas, of course, many Negroes served as household slaves: "Mammys," valets, butlers, cooks, and footmen.

The treatment of slaves differed from colony to colony, depending generally on how high a proportion of the total population was Negro and how deeply the white legislators feared a slave uprising. In South Carolina, where Negroes outnumbered whites, the slave codes were patterned after the ferociously harsh West Indian regulations. But in New England, where only about three percent of the population consisted of Negro slaves, the slave codes were so mild as to allow slaves a trial by jury and to testify under oath against whites. In New York, which had a larger slave population than any other Northern colony, it was against the law for more than three Negroes to assemble except while working.

While the basic economic foundations of slavery in colonial America can hardly be overemphasized, human attitudes dictated by ideals or fears must not be discounted. From earliest times two currents of thought appear among whites in America: prejudice and abolitionism. While it is true that both of these attitudes can be traced in large part to economic interests (prejudice as a consciously induced means of justifying ruthless economic exploitation, abolitionism as a consciously induced means of attacking the dangerous economic competition offered by slavery), both appeared before economic pressures alone could have warranted them.

Prejudice leading to anti-Negro discrimination has always been in large part based on fear. The settlers of North America, like human beings in other times and places, had much to fear. Confronted by a huge and hostile continent inhabited by what appeared to them to be fierce savages, cut off by the vast reaches of the Atlantic from immediate support from their home countries, the early settlers may well have felt inadequate to their tasks. More than that, many of them had come from near-slavery in Europe; many of them were all but slaves in the New World. Feelings of fear, inadequacy, and self-hatred or contempt are often resolved by clinging to derogatory beliefs about others. And the Negro, because of his "high visibility" (easy identification because of color), his utterly foreign cultural background, and his largely unknown place of origin, was the most obvious as well as the safest target for the uneasy settler.

Thus Virginia, many years *before* formalizing slavery, discriminated against Negroes. In 1630, for example, a Virginia court ordered one Hugh Davis to be whipped for "defiling his body in lying with a negro." In 1669 the court refused to punish a white servant because charges against him had been brought by a Negro. In 1680 (after slavery had been formalized) the Virginia legislature passed a law forbidding free Negroes from employing white servants. Since during those years (1630–1680) the Negro population of Virginia rose only from three hundred (out of fifteen thousand) to two thousand (out of forty thousand), evidently more than economic necessity lay behind Virginia law; it also expressed psychological fears.

Sincerely held religious beliefs lay at the root of early abolitionism. It was certainly not economic considerations that led Judge Samuel Sewall of Massachusetts to write *The Selling of Joseph*—the first direct attack on slavery in New England—which was published in 1701. And it was in the sincere hope of saving Negro souls that the Anglican Church's Society for the Propagation of the Gospel in Foreign Parts established a Negro school in New York City in 1705. Although Anglican efforts in the South were handicapped by direct economic interests after 1700, nevertheless the society established a second school in Charleston in which two former slaves, Harry and Andrew, helped to teach their fellow Negroes.

While the efforts of Puritans such as Judge Sewall and Cotton Mather to raise the educational level of Negroes in New England were handicapped by the fact that to admit Negroes into the Puritan churches (where most education was conducted) would automatically confer upon them the right to vote and hold political office, the Quakers of Pennsylvania faced no such problem in confronting the moral issues of slavery. From the very beginning, the members of the Society of Friends looked upon education as a means to the ultimate goal of complete emancipation of all Negro slaves. On February 18, 1688, in Germantown, Pennsylvania, the Quakers issued a formal denunciation of slavery and of the slave trade. From that time forward, Quaker agitation against slavery never ceased. Quakers John Woolman and Anthony Benezet, foremost of several, traveled the trails of colonial America urging education and emancipation of the Negroes. But independent conscience was quickly submerged by economic interest—even in Pennsylvania and New England. For if Southern plantation owners depended on the wealth produced by slave labor, New England ship builders, merchants, and seamen soon found their own profits dependent to a large degree on the trade which provided that labor.

The first colonial vessel to engage in the slave trade was the *Desire*, built in Marblehead and sailing out of Salem, Massachusetts. In 1638 the *Desire* landed an unspecified number of Negro slaves in Boston from the West Indies. The first colonial slaver to reach the coast of Africa directly was the *Rainbow* in 1645. And from this very first voyage, Yankee ingenuity and determination were evident. When the *Rainbow* reached the Guinea Coast she found several English slavers there ahead of her. They had been fruitlessly awaiting slaves for some time,

A Negro newly landed from Africa on the auction block in seventeenth century New York City (HISTORICAL PICTURES SERVICE—CHICAGO)

but apparently there were none for sale at the moment. But Captain Smith of the *Rainbow* was not to be denied. He suggested to the Englishmen a pooling of forces in order to kidnap a cargo. Accordingly, a force drawn from all the ships' crews armed with a small cannon (appropriately called a "murderer") was landed. It attacked a nearby native village, killing many of its inhabitants and carrying off a handful of slaves. With his share of this booty (two slaves) Captain Smith had to be contented.

Captain Smith's Yankee ingenuity ran head-on into the divided Yankee conscience when he returned to Boston. There, when he tried to sell his slaves, he was arrested and convicted of "murder, man-stealing, and Sabbath-breaking" (the raid had taken place on a Sunday). Smith went free because the Boston court recognized that his crimes had been committed outside its jurisdiction. But the two slaves were returned to their homes at the expense of the Massachusetts legislature.

The colonial slave trade during the first half of the seventeenth century was centered not in New England, but in the Dutch colony of Nieuw Amsterdam. The Dutch West India Company held a monopoly of the African trade then and landed its first cargo of slaves in Nieuw Amsterdam in 1625. When the English captured Nieuw Amsterdam and changed its name to New York, the slave trade there continued to prosper. But it was not until the English Royal African Company was chartered in 1672 that the North American slave trade really began to boom. Since the company was under royal patronage, it became the official policy of the British government to encourage the importation of slaves to the colonies.

Since American built, manned, and financed vessels were also licensed (usually for a fee of ten percent of their profits) to engage in the slave trade by the Royal African Company, slave trading was one of the largest factors in the rise of New England's great shipping industry and the growth of her commercial fortunes. By 1750 Newport, Rhode Island, alone had close to one hundred vessels engaged in the "triangular trade." Taking on loads of rum (as well as other colonial products) New England ships sailed to the Guinea Coast. There they traded their cargo for slaves and these they transported to the West Indies. There the slaves were sold or bartered and the ships freighted with sugar and molasses for the last leg of their journey back to Salem or Boston or Newport or New York. The sugar and molasses were distilled into rum—and the triangular voyage started anew.

But as the demand for slaves grew in North America, slavers increasingly reserved part of their slave cargo for sale (mostly in Southern ports) back home—and many found the profits from this enterprise sufficient to justify eliminating a West Indian stopover. The American slave trade grew so rapidly that the number of Negroes in British North America spiraled from 59,000 in 1714 to 298,000 by 1754. A time was coming when the African slave trade would be an all but American monopoly—but that was in the future.

During the first half of the eighteenth century the heavy influx of Negro slaves sometimes was looked upon as a mixed benefit—even among Southern plantation owners. The single greatest fear among the masters of huge slave-operated estates was of slave rebellion. Southern planters and legislators knew that there had been dozens of slave rebellions in the West Indies during the seventeenth century and that such uprisings were continuing to burst out with alarming frequency during the eighteenth century. And they knew too what the horrors of a slave rebellion might be. They had heard of the massacre of white plantation owners and all their families during slave revolts in Haiti and Surinam and Curaçao and Jamaica. They knew that since 1730 a large British expeditionary army had been unsuccessfully trying to conquer the escaped slaves in Jamaica (with whom the British were eventually forced to sign a "treaty of peace"). And as the proportion of Negro slaves among them increased, the Southerners grew increasingly nervous. The plantation owners were fairly confident that they could control the slaves they already owned and especially their descendants, who would be raised to servility from infancy, but they were apprehensive of introducing more "wild" Africans among them. Thus, while the Southern planters firmly upheld the institution of slavery itself, they grew increasingly critical of the slave trade.

In the years just preceding the American Revolution, colony after colony attempted to control or prohibit the importation of slaves. The New England colonies passed numerous anti-slave-trade measures between 1771 and 1776, as did Pennsylvania. In the South, Virginia in 1774, North Carolina that same year, and Georgia in 1775 all passed restrictive laws against the slave trade. But inevitably these measures were struck down by the British Royal Colonial governors. For although the Royal African Company had been disbanded in 1750, the slave trade was a tremendously important part of the English economy. The wealth and growth of such great ports as Bristol and Liverpool depended on it; its profits were financing the mills and factories and inventions which were producing the Industrial Revolution in England. The English Parliament, heavily influenced by British shippers, merchants, and manu-

An early engraving of the Boston Massacre, March 5, 1770. Crispus Attucks lies dead between the mob and the redcoats.

(HISTORICAL PICTURES SERVICE—CHICAGO)

facturers, was determined that the slave trade would continue and the American colonies remain an open market for it. The differing views held by Great Britain and her American colonies regarding the slave trade were to be among the chief causes of the American Revolution.

When the Continental Congress met on October 20, 1774, the second article of its agreement, which was signed by every state's representatives except those from Georgia (who signed later) stated: "That we will neither import nor purchase any slave imported after the first day of December next; after which we will wholly discontinue the slave trade." Despite the altruistic intentions of certain delegates, this was intended by the majority more as a blow against British trade than against slavery. But four years before the Continental Congress condemned the slave trade, the first American Negro slave had fallen before British guns—in defense of what? The case is curious.

In the *Boston Gazette* of Tuesday, October 2, 1750, there appeared the following advertisement: "Ran away from his master William Brown of Framingham, on the 30th of September last, a Molatto Fellow, about 27 Years of Age, named Crispas . . . Whoever shall take up said Run-away, and convey him to his abovesaid master, shall have ten pounds." No one ever collected the ten pounds. The runaway mulatto evidently made good his escape. But twenty years later, on March 5, 1770, when a British military patrol in the streets of Boston fired into a crowd of people after being baited unmercifully by the crowd, Crispus Attucks was among the first to fall, mortally wounded. It has been said that it was he who led the mob, thereby bringing on the "Boston Massacre"—an event of which Daniel Webster was later to declare: "From that moment we may date the severance of the British Empire."

For what did Crispus Attucks give his life? This is a question with no easy answer and one which was to recur again and again throughout American history. Brave Negro soldiers were to fight and die, both before and after Emancipation, to defend a land in which they were slaves, or later, little better than slaves. If many of them were perfectly able to see the dreadful irony of this, to what vision or hope did they cling to justify their suffering to themselves?

Yet Negroes had served in all the colonial wars and in the various campaigns against the Indians. They were to serve at Lexington and Concord among the Minutemen. And on the 17th of June, 1775, as the long, steady lines of British marines struggled up Bunker Hill at Boston, there were more than a few Negroes among the Yankee riflemen awaiting them at the top. Just as British Major John Pitcairn mounted the American redoubt shouting, "The day is ours!" he was shot dead by Peter Salem, a Negro soldier. In that same battle, another Negro, Salem Poor, so distinguished himself that fourteen officers commended him to the Massachusetts legislature, declaring: "[Poor] behaved like an experienced officer, as well as an excellent soldier."

In spite of all this, there were many people in the New England states and an overwhelming majority in the Southern states who feared that arming the slaves might lead to insurrection or, at the very least, that the dignity of serving in the Continental Army might give Negroes the idea that the bold words of the Declaration of Independence applied to them too. So after October, 1775, although Negroes who were already enlisted in the Continental Army were permitted to remain (at the direct insistence of Commander-in-Chief George Washington), no further enlistments of Negroes were accepted —and this policy was adopted by the state militias, North and South, as well.

While the Declaration of Independence, as promulgated in 1776, unequivocally declared that "all men are created equal," there was a significant omission. This was a paragraph which Thomas Jefferson had intended to include in the Declaration's list of grievances against King George III. The paragraph said of that hapless monarch: "He has waged cruel war against human nature itself, violating its most sacred rights of life and liberty in the persons of a distant people [Africans] who never offended him; captivating and carrying them into slavery in another hemisphere, or to incur miserable death in their transportation thither." But the Declaration of Independence, besides denouncing King George, was intended also to serve as a common rallying point for all the people of the colonies. Neither Southern plantation owners nor New England shippers and merchants would be pleased by that paragraph; it was omitted from the final document.

Not that there was any question in the minds of the leaders of the American Revolution regarding slavery. Thomas Jefferson, in his *Notes on Virginia* (1782), wrote: "The whole commerce between master and slave is a perpetual exercise of the most boisterous passions; the most unremitting despotism on the one part, and degrading submission on the other. . . . Our children see this and learn to imitate it . . . thus nursed, educated, and daily exercised in tyranny, [they] cannot but be stamped by it with odious peculiarities." John Jay, later first Chief Justice of the United States, wrote in 1785: "It is much to be wished that slavery may be abolished. . . . To contend for our own liberty, and to deny that blessing to others, involves an inconsistency not to be excused."

George Washington, in 1786, wrote: ". . . I can only say that there is not a man living who wishes more sincerely than I do to see some plan adopted for the abolition of it." Benjamin Franklin, long an abolitionist, wrote in 1789 (for the Pennsylvania Society for the Promotion of the Abolition of Slavery, of which Franklin was president): "Slavery is such an atrocious debasement of human nature that its very extirpation, if not performed with solicitous care, may sometimes open a source of serious evils." And John Adams, a few years before his death, wrote to a friend: "I have, through my whole life, held the practice of slavery in such abhorrence that I have never owned a Negro or other slave."

But these men and others who stirred the fires of revolution were considered radicals not only by the British Crown, but also by the majority of their fellow Americans. In order to win their struggle for independence they had to have the support of more conservative elements in the colonies. Thus, from the very beginning of the history of the United States as an independent nation, the rights, hopes, and dreams of Negroes were sacrificed on the altar of "unity" and expediency.

British governors and commanders in North America were quick to take advantage of this inconsistency in the American camp. As early as November, 1775, Lord Dunmore, Royal Governor of Virginia, issued a proclamation that all Negroes enlisting in the British forces would be freed. He noted, correctly, that since the colonists "were so eager to escape an imaginary slavery," he would see how they liked a proclamation which would "put an end to a very real slavery among them." They did not like it. But with the advance of American forces, Lord Dunmore was forced to flee Virginia a few weeks after his proclamation. Nonetheless, His Lordship's policy was adopted by other British commanders and proved highly successful. British Commander-in-Chief Henry Clinton declared on June 30, 1779, that any Negroes who reached the British lines would be freed. These measures were aimed at crippling the labor supply of the Southern colonies and hitting the large plantation owners where they would hurt most—in their purses. Tens of thousands of Negro slaves—mostly in the South—made their way to the British lines, and freedom. They were employed by the British as laborers, cooks, guides, and spies; and about one thousand of them served under arms. So serious did the situation become in the South that North Carolina, Georgia, South Carolina, and Virginia were forced to set up slave-catching patrols both on land and on the rivers and coasts, and to divert a large part of their militias to this profitless task.

Certain harsh facts of life were also borne in upon the Continental Congress as the war went on. Enlistments ran lower and lower, commanders cried out for more men to fill out their regiments, and, by 1779, the Congress had reversed its former policy and was urging the enlistment of Negroes in both the Continental Army and the state militias. Employed generally as cooks, laborers, orderlies, and guides, Negroes fought as stoutly as their white brothers-in-arms when given the chance. For example, the largely Negro Rhode Island First Regiment, although composed of little more than raw recruits, held its position grimly against repeated attacks by British and Hessian troops and helped turn the Battle of Rhode Island (August, 1778) into one of the rare American victories that year. But despite the promptings of Congress and the pleas of such generals as Nathanael Greene, Benjamin Lincoln, and Washington himself, the Southern colonies continued to bar Negroes from their armed forces. North and South Carolina and Georgia would accept no Negroes, Virginia would accept only free Negroes—even after the British brought the war to their very doorsteps. It was apparent that most Southerners would prefer defeat to arming their slaves.

When the Revolutionary War came to its formal end in 1783, the British were faced with the problem of what to do with the thousands of Negroes who had flocked to their lines on the promise of freedom. To their credit, the British determined to keep this promise, even over the outraged protests of the Americans. Accordingly, when Sir Guy Carleton, British commander-in-chief, ordered the final evacuation of British forces from the now independent colonies, the soldiers were accompanied by over fourteen thousand Negroes who preferred exile with freedom to returning to their former masters.

But the revolution did bring benefits to Negroes in America. Many of them had won freedom by serving with the armed

A composite mural of the Boston Massacre by Mexican artist Diego Rivera, commissioned for New York's Rockefeller Center and later destroyed for political reasons

forces — and the general triumph of radical opinion throughout the colonies gave a powerful impetus to abolitionist societies (which now proliferated throughout the North) and to anti-slavery legislation. Pennsylvania, with its strong Quaker sentiment, established a program of gradual emancipation in 1781. Massachusetts and New Hampshire abolished slavery in 1783; the following year Rhode Island and Connecticut adopted gradual emancipation laws. Even in the South, Maryland, North Carolina, and Virginia declared the slave trade illegal, if not slavery itself. And the new Continental Congress, convening after 1781, under the loose Articles of Confederation was eventually persuaded (in 1787) to abolish slavery forever north of the Ohio River throughout the new Western territories won from England. But beyond this Northwest Ordinance, the Continental Congress was unwilling to go.

The final crisis of conscience and economics surrounding the question of Negro slavery after the Revolutionary War occurred during the Constitutional Convention of 1787. To such men as Jefferson, Madison, and Hamilton, the idea of creating a national government for a democratic republic that permitted slavery was preposterous and deeply repugnant. But the alternative of disunion was even more hateful. And the states of the Deep South, Georgia, South Carolina, and North Carolina, threatened simply to walk out of the convention if any measure prohibiting slavery was adopted. Furthermore, they would not join any Federal union which attempted to suppress the slave trade. Whatever else had changed since 1776, the economies of rice, tobacco, and sugar cane remained based on slavery. And as these economies expanded after 1785, ever larger importations of slaves from Africa were required. It is interesting to note that Virginia, which was already well stocked with slaves and had a more settled economy, was willing to accept an end of the slave trade. But her sister states to the south accused her, with some justification, of arguing against the trade only to preserve her profitable traffic in selling Virginia-raised slaves farther south. The arguments over slavery were long and acrimonious. But by continuing to threaten a walk-out, the Southerners won.

Although the words "Negro" and "slave" did not appear in the United States Constitution, that document contained three provisions which bore directly on the problem. The first of these provided that runaway slaves who had escaped from any state had to be returned by any other state in which they might have sought refuge. The second forbade the Congress from making any law regarding the slave trade itself for twenty years — until 1808. The third established the principle that in

counting population in order to determine how many representatives a state might send to Congress, all free persons and
"three-fifths of all other persons" were to be counted—thus
assuring the Southern states of a larger representation in Congress than their free citizenry would otherwise have enjoyed.

What did Jefferson, Hamilton, and the other liberal framers
of the Constitution gain by these concessions? Very simply
they gained the Federal government of the United States.
Nevertheless many of them were to regret bitterly in later
years that the problem of slavery had not been fought to a
conclusion in 1787. The political blackmail practiced by the
states of the Deep South was to cost the nation dearly at a
later date.

3 The Peculiar
Institution

Legree's big house was white and green.
His cotton-fields were the best to be seen.
He had strong horses and opulent cattle,
And bloodhounds bold, with chains that would
*   rattle.*
. . . . But he went down to the Devil.

                —VACHEL LINDSAY

OF COURSE IT DEPENDED ON YOUR POINT OF VIEW. GEORGE
Fitzhugh of Virginia, an active apologist for the South's "peculiar institution," wrote:

"The Negro slaves of the South are the happiest, and, in
some sense, the freest people in the world. The children and
the aged and infirm work not at all, and yet have all the comforts
and necessities of life provided for them. They enjoy liberty,
because they are oppressed neither by care nor labor."

This viewpoint was most useful to the South's ruling class of
large plantation owners; it is familiar even today. The vision
has been celebrated in story and song and cinema with insistent
banality. There stands the old plantation house, white-pillared,
a Greek revival mansion surrounded by gently sloping green
lawns, gracefully bowing willow trees: "'tis summer, the
darkies are gay." The sun always shines in azure skies, and the
white-goateed "Ole Marse" sips his mint julep on the long
veranda, while his beautiful daughters prepare themselves for
yet another ball and "Young Marse" prances around on a thor-
oughbred horse like some knight out of the age of chivalry.
From the fields comes the happy laughter of carefree slaves,
bending over the white acres of cotton plants, while from within
the mansion can be heard the shrill scolding of "Mammy" as

she tells off the naughty scions of "Ole Missy" for dipping their fingers in the ever-present pancake batter. "Ole Missy" herself is feeling poorly, affects a touch of pallor to her languid face, and is generally napping. She is exhausted from caring for sick slaves in the cheerful row of cabins behind the Big House.

Of what does "Ole Missy" dream during her nap? What vision does "Ole Marse" glimpse through the bourbon haze of his julep? Why, of a world that never changes, of a life devoted to graceful indulgence in pleasure, to the appreciation of art, to ennobling sentiments; a life from which the need for work has been largely banished; a life in which women devote themselves only to their own beauty and men devote themselves to high politics and the noble arts of war. It has been observed of ruling classes before and since that the more precarious their position becomes, the more imminent becomes their downfall, the more they retreat from reality, thereby contributing to their own destruction.

The case of the small group of large plantation owners who, through money, influence, and simple assertion, ruled the South until 1865 is an excellent example of the pathology of decay. They had long since rationalized slavery through misreadings of the Bible, misunderstanding of history, and misinterpretation of pseudo-scientific "facts." But to continue a life based on the ruthless exploitation of other men's labor, a life without the dignity and meaning of work; to stifle consciences troubled by the "perpetual exercise of the most boisterous passions" of which Jefferson had warned; to hide the essential meaninglessness and coarseness of their society from themselves, it was necessary to create a myth—and then live it and believe in it. As usual, the root of the matter was economic.

At the Constitutional Convention of 1787, Oliver Ellsworth, delegate from Connecticut, had thought it wasteful to spend much time discussing slavery. The institution was withering away of natural causes. The expense of buying and maintaining slaves was returning less and less profit to the sugar, tobacco, and rice economy of the Southern states. "Slavery in time will not be a speck in our country," prophesied Ellsworth. But the gentleman from Connecticut had no way of foreseeing the cotton gin.

During the late eighteenth century, financed largely by profits from the slave trade, new inventions which harnessed new sources of power had revolutionized the textile industry in England. Giant steam-driven looms and mills grew up around

Leeds and Manchester and Liverpool. To keep them running a constant source of raw material was needed. Cotton would have been an ideal raw material had it not been so difficult to pick the seeds from the fluffy cotton bolls. The demand for a machine which would accomplish this was met in 1793 when Eli Whitney (an American) invented the cotton gin. Its effects on the Southern economy were immediate and profound.

Slaves returning from the fields, as imagined by the nineteenth century artist Edward Kemble in his painting "At Twilight"

(HISTORICAL PICTURES SERVICE — CHICAGO)

Suddenly it was profitable to plant cotton. The South's cotton crop in 1804 was eight times that of 1794; and from 1800 to 1860 the Cotton Kingdom expanded over virgin territories with striking speed. By 1850 the "land of cotton" extended a thousand miles, from South Carolina to Texas. The greed for new land to plant in cotton had been dominant in Southern support for annexing Texas in 1845, acquiring Florida in 1819, and Jefferson's somewhat less-than-legal purchase of the

Louisiana Territory in 1803. From 1825 to 1860, the South produced fully three-fourths of the world's cotton supply.

And cotton growing seemed made for slavery. Any slave could pick cotton, young, old, women as well as men. It required little skill and few tools. The cotton plants were low enough so that an overseer could easily keep watch over an entire gang of slaves working the rows. Furthermore cotton was a hardy plant, able to withstand careless handling, and giving year-round employment. True, the constant growth of a single crop depleted the soil, but there was always virgin land to the west. By 1860 three-quarters of all Negro agricultural workers in the South were employed in cotton cultivation.

What was it like to labor in the cotton fields? Solomon Northrup, a free Negro who had been kidnaped and then sold in 1845 to labor for twelve years on a Louisiana cotton plantation, has left an account.

"During all these hoeings the overseer or driver follows the slaves on horseback with a whip. . . . The fastest hoer takes the lead row. He is usually about a rod in advance of his companions. If one of them passes him, he is whipped. If one falls behind or is a moment idle, he is whipped. In fact, the lash is flying from morning until night, the whole day long. The hoeing season thus continues from April until July, a field having no sooner been finished once, than it is commenced again.

"In the latter part of August begins the cotton picking season. . . . An ordinary day's work is two hundred pounds. A slave who is accustomed to picking, is punished, if he or she brings in less quantity than that.

"The hands are required to be in the cotton field as soon as it is light in the morning, and, with the exception of ten or fifteen minutes, which is given them at noon to swallow their allowance of cold bacon, they are not permitted to be a moment idle until it is too dark to see and when the moon is full they often times labor till the middle of the night. They do not dare to stop, even at dinner time."

And after each slave's bag of cotton had been weighed (and whippings meted out to those who failed to collect their quota), ". . . the labor of the day is not yet ended, by any means. Each one must then attend to his respective chores. One feeds the mules, another the swine — another cuts wood, and so forth. . . . Finally, at a late hour, they reach the quarters, sleepy and overcome with the long day's toil. Then a fire must be kindled in the cabin, the corn ground in a small hand-mill, and supper, and dinner for the next day in the field, prepared. All that is allowed them is corn and bacon. . . . Each one receives as his weekly allowance, three and a half pounds of bacon, and corn enough to make a peck of meal. That is all."

What about that cheerful row of cabins behind the Big House? Northrup describes them: "The softest couches in the world are not to be found in the log mansion of the slave. The one whereon I reclined year after year, was a plank twelve inches wide and ten feet long. My pillow was a stick of wood. The bedding was a coarse blanket, and not a rag or shred beside. . . .

"The cabin is constructed of logs, without floor or window. The latter is altogether unnecessary, the crevices between the logs admitting sufficient light. In stormy weather, the rain drives through them, rendering it comfortless and extremely disagreeable. . . .

"An hour before daylight the horn is blown. Then the slaves arouse, prepare their breakfast, fill a gourd with water . . . and hurry to the field again. It is an offense invariably followed by a flogging, to be found at the quarters after daybreak. Then the fears and labors of another day begin; and until its close there is no such thing as rest."

While Northrup's description was perfectly valid for a tremendous proportion of the South's slaves, it is difficult to generalize about the actual lot of any given slave. They lived in regions as different as the Eastern Shore of Maryland and the vast plains of Texas. While many of them worked on cotton plantations, others worked growing rice, sugar, hemp, or tobacco; and each crop dictated its own harsh rigors of work. Then, too, much depended on the personality of the slave's master. There is no doubt that there were some masters to whom the welfare and happiness of their slaves were important—rarely important enough to grant them freedom, but of sufficient concern to spare them the worst conditions of labor and punishment. Although each state had its own code of laws dealing with slaves, a master's power was absolute: in regard to his slaves he was the law.

Perhaps the best-off slaves were those who lived in towns. In order to profit from his slaves, a town-living master had to hire them out to do whatever work they could, and the more skilled they were at various crafts, the more hire-money they were worth. Therefore many city slaves were trained as carpenters, mechanics, clerks, and servants. Furthermore, it was often easier to allow a trained slave to go out to seek his own employment in a town. On occasion a slave could earn a little money for himself in this way and perhaps even save up enough to purchase his own freedom, though this was very rare.

On the plantations the slaves who fared best were the house

servants: the "Mammy," the butler, the cook, the maids, the
coachmen. For the sake of their masters' appearances they
were generally dressed better, in fancy uniforms; since they
usually ate in the kitchen they often shared their masters' food;
and sometimes they slept in a wing of the big house. It was
customary to pretend that they enjoyed the confidence of their
master, that they were, in a sense, like his children. Often
enough they were. And in their privileged positions they often
did develop ties of loyalty to their owners that led them to
betray their fellow slaves. For example, on June 7, 1802, a
Mr. Mathews of Norfolk, Virginia, received an anonymous
warning of a slave uprising:

"White pepil be-ware of your lives, their is a plan now form-
ing and intent to put in execution this harvest time—they are to
commence and use their Sithes as weapons until they can get
possession of other weapons . . . the scream is to kill all before
them, men, women, and children . . . I am a favorite Servant of
my Master and Mistis, and love them dearly."

At the urging of President Jefferson that the United States
withdraw from "all further participation in those violations of
human rights which have been so long continued on the un-
offending inhabitants of Africa," the foreign slave trade had
been declared illegal beginning on January 1, 1808, by action of
Congress. But the enforcement of this law was difficult. The
cotton planters in the new territories of the Southwest—Texas
and Mississippi—demanded slaves and more slaves, and for
the New York and New England shipping merchants the profits
were as great as ever. American-owned slave ships continued
their trade and smuggled not less than five thousand Africans
each year into Southern ports. Ships flying other flags, notably
the Brazilian and the Portuguese, multiplied this number.
Nevertheless, the overall import figures were drastically reduced, and the states of the lower South where new plantations were being opened were forced to buy their slaves on the
domestic market—from Virginia, Maryland, and Kentucky,
which had surpluses. A large and flourishing industry, the
domestic slave trade, sprang into existence.

Masters in Virginia, for example, who wished to sell slaves
contacted licensed traders who bought and sold slaves on
speculation. The traders would inspect the slaves offered for
sale (many of them at public auction in the local county court-
house) and then offer a price. If their bids were accepted, the
male slaves were chained together and, followed by the women
and children, were marched off overland or transported on
Mississippi River steamers to the Deep South—especially to

New Orleans, which became the center of the domestic slave trade. Besides the many slave showrooms the city boasted, it also had about two hundred slave-auction markets. It has been estimated that 740,000 slaves were "sold South" from 1800 to 1860.

Being "sold down the river" (Mississippi) was a fate much dreaded by the slave. However hard or tiresome his life might have been on a plantation in Kentucky or Virginia, it was as nothing compared to the exploitive cruelty he faced on the vast "factory plantations" of Louisiana or Texas. But perhaps worse than this was the near certainty that families would be broken up, the husband and wife and children going to different new masters. Solomon Northrup, the kidnaped Negro who was sold into slavery at New Orleans in 1845, has described a scene that was common to the auction markets of that city:

"An old gentleman, who said he wanted a coachman, appeared to take a fancy to me. . . . Freeman [Theophilus Freeman, owner of the auction market] asked him fifteen hundred dollars for me. The old gentleman insisted it was too much as times were very hard. . . . During the day however a number of sales were made. . . . Sethe [a Negro who had traveled South with Northrup] was sold to a planter of Baton Rouge, her eyes flashing with anger as she was led away.

"The same man also purchased Randall. The little fellow was made to jump, and run across the floor, and perform many other feats, exhibiting his activity and condition. All the time the trade was going on, Eliza [Randall's mother] was crying aloud and wringing her hands. She besought the man not to buy him, unless he also bought herself and Emily [Randall's sister]. She promised, in that case, to be the most faithful slave that ever lived. The man answered that he could not afford it, and then Eliza burst into a paroxysm of grief, weeping plaintively. Freeman turned around to her, savagely, with his whip in his uplifted hand, ordering her to stop her noise, or he would flog her. He would not have such work — such sniveling; and unless she ceased that minute, he would take her to the yard and give her a hundred lashes. . . . Eliza shrunk before him, and tried to wipe away her tears, but it was all in vain. She wanted to be with her children, she said, the little time she had to live. . . . But it was of no avail; the man could not afford it. The bargain was agreed upon and Randall must go alone. Then Eliza ran to him; embraced him passionately; kissed him again and again; told him to remember her — all the while her tears falling in the boy's face like rain.

"Freeman damned her, calling her a blubbering, bawling

wench. . . . He swore he wouldn't stand such stuff but a little longer.

"The planter from Baton Rouge, with his new purchase, was ready to depart.

"'Don't cry, Mama, I will be a good boy. Don't cry,' said Randall, looking back as they passed out of the door.

"What has become of the lad, God knows. It was a mournful scene indeed. I would have cried myself if I had dared."

If any further evidence were needed to dispel the ridiculous myth of the kindly, sunny old South of contented slaves, it would be that of Frederick Douglass, a Negro who was to become a great leader in the cause of abolition. Douglass was sold by his Baltimore owner in 1834 to a man named Covey, whose profession it was to "break" slaves so that they would be physically and mentally conditioned for the hard life of the plantations in the Deep South. Douglass' description of his life with Covey reveals the central anguish of the slave's life:

"If at any one time of my life, more than another, I was made to drink the bitterest dregs of slavery, that time was during the first six months of my stay with this man Covey. We worked all weathers. It was never too hot, or too cold; it could never rain, blow, snow, or hail too hard for us to work in the field. . . . The longest days were too short for him, and the shortest nights were too long for him. I was somewhat unmanageable at first, but a few months of this discipline tamed me. Mr. Covey succeeded in *breaking* me—in body, soul, and spirit . . . the dark night of slavery closed in upon me, and behold a man transformed to a brute!

". . . I shall never be able to narrate half the mental experiences through which it was my lot to pass, during my stay at Covey's. I was completely wrecked, changed, and bewildered; goaded almost to madness at one time, and at another reconciling myself to my wretched condition.

". . . I suffered bodily as well as mentally. I had neither sufficient time in which to eat, nor to sleep, except on Sunday. The overwork, and the brutal chastisement of which I was the victim, combined with that ever-gnawing and soul-devouring thought—*'I am a slave—and a slave for life—a slave with no rational ground to hope for freedom'*—rendered me a living embodiment of mental and physical wretchedness."

Who benefited from all this cruelty? Certainly not the majority of Southern whites. In 1850 (a typical year) only about one-third of the population of the Cotton Kingdom owned any slaves, or worked on slave-operated plantations. And of that third only four thousand families, who possessed the choice lands, could be said to profit from the institution. One thousand

Southern families had a combined income of $50,000,000 in 1850 — as much as the combined income of *all other families living in the South.* A large factor in this financial situation was the inability of small-holding independent farmers to compete with slave labor. A Southerner from Madison County, Alabama, reported in 1850: "In traversing that county, one will discover numerous farmhouses, once the abode of industrious and intelligent freemen, now occupied by slaves . . . and will find that 'only one master grasps the whole domain' that once furnished happy homes for a dozen white families."

It might be supposed that the despoiled white farmers of the South would have been among the foremost opponents of slavery as the means whereby a tight oligarchy of ruling families imposed economic exploitation upon them. Certainly their way of life — their rough-hewn log cabins, their diet of corn and bacon, the hard labor they underwent trying to scratch a living from their small farms — was little better than that of the slaves. But from every pulpit, from every newspaper, from their political leaders came an incessant barrage of proslavery propaganda. The Negro, they were told, was biologically inferior to the white; the Negro was a potentially dangerous savage who, if set free, would run amuck, killing and burning; the Negro, if free to compete with them economically, would bring unemployment and ruin to their meager lives. And, if the poor whites were not superior to the Negro, to whom were they superior? Besides a small farmer might live in hope that someday, somehow, he would be able to save up the purchase price (about $1,500 in 1850 — equal to many times that much today) of a slave and thereby rise in the social and economic scale.

There had once been a dream — in the South as in the North — that all men were created equal, that from the virgin wilderness of the New World a man might wrest a living on his own merits, that with the riches of an entire continent to exploit all men might live in comfort and economic security. But somehow this dream, especially in the South, had turned into a far different reality. Somehow all the best land was owned by a few families; somehow riches and even a modest security had eluded the great majority of Southerners. This must mean that all men were *not* created equal — that the rich man was created more industrious, more intelligent than the poor man. Such was the view of the South's greatest apologist, Senator John C. Calhoun, and of most Southern leaders. And if this were so, then the poor man had only himself to blame for his poverty in the "land of opportunity" and only himself to hate for it.

But self-hate, self-contempt, is the psychological foundation for hatred of others. And the most apparent and safest object of hate in the South was the Negro. When onto this foundation of externalized hatred carefully nurtured fears were piled—the fear that Negro freedom, by bringing about everything from extravagant competition in the labor market to intermarriage, would somehow reduce the poor Southern white to slavery himself—a strange phenomenon was created. The majority of poor Southerners were turned into the most violent advocates of the very system—slavery—which kept them poor. They became the most vociferous supporters of anti-Negro legislation, the most vicious enemies of Negro hopes.

The fact that the Southern aristocracy (for such it was in all but name) honestly believed in all the lies it dinned into its countrymen's ears about Negroes and about slavery does not mitigate the objective fact that its propaganda was aimed at creating a state of mind which would accept its economic exploitation of all the poorer people of the South, white as well as black. And if it seems strange that the poor people of the South could not recognize who their real enemies were, it would be well to remember that the same system of misdirection—of offering the Negro as a scapegoat for misery and a lightning rod for thwarted hopes and potential rebelliousness—is still in use today in the North as well as in the South.

While propaganda was relied upon to keep poor whites in line, the controls brought to bear on slaves were not simply those of overwork and the lash. There were legal and psychological controls also. One of the most favored was religion; but this was sometimes a two-edged weapon. Masters made sure that Sunday sermons included repetition of the idea that whites derived their right to rule over blacks from God. To question this right was to question the will of God and incur divine wrath. Catechisms for the instruction of slaves in the Christian religions often contained such passages as:

Q. Who gave you a master and a mistress?
A. God gave them to me.
Q. Who says that you must obey them?
A. God says that I must.

But Christianity had come into being as the religion of the slaves of the Roman Empire. Nearly two thousand years before the Cotton Kingdom it had been a revolutionary doctrine and its tenets had helped to overthrow the ancient empire. Slaves in Dixie were quick to identify themselves with the oppressed Hebrews of old. Nor were the Christian doctrines of equality before God, love of one's fellowmen, and the innate worth of each human soul lost upon black congregations.

Since no direct reference to the real hell-on-earth in which they lived was allowed in sermons or hymns, slaves used the language of religion as a disguise to voice their complaints and hopes. References to the "promised land" and the far side of the river Jordan meant to them the North, Canada—any place in which they might be free. Their Southern masters were equated with the ancient Egyptians who had held the Hebrews in bondage before Moses:

> *Go down, Moses,*
> *Way down in Egypt's land.*
> *Tell ole Pharaoh*
> *To let my people go.*

And in the hardly less obvious spiritual:

> *O Mary, don't you weep, don't you mourn,*
> *O Mary, don't you weep, don't you mourn;*
> *Pharaoh's army got drownded,*
> *O Mary, don't you mourn.*

The legal position of the Negro in the South varied in detail from state to state but was based everywhere on the assumption that he was property. Courts, even when they attempted to lighten the slave's burden, were clear about this. A Virginia judge stated in 1825: "Slaves are not only property, but they are also rational beings and entitled to the humanity of the court, when it can be exercised without invading the rights of property."

To enforce their laws, the Southern states maintained armed militias and adopted "slave codes" aimed at preventing organized opposition to white supremacy. There was, for example, no freedom of assembly—not more than four or five Negroes could meet together at one time except under white supervision. Firearms and weapons of any kind were strictly forbidden, of course. Slaves were not even allowed to beat drums or blow horns for fear they might use these instruments as a means of signaling. In the towns and cities there was a curfew for Negroes, usually 9 P.M.; and the local constables were required to enforce it. Negroes could not move from place to place, even on their masters' business, without valid passes; and woe to the Negro caught without one by a constable or by the slave patrols.

The slave patrols, organized like militias, were composed of armed and mounted whites who patrolled the roads and paths of the countryside to prevent Negro escapes and guard against slave uprisings. A Negro who fell into their hands without a pass was sure to be punished severely. He might be whipped or branded with a red-hot iron on his face; or if white nerves were taut, he might be lynched on the spot. It might be supposed that the slave codes and their armed enforcers, even if supposedly legal within the framework of state law, would certainly be considered unconstitutional and struck down by the Federal courts or by the United States Supreme Court. But such was not the case.

In July, 1847, a Negro resident of Missouri named Dred Scott brought suit in a Federal court for his freedom.

"Your petitioner, Dred Scott, a man of color, respectfully represents that sometime in the year 1835 your petitioner was purchased as a slave by one John Emerson, since deceased, who . . . conveyed your petitioner from the State of Missouri to Fort Snelling [Illinois], a fort then occupied by the troops of the United States and under the jurisdiction of the United States."

Dred Scott was claiming that since he had been transported into territory (Illinois) in which slavery was forbidden by Act of Congress as well as state law, he was now a free man. His case, which was seized upon as a "test case" by Northern abolitionists, took ten years to reach the Supreme Court. When that august body spoke, in early March, 1857, through the voice of its aged Chief Justice, Roger Taney, it denied Dred Scott's claim on three basic grounds: (1) Illinois laws could not affect his position as a slave in Missouri; (2) the Act of Congress that had declared territory north of 36°30′ latitude to be prohibited to slavery was itself unconstitutional; (3)—and this was the part of the decision that most outraged Negroes—"people of African descent are not and cannot be citizens of the United States, and cannot sue in any court of the United States. . . ."

The dark night of slavery seemed to close permanently over Southern Negroes with this decision. To Southern whites it was simply further confirmation of the righteousness of a centuries-old institution. But secure as the South's "peculiar institution" seemed to be to those who benefited from it, the struggle against slavery was equally old; and led primarily by Negroes themselves, South as well as North, slave as well as free, the fight for freedom steadily gained strength. As early as 1808 an anonymous Negro member of the African Society in Boston had written:

"Men have exercised authority over our nation as if we were their property, by depriving us of our freedom, as though they had a command from heaven thus to do. . . .

"Your petitioner, Dred Scott . . ."
(HISTORICAL PICTURES SERVICE — CHICAGO)

"Freedom is desirable; if not, would men sacrifice their time, their property, and finally lose their lives in the pursuit of it? . . . Yea, I say there is something so dreadful in slavery that some had rather die than experience it."

And many did die, while many more devoted long lives of incessant labor, thought, risk and pain to the cause of freedom. The story of the Negro's fight for emancipation against all but insuperable obstacles is a proud chapter in his history. If many Southern whites envisioned a world returned to feudalism and knightly chivalry, Negroes clung to a vision of freedom which burned as steadfastly in their minds as the North Star in the heavens. Both dreams could not exist in the same nation — and the one more firmly rooted in reality would sooner or later triumph.

4 The Freedom Road – I

*The Lord has not taught the Americans that we
will some day or other throw off their chains and
handcuffs, from our hands and feet, and their
devilish lashes (which some of them will have
enough of yet) from off our backs.*

— DAVID WALKER'S "Appeal" *(1829)*

BUT THE LORD HAD TAUGHT SOME AMERICANS. HE HAD IN-
structed the religious revivalist, Charles G. Finney, prompted
such men as Theodore Weld, James G. Birney, and the rich
New York merchants Arthur and Lewis Tappan, "shown the
light" to Angelina and Sarah Grimké (former slave owners
themselves), inspired intellectuals and poets such as John
Greenleaf Whittier and Ralph Waldo Emerson. In fact the
thunders of the Almighty himself seemed to echo in the words
of William Lloyd Garrison, who wrote in the first issue of his
new abolitionist newspaper *The Liberator*, on January 1, 1830:
"On this subject I do not wish to think, or speak, or write, with
moderation. . . . I will be as harsh as truth and as uncompro-
mising as justice. . . . I am in earnest – I will not equivocate –
I will not excuse – I will not retreat a single inch. AND I WILL
BE HEARD."

Since the earliest days of the Republic, the American conscience – especially the Northern conscience – had remained
uneasy over the compromise which had made slavery an unwritten article of the United States Constitution. The words
of the Declaration of Independence, the admonitions of Washington, Franklin, Jefferson, Adams, and others of the Founding
Fathers, had continued to echo, however faintly, in the minds
of many. Irritation against slavery continued to grow, too, because of the disproportionate number of representatives
Southern states were allowed to send to the House of Representatives, based on the "three-fifths clause" of the Constitution. But by far the most important grounds for opposition to

Masthead of William Lloyd Garrison's abolitionist newspaper
(HISTORICAL PICTURES SERVICE — CHICAGO)

slavery lay in the vexing question of who should control the new West.

Northern capitalists, merchants, and industrialists viewed the West as a great storehouse of raw materials and a potential area for profitable expansion of the growing manufactury of New England and the East. They dreamed of transcontinental railroads, of mines and mills pouring forth endless wealth. To the common people of the North, the West was where a man could go when he could find no work back East, a place for homesteaders and small, independent farmers, a safety valve to the brutal beginnings of the Industrial Revolution. Southerners, on the other hand, saw in the West a huge and fertile region for the spread of the profitable cotton plantation system. Western lands, tilled by slaves, would form a great new bastion for the aristocratic society of which they dreamed.

Since free Northern farmers and slave-manned plantations could not coexist within the same immediate economic area, a clash between two visions of the future became inevitable. Every time a new state was admitted to the Union a bitter fight developed over whether it would be admitted slave or free. Despite the ingenious compromises worked out by such men as Daniel Webster and Henry Clay to keep the political power of Southern and Northern states in balance (for example, when Missouri was admitted as a slave state in 1821, Maine was

admitted as a free state), each new crisis revealed greater bitterness and a deeper chasm between the two sections. Basically the struggle was between those in the North who wished to build a capitalist-industrial society and those in the South who intended at all costs to preserve a semifeudal, agricultural society. The battle flared for half a century on every issue from tariffs to foreign policy, but its central theme remained slavery. It was against this background of economic and political warfare that the struggle for abolition took place.

Despite the fact that the most famous abolitionists, from William Garrison to John Brown, were whites, the movement was overwhelmingly based on the agitation, leadership, and sacrifice of Negroes themselves. Without the many slave uprisings in the South, the constant stream of runaway slaves to the North, the incessant preachings of the free Negro churches, the hundreds of organized Negro petitions to Congress, the incisive writings of Negro intellectuals such as Benjamin Banneker and Frederick Douglass, the demonstrations in Northern cities, the arousing of liberal opinion throughout Europe—all of which was accomplished by Negroes—there would have been no abolitionist movement. Emancipation was not a gift to the Negro when it came—it was something for which he had struggled for many decades.

The most direct means of protesting slavery was to rebel

against it. And despite the laws, militias, slave patrols, and gallows of the Southern states, more than four hundred slave uprisings took place between 1750 and 1850. Most of them were of minor importance, involving a handful of slaves maddened by harsh treatment who would rise up, burn the plantation houses, and murder their masters' families. Such slave rebellions were terribly feared by Southern whites. Having reduced their Negroes to a state of brutishness and desperation, they feared the wild, blind fury of rebellious slaves—a fury which would not, indeed could not, distinguish between "good" and "bad" whites or among men, women, and children as it vented itself. And since Negro slaves far outnumbered whites in many Southern districts, the whites feared, above all, a conspiracy which might lead to a wholesale uprising. One such conspiracy, of truly formidable proportions, was uncovered in the year 1800. Our knowledge of its details comes only from the court records of interrogations of captured slave subordinates in the conspiracy—its leader refused to testify.

During the summer of 1800, a twenty-four-year-old Negro slave named Gabriel, the property of Thomas Henry Prosser of Henrico County, Virginia, began sending word throughout the plantations that the time had come for slaves to strike for their freedom. Gabriel, a tall and powerful man (he stood six feet two inches) appointed himself general of the projected uprising. His plan was simple and direct—and not without merit. On an appointed day (August 30th) all the slaves in Henrico County were to rise up simultaneously, murder their masters and any other whites who crossed their paths, and then march on Richmond. There they would offer the whites a chance to surrender; but if they refused, then all would be put to death except Quakers, Methodists, and Frenchmen—and even if they did surrender, the slaves would "at least cut off one of their arms." Once in command of Richmond (and the state treasury and arsenal), Gabriel felt confident of being able to defend himself against all comers.

Gabriel's resources for all this consisted of exactly twelve shillings (which he gave to his recruiting agents), twelve dozen handmade swords (the blades were made by a slave named Solomon, the handles whittled by Gabriel himself), about one peck of bullets (hand-cast by Gabriel), and ten pounds of gunpowder. Until they could seize their masters' weapons, the slaves were to fight with scythes, axes, shovels—anything that came to hand.

Gabriel's agents diligently spread the word from plantation to plantation all during the summer of 1800. So effective was their work that by August more than ten thousand slaves had agreed to join the uprising, one thousand of them in Richmond itself. And so secretly did the conspiracy spread that no hint of it reached the whites—until the day set for the rising, when a Negro informer betrayed his comrades. The whites moved swiftly to round up the leaders of the conspiracy, and they were helped by the fact that a tremendous storm and floods on August 30th made it all but impossible for the slaves to gather. Gabriel himself was captured, along with thirty-five of his lieutenants. All were speedily tried and hanged during September and October.

One of the largest slave conspiracies in American history was organized in 1822 by Free Negro Denmark Vesey of Charleston, South Carolina. He enlisted slaves not only from Charleston, but as far distant as eighty miles. Many thousands were involved, but exactly how many and their precise plans were never determined, since the leaders of the conspiracy died with sealed lips. Once again, a Negro informer betrayed the conspiracy, on May 30, 1822. Shortly thereafter 131 Negroes and four whites were arrested. The whites, convicted of sympathizing with the Negro rebels, were fined and jailed; of the Negroes, thirty-seven, including Denmark Vesey, were hanged, while various other punishments were meted out to the rest. The informer in the case, a "favorite and confidential slave" named Peter, property of Colonel J. C. Prioleau, was rewarded by the state of South Carolina with a pension of $50 a year, which was raised to $200 a year in 1857.

Of all the slave revolts in the old South, none equaled in consequence the rebellion led by Nat Turner. Nat, a slave owned by Joseph Travis of Southampton County, Virginia, was a preacher and something of a religious fanatic. Having read deeply in the Old Testament, he believed he had been chosen by God to lead his people out of bondage, just as Moses had led the Hebrew children out of Egypt. Since he felt himself divinely elected, Nat Turner did not bother to enlist a large force—he simply prayed and awaited a sign from Heaven. The sign came in February, 1831, when a total eclipse of the sun took place. Knowing the time had come to strike, but still uncertain as to his means, Nat conceived and rejected various plans and procrastinated for six months. But finally, on August 20, 1831, Nat led a party of eight slaves in murdering his master and his family—the beginning of his crusade. Seizing weapons when possible, the small group pushed its way through the countryside, proclaiming Judgment Day and gathering slave recruits as it went until the party numbered seventy. In a statement made before his death, Nat Turner himself described what followed:

"I took my station in the rear [of the slaves], and, as it was my object to carry terror and devastation wherever we went, I placed fifteen or twenty of the best-armed and most to be relied on in front, who generally approached the [plantation] houses as fast as their horses could run. This was for two purposes — to prevent their [the whites] escape, and strike terror to the inhabitants. . . . I sometimes got in sight to see the work of death completed; viewed the mangled bodies as they lay, in silent satisfaction, and immediately started in quest of other victims. . . .

"The white men pursued and fired on us several times. Hark [one of Nat's lieutenants] had his horse shot under him . . . five or six of my men were wounded, but none left the field."

The white plantation masters in their path were taken by surprise; nearly sixty of them were killed. But by now the entire countryside was aroused. The whites hastily gathered together in volunteer companies and called out the state militia. They cut the roads ahead of Turner's band and then began sweeping the fields with cavalry patrols and bloodhounds. Turner's party dispersed, his men were captured one by one, and Nat himself abandoned hope:

". . . after having supplied myself with provisions . . . I scratched a hole under a pile of fence-rails in a field, where I concealed myself for six weeks, never leaving my hiding place but for a few minutes in the dead of night."

But an overinquisitive dog betrayed Nat's hideout:

"I immediately left my hiding place, and was pursued almost incessantly, until I was taken, a fortnight later, by Mr. Benjamin Phipps, in a little hole I had dug with my sword."

Nat was sentenced to be hanged on November 11, 1831:

". . . I am here loaded with chains, and willing to suffer the fate that awaits me."

Nat Turner's rebellion cost the lives of nearly one hundred slaves, of whom only nineteen received a trial before execution. Newspapers from every part of the nation reported the affair and Nat's confession. Disgust at the entire institution of slavery was reinforced throughout the North, while widespread fear of further uprisings swept through the South, amounting at times to mass hysteria. Repressive laws were strengthened throughout the Southern states; Negro slaves were arrested, questioned, and lynched on the slightest hint of conspiracy; and it became impossible for moderate Southerners to criticize slavery itself without seeming to sanction such tragedies as had occurred in Southampton County.

While rebellion seemed hopeless to the majority of slaves, there was another means of gaining freedom which worked for

An imaginary (and none too sympathetic) illustration of Nat Turner preaching to his followers in a Virginia swamp   (CULVER PICTURES, INC.)

thousands—flight. If a slave could reach the Northern states and was not betrayed or seized by local law officers, he was free. If he could reach Mexico or Canada, he was completely secure. But the flight was dangerous—if caught, a runaway slave could expect the lash and the auction block as the least of his punishments. Only the most compelling necessity could drive a slave to leave his familiar surroundings, often his loved ones, and strike out on a dangerous journey to an unknown destination. Henry Bibb, an escaped slave, in replying to a letter he had received from his former master, W. H. Gatewood of Bedford, Kentucky, wrote:

"You may perhaps think hard of us for running away from slavery, but as to myself, I have but one apology to make for it, which is this; I have only to regret that I did not start at an earlier period. . . .

"To be compelled to stand by and see you whip and slash my wife without mercy, when I could afford her no protection, not even by offering myself to suffer the lash in her place, was more than I felt it to be the duty of a slave husband to endure, while the way was opened to Canada. My infant child was also frequently flogged by Mrs. Gatewood, for crying, until its skin was bruised literally purple."

Many slaves made their way north with the aid of passes and "free papers" which they had forged. But most, with nothing but the North Star to guide them, took to the woods. They would travel by night and hide out in caves or holes during the day, taking the most unlikely routes — preferably through swamps. They survived on nuts and berries and an occasional stolen chicken. If they lived near a river, they might pole their way north in canoes or skiffs; if they lived on the coast, they might stow away on a northbound boat, posing as servants as they went up the gangplank. One of the most original escapes was that carried out by slaves William and Ellen Craft of Macon, Georgia.

In January, 1849, William, a cabinetmaker who had saved his meager earnings for years, bought a man's suit for his wife, Ellen. Since Ellen was very light-skinned, she was to play the part of a slave-owning planter, with William as her personal servant. Pretending to be hard of hearing so that no one could converse with her, Ellen also wore bandages on her arm so that she would not be asked to sign a steamboat or hotel register (she was unable to read or write). In this disguise the slave couple traveled first class all the way. Ellen, the rich but ailing planter going North for medical treatment, William the faithful slave seeing to his "master's" every need. They put up at the best hotels, and carried themselves with an irreproachable air of genteel swagger. When they arrived at Philadelphia, they

The marvelous resurrection of Henry Brown
(PICTURE COLLECTION, NEW YORK PUBLIC LIBRARY)

Fugitive slaves arriving by ship from Norfolk, Virginia, find safety and a helping hand in Philadelphia. (HISTORICAL PICTURES SERVICE—CHICAGO)

were taken care of by one William Wells Brown, a Negro abolitionist, who accompanied them to Boston.

Slave Henry Brown of Richmond, Virginia, devised a somewhat more rigorous means of escape. He ordered a specially designed box to be made; it was two feet wide and three feet long, and contained ingenious receptacles for food and water. Carefully marking one end of the box "THIS SIDE UP" Brown climbed in, had the lid sealed, and was shipped north via Adams Express Company. The trip lasted twenty-six hours from Richmond to Philadelphia. There, four men anxiously awaited the arrival of the crate. One of them, William Still, reported that when they had pried off the lid, "the marvelous resurrection of Brown ensued. Rising up in his box, he reached out his hand, saying, 'How do you do, gentlemen?'"

Since the road north was beset by perils, most runaway slaves needed outside help. From a small beginning during the 1820's a system of receiving, concealing, and forwarding escaped slaves grew to large proportions. It was known as the Underground Railroad, and between 1830 and 1860 it helped no less than seventy-five thousand slaves to find freedom. Manned by Negroes and white abolitionists, the Underground Railroad had established routes and way stations in every Southern state and in most Northern states as well.

The first contact with potential runaways was made by a white "field agent" who traveled through the plantations posing as a peddler, or a surveyor, or perhaps a census taker. When any slave showed his willingness to escape, the field agent

would put him in the hands of a "conductor," generally a free
Negro, who took the escapee to the first way station. There the
runaway was fed, rested, and often given a disguise. Traveling
was done at night—the way stations being about twelve hours
journey apart. During the day the runaway was hidden in a
barn or basement or nearby cave. In nightly stages the journey
was accomplished until the slave reached Ohio or Connecticut
or any other of the strongly abolitionist states, where he was
sure of food, lodging, and transportation to Canada, if he
wished.

Underground Railroad "conductors" in the South faced
harsh treatment if they were caught. Calvin Fairbanks, one
such "conductor," spent a total of seventeen years at hard
labor for his activities.

The most famous of all Underground Railroad operators was
undoubtedly Harriet Tubman. A small and frail lady of tremendous courage, she was born a slave in Dorchester County,
Maryland, around 1823. Her maiden name was Araminta Ross,
but she married slave John Tubman and ran away when she
was still quite young. Harriet returned to the slave states
nineteen times as a "conductor" on the Underground Railroad and conveyed more than three hundred slaves to freedom
in the North. She would organize her slave followers into small
groups and warn them that if any of them attempted to turn
back or lost his nerve, he would be put to death immediately.
But this threat was never put to the test. Harriet seemed to
lead a charmed life. She was never caught during her Underground Railroad days, nor was she caught when she acted as a
Northern spy in the South during the Civil War.

The Southern response to the serious drain on "property"
represented by individual runaways and the operations of the
Underground Railroad was to press in Congress for the strict
application of the fugitive slave laws. The right of a master in
one state to reclaim his "property" in another had been written
into the Constitution. It was part of the compromise whereby
certain Southern states were appeased in their objections to
joining a Federal union. But increasingly, Northern states were
refusing to apply fugitive slave laws, refusing to punish their
citizens who aided runaways, refusing to extradite escapees. In
1850, Southerners in Congress forced through a new and
stricter Fugitive Slave Law. It was a part of the compromise of
that year whereby California was admitted to the Union as a free
state and New Mexico and Utah territories were organized on
the principle of popular sovereignty—that is, the question
of slavery would be left to the inhabitants. The Southerners
had thus paid much for their Fugitive Slave Law, and they ex-

Harriet Tubman (SCHOMBURG COLLECTION, NEW YORK PUBLIC LIBRARY)

pected much from it. They were to be sorely disappointed.

When Ralph Waldo Emerson heard of the new Fugitive Slave Law he announced, "I will not obey it, by God!" And he voiced the sentiments of an increasing number of people in the North. Northern states responded to the law by passing "personal liberty" laws of their own which threw a protective net of legal restrictions around Negroes living within their borders. Some Northern legislatures simply declared the Fugitive Slave Law "null and void," thereby legally placing themselves in rebellion against the Federal government.

In 1854, Anthony Burns, a fugitive slave, was apprehended by Southern agents in Boston, and local authorities were forced to imprison Burns while he awaited shipment back to Virginia. But a large mob of Bostonians, inflamed by the oratory of abolitionists Theodore Parker and Wendell Phillips, attacked the jail where Burns was put in an attempt to rescue him. The attempt failed, but it took a formidable display of military strength—infantry, marines, and artillery—to get Burns from the jail to the ship which was to carry him back to slavery. Fifty thousand enraged citizens lined the streets through which Burns was led, cursing the soldiers and screaming, "Kidnapers! Kidnapers!" Buildings were hung in black crepe, and the churches of Boston tolled their bells in mourning.

In the face of Northern resistance to reclaiming slaves, Southerners had resorted for many years to simple kidnaping. Rewards were generally posted for runaway slaves; and slave catchers, a class of ruffians among whom many criminals were to be found, made little distinction between escaped slaves and legally free Negroes. The tragic case of John Read is illustrative of their methods.

On December 14, 1820, two white men named Griffith and Shipley tried to force their way into Read's house in Kennett Township, Pennsylvania. Read was a Negro who had arrived in Pennsylvania from Maryland about three years previously. He claimed to be free, but went in constant fear of slave agents. He had married in Pennsylvania and had one child and supported himself as a neighborhood handyman. According to the court records:

"On the night of the 14th of December, 1820, his [Read's] wife was from home. . . . About midnight he thought he heard persons walking around the house, one at length rapped smartly on the door. He asked what was wanted; the person answered they had a search warrant for stolen goods. Read told them to go away; he believed them to be kidnappers, and if they were not, he had no stolen goods, and if they would wait until morning they might search the house. Soon after they began to force the door. He rolled a barrel of cider against it and told them if they attempted to come in he would kill them. They pried the door off the hinges, and it fell over the cider barrel; at the instant he heard the click of a pistol, and called out, 'It is life for life!' One of the persons said, 'Rush on, Shipley; damn the Negro, he won't shoot.' A person attempted to enter, he shot him; another attempted to come in, he struck him with a club."

On the bodies of Griffith and Shipley were found handcuffs, pistols, a rope, and a whip. There was no question as to their intent. Read, who made no effort to escape prosecution, was sentenced to nine years in jail for manslaughter.

But the kidnapers were often successful. An article which appeared in the *New York Sun* reported the kidnaping of a free Negro on July 23, 1836:

"On Saturday, 23rd instant, about 12 o'clock, Mr. George Jones, a respectable free colored man, was arrested at 21 Broadway, by certain police officers, upon the pretext of having committed 'assault and battery.' Mr. Jones, being conscious that no such charge could be sustained against him, refused to go with the officers. His employers, placing high confidence in his integrity, advised him to go and answer to the charges. . . .

"Between the hours of 1 and 2 o'clock, Mr. Jones was carried before the Hon. Richard Riker, Recorder of the City of New York. In the absence of his friends, and in the presence of several notorious kidnappers, who . . . by oath sustained that he was a runaway slave, poor Jones . . . was by the Recorder pronounced to be a slave!

"In less than three hours after his arrest, he was bound in chains, dragged through the streets like a beast to the shambles!"

Negro abolitionist William Wells Brown reported from Georgetown, Ohio, on September 27, 1844:

"I learned that about ten o'clock at night, five or six men went to the house of a colored man by the name of John Wilkinson, broke open the door, knocked down the man and his wife, and beat them severely, and seized their boy, aged fourteen years, and carried him off into slavery. After the father of the boy had recovered himself, he raised the alarm and with the aid of some of the neighbors, put out in pursuit of the kidnappers, and followed them to the river; but they were too late. The villains had crossed the river, and passed into Virginia."

Against these acts of lawlessness, Negroes could not afford to depend entirely on the assistance of sympathetic whites or on corruptible local police officials. In several instances they formed Negro Vigilance committees, whose members were bound to guard themselves and other Negroes against kidnapers.

Between the time when Mr. George Jones could be led through the streets of New York by his kidnapers, "bound in chains," and the day when fifty thousand people tried to free Anthony Burns on the streets of Boston, a tremendous change had come about in Northern public opinion. And largely responsible for this shift in sentiment were the untiring labors of several generations of free Negroes.

5 The Freedom Road – II

Then, come, dear brethren,
If we would be free,
We must demand our liberty,
And strike the blow with all our might,
For Liberty is the Balm of Life.

—MINUTES OF THE STATE CONVENTION OF THE
COLORED CITIZENS OF THE STATE OF
MICHIGAN (1843)

THE SOUTH HAD ALWAYS RECOGNIZED THE THREAT TO ITS
institutions of the free Negro. By 1860 there were no less
than 250,787 free Negroes to be found in the Southern states
(the slave population amounted to about three million); and
their lives were as hedged about with laws, restrictions, and
codes as if they were an army of potential saboteurs, which, of
course, they were. Aside from helping the activities of the
Underground Railroad, leading (as had Denmark Vesey) slave
uprisings, purchasing freedom for friends and relatives when
they could, and maintaining a subdued but constant agitation
for equality, their very existence—a constant reminder to
slaves that Negroes could be free—was an implicit act of
sabotage in Southern society.

The primary means of controlling free Negroes in the South
were the laws maintained by every Southern state against the
immigration of non-slave Negroes. Maryland's statutes were
typical. Any free Negro entering the state would be fined $20
for the first offense, $500 for the second; and if he could not pay
these fines he would be auctioned off and sold to the highest
bidder as a slave.

Free Negroes had to observe the same curfew laws as slaves
and, like slaves, they could not vote, own firearms without a
special permit, assemble in groups of more than three or four
(except in church), testify in court against a white person (except in Louisiana), or even buy a drink in most areas without

the recommendation of some white. Worst of all, the burden of proving that he was, in fact, free rested entirely upon the Negro.

To prove that he was not a slave, a free Negro had to carry around with him a certificate of freedom. These so-called "free papers" were documents that were numbered, registered, and issued by local courts. They had to be renewed from time to time for a set fee. Except in Virginia, a free Negro who lost his "papers" had no recourse at law — he was considered a fugitive slave and sold at auction. The Virginia Supreme Court of Appeals held that "In the case of a person visibly appearing to be a Negro, the presumption is that he is a slave . . . the plaintiff in a suit for freedom must make out his title against all the world."

The free Negro class had come into being in a variety of ways. First of all, there were the descendants of those Negroes who had served out their terms as indentured servants before their entire race had been reduced to slavery. There were also, as we have seen, the thousands who ran away. Many had won freedom by serving in the army or navy during the Revolutionary War. A large part of the free Negro population was composed of slaves (and their descendants) who had been set free by liberal masters. But in these cases it was often because the master was also the father of the slave — in 1850, for example, the percentage of mulattoes among free Negroes was more than fifty percent. Finally, many Negroes had purchased their own freedom and the freedom of relatives or friends.

Buying freedom for oneself or another represented years and years of hard work for scant pay and untold self-denial. And except for a handful, only those Negroes living in cities or towns had any chance of earning any kind of wage at all. And of these there were but few whose masters did not simply seize all their pay. Free Negroes living in the North sometimes raised the money to purchase freedom for loved ones through public appeals, as the following advertisement (from the December 16, 1836, issue of Garrison's *Liberator*) shows:

"George Potter and Rosella, his wife, would take this opportunity to express their gratitude to God, and under him, to the benevolent individuals who generously contributed in aiding them to redeem their two children from Slavery. They have the unspeakable happiness of informing the generous donors that, on the 12th inst. they received their children, aged eleven and seven years, raised from the degradation of Slavery to the rank of Freemen."

In spite of the restrictions and oppressions which surrounded them, there were some free Negroes in the South who managed to become wealthy. The free Negro throughout the South was allowed to make contracts and to own property. And since the

tide of white immigration from Europe flooded into the Northern rather than the Southern states (because immigrants did not
care to compete with slave labor), there was a chronic shortage
of skilled labor in Southern areas which an ambitious free
Negro could exploit. In Southern cities much of the mechanical
work was done by free Negroes, and free Negro proprietors of
hotels and restaurants flourished. In Charleston, South Carolina, for example, free Negro hotel owner Jehu Jones owned
property valued at $40,000. The richest Negro in the pre-Civil-
War South was Thomy Lafon of New Orleans, who owned
$500,000 worth of real estate. Among them, New Orleans'
eighteen thousand free Negroes owned more than $15,000,000
worth of taxable property. How Southern apologists squared
these facts with their incessant propaganda about the Negro's
inability to take care of himself as a free man was a curious feat
of mental gymnastics.

Strictly speaking there were no free Negroes in the North,
since, after 1830, there were no slaves there; there were simply
Negroes—about 250,000 of them. But although their lot was
easier than that of their Southern brethren it was far from
paradise. Northerners clung to the theory of white supremacy
almost as tenaciously as Southerners, and the Negro among
them was regarded as an inferior and a threat to the general
welfare. Only in Maine, Massachusetts, New Hampshire, and
Vermont could a Negro vote, and in New York, if he owned
$250 worth of real estate. In California, Illinois, Indiana, Iowa,
and Ohio a Negro could not testify against a white in court, and
everywhere except Massachusetts he was debarred from jury
duty. Some states attempted to prevent Negroes from immigrat-
ing. Ohio required a Negro entering its borders to post a
bond of $500 for his good conduct; in Illinois the bond was set
at $1,000. Indiana and Oregon simply forbade new Negro im-
migrants to enter their territories at all.

Economically, the Negro in the North was not vastly better
off than the free Negro in the South. Craftsmen's guilds and
trade unions were unwilling to take Negro members; and in
such unskilled work as portering, waiting on tables, ditch-dig-
ging, and house service, the Negro faced stiff competition from
the millions of European immigrants who flocked to the North
between 1830 and 1860. There were, of course, a few Negroes
who became rich. Cincinnati Negroes owned $500,000 worth
of property in 1852, while in Rush County, Indiana, there were
forty-six Negro farmers who owned three thousand acres of
good land among them. However, the large majority of Negroes
in the North lived in abysmal poverty.

Nevertheless, the Negro in the North enjoyed freedom—

and he was able to organize, protest, and agitate to improve his lot. He could speak through petitions and resolutions and his own newspapers. He could continue to irritate the white conscience and, above all, he was free to give meaning, support, and leadership to the abolitionist movement. While slaves rebelled in the South or fled in the thousands, the Northern Negro waged a ceaseless campaign for freedom and equality — and it was this untiring struggle which eventually brought emancipation.

The Negro agitation against slavery in America went back to pre-Revolutionary days. As early as 1661 Anthony Pieterson successfully petitioned the Governor of Nieuw Amsterdam for recognition as a free man; and individual and group petitions for freedom multiplied during the Revolutionary War. In 1780, seven Dartmouth, Massachusetts, Negroes sent a protest to the colonial legislature pointing out that while Massachusetts Colony was in a state of rebellion against George III, partly because of parliamentary policies of "taxation without representation," Massachusetts Negroes were taxed and yet could not vote. By 1783 Massachusetts courts had granted the vote to all Negroes who paid taxes. In 1787 the Negroes of Boston complained that although they paid taxes, their children were denied the right to attend the city's public schools. But this complaint went unheeded.

One of the most influential voices for Negro freedom in eighteenth century America was that of Benjamin Banneker. A free Negro born in Maryland in 1731, Banneker was a mathematician and scientist of international repute; his yearly *Almanacs* were highly prized throughout America in the 1790's and he was one of the team of three men which was appointed by Congress to survey and plan the site for the city of Washington, D.C. In 1791 Banneker sent one of his *Almanacs* to Thomas Jefferson and took the occasion to remind Jefferson of some of his oft-proclaimed observations regarding slavery:

"Sir, suffer me to recall to your mind that time, in which the arms and tyranny of the British crown were exerted, with every powerful effort, in order to reduce you to a state of servitude: look back, I entreat you, on the variety of dangers to which you were exposed. . . .

"This, Sir, was a time when you clearly saw the injustice of a state of slavery, and in which you had just apprehensions of the horror of its condition. It was now . . . that you publicly held forth . . . 'We hold these truths to be self-evident, that all men are created equal.'"

Although Jefferson's conscience hardly needed pricking on the subject of slavery, Banneker clearly saw that no white

conscience could be allowed a moment's respite. Until the end
of his life (in 1806) the Negro scientist kept up a constant flow
of correspondence on the subject with his influential white
friends. Negro petitions to Congress against slavery, the fugitive slave laws, and various restrictive state laws started to
appear almost as soon as that body first convened. Although
most of these petitions were simply resealed and returned to
their senders as unacceptable, they did, on occasion, bring
about debate in the House of Representatives. A petition from
the free Negroes of Philadelphia in 1800, for example, was rejected by the House as having "a tendency to create disquiet
and jealousy," but only after a heated debate; and every such
debate emphasized the widening gap between representatives
from the slave states and those from the free. Over the next
fifty years Negro petitions to Congress grew to flood proportions and continued, as they were designed to do, to excite
ever-greater "disquiet and jealousy."

To carry on the fight for freedom, Negroes formed many
mutual aid societies. The earliest of these was the Masonic
order—founded in 1787 in Boston by Prince Hall, a free Negro
from Barbados. Since the American Masonic lodges would not
accept Negro members, a charter was obtained from the
Masonic Grand Lodge in England. Likewise the Negro branch
of the Grand United Order of Odd Fellows was formed through
a charter granted by the English branch in 1843, after the
American Odd Fellows had excluded Negroes. By far the most
famous and effective of the Negro societies was the Free African Society of Philadelphia, founded in 1787. Its purpose was
not only to agitate for freedom, but, like most Negro societies,
to educate its own members. When the great yellow fever
epidemic of 1793 swept through Philadelphia, carrying off untold thousands of people, the Free African Society, under its
leaders, Richard Allen and Absolom Jones (both former slaves),
supplied nurses to aid Dr. Benjamin Rush in his all-but-hope-
less fight against the pestilence. Free African Society members
worked around the clock for weeks, visiting plague-stricken
homes by day and carting away and burying the dead by night.
Their sacrifices were not forgotten by some, at least, of the
white citizens of Philadelphia, which later became one of the
strongholds of abolitionism.

At a very early date, the Negro in America reached a basic
decision: he would remain in America. Ever since the institution of slavery in the South (and its attendant problem of Negro
second-class citizenship in the North) had exercised the consciences of the delegates to the Constitutional Convention,
certain "humanitarians" had thought to solve the problem and

salve their consciences by simply shipping the Negro back to Africa. What an American bred and born Negro was to do on the fever-ridden coasts of an utterly foreign continent, except perish, remained an unanswered question. The American Colonization Society, composed of prominent "humanitarians," had been formed in 1817. Enlisting the aid of Congress (which appropriated $100,000 for the society) and of President James Monroe, the society founded the colony of Liberia in 1822, on the old Grain Coast in Africa. Unfortunately for the aims of the society, however, American Negroes did not share its enthusiasm for a return to semibarbarism. By 1852, less than eight thousand Negroes had gone to Liberia; and of these thirty-six hundred were slaves who could only gain their freedom by promising to emigrate, while another thousand were Africans taken from captured slave ships. A major reason why free Negroes would not emigrate was their realization that the colonization scheme was a means whereby slavery as an institution could be made secure through the deportation of the troublesome free Negro. But basically their attitude was summed up by Negro leader Robert Purvis: "A few may go," he wrote, "but the colored people as a mass will not leave the land of their birth."

All during the decades preceding the Civil War Negro societies proliferated throughout the North. In every city, and in almost every town there were branches of antislavery societies, abolitionist societies, mutual aid societies and vigilance committees. These groups agitated for Negro freedom through resolutions, petitions to Congress and to state legislatures, the subscription of money for fugitive slaves, the enlisting of agents for the Underground Railroad, and the mass support of the white abolitionist movement. In 1831 representatives of such groups met at the first annual Negro Convention, held in Philadelphia, June 6–11. The convention passed various resolutions, especially regarding the establishment of schools for Negro children throughout the North. National conventions were held annually in various cities from 1831 to 1837, and somewhat erratically thereafter, at Buffalo in 1843, Troy in 1847, Cleveland in 1848, and Rochester in 1853. At this last convention a resolution was adopted which eloquently and simply summed up Negro aims: "We ask that in our native land we shall not be treated as strangers, and worse than strangers."

Of the many Negro organizations, however, none had greater influence than the various Negro churches. Negroes had been accepted as members by most white churches—the Methodist, Anglican, Catholic, and Presbyterian—since

Revolutionary and pre-Revolutionary days. But Negro churchgoers had to worship from special "colored pews" in the rear of the church, could not become church officials and, in those churches which celebrated communion, had to wait for their wine and wafers until after the whites had been served. It was an anti-Negro incident in one of Philadelphia's churches that sparked the drive for an independent Negro church.

One wintry morning in the year 1787, Richard Allen and Absolom Jones (who a few months earlier had founded the Free African Society) were kneeling in prayer in Philadelphia's St. George's Methodist Episcopal Church. A church trustee came upon them, pulled Jones up by the arm, and brusquely informed the two Negroes that they would have to do their praying from the rear of the church. When the Negroes asked to at least be permitted to finish their prayers, the trustee refused. Allen and Jones walked out of St. George's, never to return. Instead they set about founding their own churches—Jones organizing the St. Thomas Protestant Episcopal Church in 1794, and Allen founding the Bethel African Methodist Episcopal Church in that same year.

Negro churches quickly arose throughout the country and were as sect-ridden and suspicious of each other's religious doctrines as were the white churches. In 1816 the Negro Methodist Churches organized an entirely separate branch of Methodism to be known as the African Methodist Episcopal Church, its first bishop being Richard Allen. New York Negroes formed their own African Methodist Episcopal Zion Church, which kept aloof from Allen's organization. Other Negroes, opposed to any kind of Methodism, under the leadership of the Reverend Thomas Paul, established separate Negro Baptist churches in various Northern cities between 1805 and 1810.

The independent Negro churches performed many tasks in the Negro community. They were educational institutions where Negro children could be taught to read and write, they served as meeting places for various Negro societies, they gave great financial and moral support to the abolitionist crusade, and more than a few of them served as stations on the Underground Railroad. Furthermore, the Negro church, as a place where Negroes could express themselves freely, served as a training ground for Negro leaders in all walks of life. It also trained and then supported those Negroes who fought for freedom through the Negro press. The first Negro newspaper was founded in 1827, three years before William Lloyd Garrison's *Liberator* began publication with the great abolitionist's *"I will be heard"* statement. Its aims were expressed in its title,

Freedom Journal, and its editorial policies were violently abolitionist. Thereafter, despite financial handicaps, Negro newspapers appeared in almost every city or town that boasted a Negro population large enough to support them. Their abolitionist sentiments were revealed in some of their titles, *The Rights of All, Mirror of Liberty, Herald of Freedom.*

From its beginnings, the Negro abolitionist movement understood that American militarism and imperialism abroad were important and dangerous enemies of Negro aspirations. When the United States fell upon the hapless Mexicans in 1848 (to the disgust of such white Americans as Abraham Lincoln, Henry Thoreau, and James Russell Lowell), American Negroes were vociferous in their denunciations of what they considered an unjust war fomented by the very apostles of slavery who were their bitterest foes. Frederick Douglass, writing in his newspaper, *North Star*, on March 17, 1848 (one week after peace had been concluded with Mexico), expressed the common attitude of Negroes:

"In our judgement, those who have all along been loudly in favor of a vigorous prosecution of the war, and heralding its bloody triumphs with apparent rapture, and glorifying the atrocious deeds of barbarous heroism on the part of wicked men engaged in it, have no sincere love of peace, and are not now rejoicing over *peace*, but *plunder*. They have succeeded in robbing Mexico of the most important and valuable part of her territory . . . we are not the people to rejoice, we ought rather to blush and hang our heads for shame."

The Negro abolitionist movement also understood from the first the importance of foreign — especially English support. Negro apostles of freedom were many in the British Isles during the pre-Civil-War decades. Their activities and how they fared generally were reflected in the report sent home by Reverent Nathaniel Paul, a Negro abolitionist and friend of William Lloyd Garrison, who arrived in England in 1832 with the intention of raising funds for the abolitionist crusade. On April 10, 1833, Reverend Paul wrote to Garrison:

"I have been engaged, for several months past, in traveling through the country and delivering lectures upon the system of slavery as it exists in the United States, the condition of the free people of color in that country. . . . My lectures have been numerously attended by two to three thousand people, the Halls and Chapels have been overflown, and hundreds have not been able to gain admittance. I have not failed to give Uncle Sam due credit for his 2,000,000 slaves; nor to expose the cruel prejudices of the Americans to our colored race. . . . And is this, they say, republican liberty? God deliver us from it.

Frederick Douglass

"And now, to contrast the difference in the treatment that a colored man receives in this country, with that which he receives in America. . . . Here, if I go to church, I am not pointed to the 'Negro' seat in the gallery; but any gentleman opens his pew door for my reception. If I wish for a passage in a stage, the only question that is asked me is, 'Which do you choose, sir, an inside or an outside seat?' If I stop at a public inn, no one would think of setting a separate table for me; I am conducted to the same table with other gentlemen."

England had abolished slavery in 1772, the slave trade in 1806, but it was not until 1820, as a part of the Missouri Compromise, whereby that state entered the Union as a slave state, that the American Congress had passed a law defining slave trading as piracy, punishable by death. But neither the Northern merchants and shipowners who made such tremendous profits through the trade nor the Southern slave dealers who received the black cargoes were disposed to take this law seriously. Enforcement was all but nonexistent. The United States Navy was much too small to capture more than a handful of the thousands of American slavers who put to sea, and when a slave ship was by chance seized, the courts were not disposed to interpret the law strictly. No American slaver was hanged for his crime in the United States until after the beginning of the Civil War. The greatest obstacle to the suppression of the slave trade was the fact that successive American governments, jeal-

ous of the rights of "freedom of the seas" for which the United
States had fought England in 1812, absolutely refused to co-
operate with the Royal Navy in its efforts to stamp out the
trade. Any ship which could produce papers identifying her as
an American vessel was secure from British men-of-war. Between 1820 and 1860 hundreds of thousands of "contraband"
Negroes were sped across the Atlantic in swift American clip-
per ships and smuggled into the Southern states.

And those white Americans who protested too openly were
liable to rough treatment. Elijah Parish Lovejoy, whose newspaper was violently antislavery, was shot to death in Alton,
Illinois, in November, 1837, when a mob seized his printing
presses and threw them into the river. Anti-Negro violence
erupted even in abolitionist-minded Philadelphia. Mobs of
whites killed and pillaged throughout the Negro section of the
city in August, 1842. Troops finally had to be called to quell the
riots. Nevertheless the agitation for freedom continued. More
and more white Americans were being drawn into the abolitionist crusade, and many who were not yet committed were
pondering the words of such brilliant Negro abolitionists as
Frederick Douglass, who, in a lecture delivered in Rochester,
New York, on December 8, 1850, warned:

"While slavery exists, and the union of these states endures,
every American citizen must bear the chagrin of hearing his
country branded before the world as a nation of liars and
hypocrites. . . .

". . . I would warn the American people, and the American
government to be *wise* in their day and generation. I exhort
them to remember the history of other nations . . . prouder and
stronger governments than this have been shattered by the bolts
of a just God."

Just four months before Douglass gave this lecture Congress
had passed the compromise acts of 1850 under which the new
and much stronger Fugitive Slave Law that Emerson said he
would not obey went into effect. It was the adoption of this
law which irritated Harriet Beecher Stowe into writing *Uncle
Tom's Cabin*, published in 1852. While it romanticized some
aspects of Southern life and was perhaps something less than
a literary success, its popularity was sensational. In less than a
year it sold over three hundred thousand copies, and sales
multiplied thereafter until throughout the North it became almost as popular a seller as the Bible. Millions of people
shivered as 'Liza crossed the ice floes in her dash for freedom
to the North and wept as faithful old Uncle Tom died beneath
the savage blows of Simon Legree's whip. Years later, when
Mrs. Stowe was presented to President Abraham Lincoln, the

UNCLE TOM'S CABIN;

OR,

LIFE AMONG THE LOWLY.

BY

HARRIET BEECHER STOWE.

VOL. I.

The title page of the first edition of a classic

Great Emancipator said, "So this is the little lady who started the big war!"

And in Lincoln's remark there was a truth that was sometimes obscured by the conflict of various interests which precipitated the Civil War. While it was true that the Civil War was something of an economic revolution in the North, and while it was supposedly fought solely to preserve the Union, and although the underlying economic causes were complex and materialistic, nonetheless basic was the question of slavery. It was basic to the economic conflict and above all it was paramount in the minds of the people of that time. And for this, the largest share of the credit must be given to the ceaseless activities of the abolitionists, with Negroes in the forefront of the movement.

When, in 1854, Congress passed another of its compromise measures on the admittance of new states, the Kansas-Nebraska Act, which repealed the old Missouri Compromise of 1820 by throwing the new territories open to an extension of slavery, anger in the North was unlimited. The North was further angered in 1857 by the Supreme Court's ruling in the Dred Scott case that Negroes could not be citizens of the United States. A new political party, the Republican Party, began to gain strength in the North with the slogan "Free Speech, Free Press, Free Soil and Free Men!" The Southern reaction to increased Northern sentiment for abolition was expressed by an angry Virginia newspaper editor who wrote, "We have got to hating everything with the prefix *free*—from free negroes up and down the whole catalogue—*free farms, free labor, free society* . . . and *free schools*—all belonging to the same brood of damnable *isms!*"

But in the North there were men who were now willing to fight to eradicate slavery in the United States. One of them, and the most famous, was John Brown, whose war against slaveholders in Kansas had already earned him the title "God's angry man." Supported by various abolitionists in the Eastern states, Brown planned to invade the South and free the slaves. He and his abolitionist backers hoped that one act of violence would rouse the Southern slaves to rebel *en masse* and strike for their liberty.

On the night of October 16, 1859, moving in strict silence under overcast skies, Brown took a group of twenty-one men, including his own sons and five Negroes, to seize the government arsenal at Harper's Ferry. The raiders carried the arsenal in a rush, but there they were trapped by the hurriedly summoned Maryland and Virginia militia. After a brief siege, Colonel Robert E. Lee stormed the arsenal with a company of U.S.

John Brown on his way to the gallows
(COURTESY OF THE PENNSYLVANIA ACADEMY OF THE FINE ARTS)

Marines and captured Brown and a handful of survivors. Brown's subsequent trial in Virginia for insurrection, murder, and treason, his conviction on October 31, 1859, and his execution on December 2nd, stirred the North to a paroxysm of rage, self-righteousness, and determination. The martyr's (for so he appeared to most Northerners) last words were quoted and requoted. Not so well known, but perhaps more pertinent, were the words of John A. Copeland, a free Negro who had taken part in Brown's raid and who was hanged on December 16, 1859. In a last letter to his family, written on the eve of his execution, Copeland said:

"It was a sense of the wrongs which we have suffered that prompted the noble but unfortunate Captain John Brown and his associates to give freedom to a small number, at least, of those who are now held by cruel and unjust laws. . . . And now, dear brother, could I die in a more noble cause? . . . I imagine that I hear you, and all of you, mother, father, sisters and brothers, say—'No, there is not a cause for which we, with less sorrow, could see you die.'"

Less than a year later Abraham Lincoln, candidate of the Republican Party, was elected President. Southern states began to leave the Union. The long battle for abolition had entered its final crisis, and to the tune of "John Brown's Body," Northern volunteers were on the march. With them were to march hundreds of thousands of Negroes ready and able to fight for their own freedom. And with them too marched the spirits of the millions of slaves who had suffered over the centuries—voiceless, perhaps, but eloquent in memory—for that New Birth of Freedom which was now to be won with the sword.

6 Terrible Swift Sword

> *By every consideration which binds you to your enslaved fellow-countrymen, and the peace and welfare of your country; by every aspiration which you cherish for the freedom and equality of yourselves and your children . . . I urge you to fly to arms, and smite with death the power that would bury the government and your liberty in the same hopeless grave.*
>
> —FREDERICK DOUGLASS

BUT BEFORE NEGROES COULD FLY TO ARMS THEY FACED STILL another fight: to convince the North, and President Lincoln in particular, that the Civil War was basically a war against slavery and that Negroes were both needed in the battle lines and capable of fighting once they got there.

The attitude of Lincoln, and of many influential Northerners, was that the war was being fought to preserve the Union, to put down a rebellion on the part of "combinations too powerful to be suppressed by the ordinary course of judicial proceedings." In Defense Department records the Civil War is still referred to as the War of the Rebellion. It was, in fact, a revolution that occurred on several levels at once. If the Republican Party's program of Free Soil and Free Men was to be carried out and maintained, then the Southern aristocracy, whether within or temporarily without the Union, had to be suppressed. And in an overall view, the Civil War was also a revolution which would increase the scope of liberty for all segments of the American population. But to the men charged with the conduct of the war, an overall view was veiled by pressing and immediate necessity. Lincoln and his associates would grow in stature and understanding as the struggle progressed, but meanwhile they thought that the more limited their objectives, the easier victory would be. By waging a war with the limited aim of simply reasserting Federal authority over the Southern states, Lincoln felt that he was also limiting potential enemies. Nor was this view entirely mistaken.

From the beginning of the war, Lincoln understood that the attitude of the border slave states was vital. To lose Kentucky, said Lincoln, "is nearly . . . to lose the whole game. Kentucky gone, we cannot hold Missouri, nor, as I think Maryland. These all against us, and the job on our hands is too large for us." To have stated that the Civil War was being fought to free the slaves would almost certainly have lost the border states to the Confederacy. Silence on this subject kept them within the Union (although as many of their men fought for the South as for the North). Also, Lincoln understood that victory (both for the principles of Federal union and abolitionism) would first have to be won in the minds of men before it could be won on the battlefield. "This," he said, "is essentially a people's contest. On the side of the Union it is a struggle . . . to elevate the condition of men — to lift artificial weights from all shoulders . . . to afford all an unfettered start, and a fair chance in the race of life." But words alone would not be convincing enough; the lessons which would convert a struggle to subdue rebellion into a social revolution had to be learned on the battlefields.

But to American Negroes, the goals of the Civil War were clear from the start. They saw in the conflict the seeds of their own emancipation. Since the war had been precipitated by the desperate class of Southern slaveholders, the abolition of slavery would sooner or later be used as a weapon against this class. And when, on April 15, 1861, President Lincoln issued his call for seventy-five thousand volunteers, Northern Negroes fully joined in the great wave of enthusiasm which came to be known as "the rising of the North." From cities and hamlets across the country, Negroes volunteered for service. In Boston, Negroes met and pledged their "lives and fortunes" to the cause; in Providence a Negro company was ready to march with the First Rhode Island Regiment; New York Negroes offered three regiments, fully equipped, for the fight; in Philadelphia two Negro regiments began drilling at Masonic Hall; in Pittsburgh the all-Negro Hannibal Guards volunteered to a man; in Detroit, Cleveland, Chicago — everywhere throughout the North — the Negro was ready to march. Unfortunately, neither the governors of the Northern states (who were responsible for raising men for the Federal army) nor the War Department had any intention of employing Negro troops. For nearly two years, the large and eager source of manpower represented by Negroes went untapped.

Opposition to the use of the Negro as a soldier was rooted

in prejudice. It was assumed that Negroes could not stand and fight against white men, especially Southern whites, who could be expected to show Negro troops no mercy. Besides, arming the Negro would be admitting that white soldiers alone were not sufficient to win victory; it would also, in unforeseeable ways, change the status of the Negro in American society. And among the conservative politicians of the Northern states and cities, as well as in apprehensive Washington, to change the status of the Negro was to complicate an already hugely complicated struggle. The fact that Negroes had served with distinction both on land and sea in every American war was overlooked. Time and a series of costly defeats would teach the North it needed all its sons—but for many agonizing months Negroes were to be excluded from the struggle.

One immediate victim of the opening of the Civil War was the American slave trade. All during the decades preceding the war, the British fleet had carried on its valiant struggle to suppress the trade, which was normally as illegal for Americans under American law as for the English themselves. But despite the occasional presence of a few American warships supposedly cooperating with the British squadrons off the African coast (but in reality more concerned with protecting American-flag ships from British search parties), the trade had boomed, with American connivance. There were times when war between Britain and the United States over the slave trade seemed perilously close.

It was British opposition to the trade which was paramount in causing the slave trade to be prohibited by the Confederate Constitution. Without such a prohibition, the Confederates realized, they stood little chance of recognition by Her Majesty's Government. And English recognition and potential support against the North was one of the most vital of Southern hopes. More effective than the words of the Confederate Constitution in suppressing the trade, however, was Northern realization that slaves were, to the South, implements of war production.

In August of 1860, the 476-ton American ship *Erie*, out of Warren, Rhode Island, commanded by Captain Nathaniel Gordon (of Portland, Maine), left the mouth of the Congo with a cargo of 890 slaves (including 612 children). Fifty miles off the African coast she was intercepted by the U.S. steam sloop of war *Mohican*. The slaves were put ashore in Liberia, and Gordon was carried to New York for trial. At first it seemed that this case, like every case of a captured slaver before it, would end with a fine or with the captain's escape. And when Gordon's trial produced a hung jury, nobody was surprised.

Abraham Lincoln (PICTURE COLLECTION, NEW YORK PUBLIC LIBRARY)

But since Gordon's capture one very important change had occurred; the United States had gone to war against the Southern slaveholders. The new district attorney in New York City looked upon himself as a soldier of a government fighting for its life. He called for a new trial. The second trial, in November, 1861, lasted but two days before the jury returned a verdict of guilty. Gordon was hanged on February 21, 1862. He was the first and the last American captain to suffer the legal penalty established in 1821 for slave trading; but the example of his death was sufficient. There are records of some subsequent slaving voyages by American vessels; but in 1862, the United States finally accorded British vessels the right to stop and search suspected American slavers, and by 1867 the British were able to withdraw their Atlantic Slaving Squadron as no longer necessary. The trade had lasted four centuries, involved the transport of at least fifteen million Negroes into slavery, and cost the lives of an estimated thirty-five million others in the process.

If the fear of British intervention on the side of the South was an important argument for Federal cooperation in suppressing the slave trade, the labors of white and Negro abolitionists in England all during the years preceding the Civil War now also bore fruit. Although many members of England's ruling aristocracy, fearing and disliking the egalitarian ideals of the American republic, would have been happy to help in its disruption, and the rich mill owners of England faced ruin when the Federal blockade cut off their vital supplies of Southern cotton, it was now demonstrated that England was inhabited by others besides aristocrats and mill owners. There was a huge laboring class and a large middle class—many of whom had listened to the words of American abolitionists over the years. They were strongly antislavery and they had effective leadership in Parliament. No British government could disregard their views.

English liberals were aware of the meaning to themselves of a Northern victory. "The success of free institutions in America," one such group declared, "is a political question of deep consequence to England. . . . [We will] not tolerate any interference unfavorable to the North." And although the Federal blockade did in fact shut down mills throughout England, the very workers who were thrown out of work flocked by the thousands to pro-Northern meetings and rallies. Henry Adams, who was present at one such pro-Union meeting in Manchester (one of the areas in England hardest hit by the Federal blockade), wrote: "I never quite appreciated the moral influence of American democracy . . . until I saw directly how it works." And the fact that it worked must be attributed in no small degree to the incessant agitation and propaganda carried on in England by hundreds of American abolitionists, white and Negro, before and during the Civil War.

In the United States, the war, which many had expected to be over in thirty days, quickly developed into a "people's contest" as Lincoln had predicted, involving hundreds of thousands of troops and the active participation of the entire populations of the North and the South. Northern defeats at the hands of brilliant Southern generals multiplied. Militant abolitionists in and out of Congress called upon Lincoln to strike a blow against the slaveholders where it would hurt them most, in their purses, by emancipating their slaves. Horace Greeley's *New York Tribune* on August 20, 1862, editorially urged the President to take strong antislavery measures. But Lincoln, who had many times expressed his personal detestation of slavery, was not convinced that an American president had the constitutional right to abolish it (he did not, in fact), nor was it yet clear that abolition (or really "social revolution") was the basic definition of the war. Replying to Greeley's editorial, Lincoln wrote:

"My paramount object in this struggle, is to save the Union, and is not either to save or destroy slavery. If I could save the Union without freeing any slave, I would do it; and if I could save it by freeing all the slaves, I would do it, and if I could save it by freeing some and leaving others alone, I would also do that. What I do about slavery and the colored race, I do because I believe it helps to save the Union; and what I forbear, I forbear because I do not believe it would help to save the Union."

Lincoln, who reasoned that abolition would find more acceptance both North and South if there was a place outside the United States to which freed slaves could be sent, long favored the scheme of colonization for American Negroes. At his insistence, Congress had appropriated a large sum of money at the beginning of the war that he could use as he saw fit to further Negro colonization. At Lincoln's request, Liberia (which had been set up as a sovereign nation by the American Colonization Society in 1847) declared itself willing to receive any number of American Negro settlers. Other locations in Central America and the Caribbean (especially the Republic of Haiti) suggested themselves. But the great obstacle to Lincoln's plans for colonization was the fact that Negroes refused to go.

On August 14, 1862, Lincoln invited a delegation of Negro leaders at the White House to hear his views on colonization. The reaction was immediate and strong. A Newton, Long Island, mass meeting of Negroes on August 20, 1862, resulted in the following declaration: "This is our native country; we have as strong attachment naturally to our native hills, valleys, plains, luxuriant forests, flowing streams, mighty rivers, and lofty mountains, as any other people." Shortly thereafter, a protest meeting in Philadelphia resolved: "Many of us, in Pennsylvania, have our own houses and other property, amounting, in the aggregate, to millions of dollars. Shall we sacrifice this, leave our homes, forsake our birthplace, and flee to a strange land, to appease the anger and prejudice of the traitors now in arms against the Government?" Although a handful of Negroes accepted Lincoln's offer (and a few actually settled in the short-lived colony of Cow Island near Haiti), the overwhelming answer to this question was No.

But even as Lincoln received his Negro guests at the White

House (the first time a Negro delegation had been there), he had already steeled himself for the step which would recognize the Civil War for what it was: a great social revolution. If there had been no other factor involved, military necessity alone was reason enough for an emancipation act.

By the summer of 1862 there were few in the North who did not realize that victory over the Confederacy would be a long, bloody, and bitter struggle. Weak in manufacturing, communications, population, and supplies, the South was rich in a native genius for war. Moreover, a far larger proportion of her eligible young men were freed to fight than in the North by the employment of Negro slaves in farming, hauling, manufacturing, and military construction. General Ulysses S. Grant observed that because Negro slaves were forced to work, without regard to age or sex, "the four million of colored non-combatants were equal to three times their number in the North, age for age, sex for sex." That an emancipation act would strike a heavy blow against the South's slave resources was already being demonstrated by the number of slaves who were fleeing to Union camps whenever they could.

Most of the military operations of the war were conducted on Southern territory. And whenever Union armies appeared in any given area, the slaves for miles around would pour into the Yankee lines. Since no official policy regarding them had been established by Washington, they proved at first to be an embarrassment to Union commanders. Soon, however, it was found that runaway slaves often brought vital military information, made excellent guides to the local terrain, were expert at foraging for food and wood, and were willing to work as cooks, nurses, and in whatever capacity they could to aid the troops. Union commanders generally refused to return fugitive slaves to their masters—and the word spread quickly throughout the South; any slave who succeeded in reaching the Union lines would be a free man. Thousands took the opportunity.

So vital was the slave to the Southern war effort, and so serious the drain caused by slaves escaping to Northern lines, that before the war ended General Robert E. Lee would suggest to Confederate President Jefferson Davis that Negro slaves be formed into fighting regiments and emancipated for their efforts. But this was a suggestion that no Confederate government could have accepted, even in desperation.

Congress, under the influence of such "radical" Republicans as senators Benjamin Wade of Ohio and Zachariah Chandler of Michigan, had already made some preliminary steps toward full emancipation. In April, 1862, slavery was abolished in the District of Columbia and a resolution adopted which stated

that Federal funds should be used to recompense the citizens
of any state which adopted a plan for the gradual abolition of
slavery. This offer was turned down by the slaveholding border
states.

In June, 1862, Congress abolished slavery in the territories;
in July it announced that all slaves coming into Union lines
would be considered prisoners of war and set free. At the same
time Congress authorized Lincoln to receive Negroes into the
service of the United States to perform "any labor or any war
service." If the Negro had been a slave, his mother, wife, and
children would also be set free. There was little doubt that full
emancipation was coming—but when?

Lincoln felt he needed a military victory in order to issue a
proclamation of emancipation, and Northern military victories
were scarce. Then, on September 17, 1862, the Union and Confederate armies clashed in the bloody battle of Antietam. The
Confederate Army escaped the destruction it might have
suffered at the hands of a better Union commander, but Antietam was a Union victory, at least enough of a victory for
Lincoln. On September 22, 1862, he issued a preliminary
proclamation of emancipation which stated that as of January 1,
1863, all slaves would be free in those states or parts of states
which were still in rebellion against the Federal government.
As a threat to the South, this preliminary declaration was
completely ineffective, but as a morale booster for the North
its impact was tremendous. At last the terrible struggle had
found its truest, deepest channel.

The agonizing wait between September 22, 1862, and January 1, 1863, on the part of Northern Negroes, who had known
too many broken promises in the past, went on until the last
moment. In Boston Frederick Douglass waited with hundreds
of Negro friends for the flicker of the telegraph key which
would carry the news—

"Eight, nine, ten o'clock came and went, and still no word. . . .
At last, when patience was well-nigh exhausted and suspense
was becoming agony, a man (I think it was Judge Russell)
with hasty step advanced through the crowd, and with a face
fairly illumined with the news he bore, exclaimed in tones that
thrilled all hearts, 'It is coming!' 'It is on the wires!'

"The effect of this announcement was startling beyond all
description, and the scene was wild and grand. . . . My old friend
Rue, a Negro preacher, a man of wonderful vocal power expressed the heartfelt emotion of the hour, when he led all voices
in the anthem, 'Sound the loud timbrel o'er Egypt's dark sea,
Jehovah hath triumphed, his people are free!' "

The Emancipation Proclamation itself was a rather dry

document, and it was still partial—emancipating only slaves in states "presently in rebellion" against the Federal government —and it had still to be enforced. But Negroes read the words "thenceforward, and forever free" and knew that slavery was at an end. It was the jubilation with which Negroes hailed the Proclamation that gave it that dignity which has come to associate it in men's minds with the Declaration of Independence, the Magna Carta, and other historic documents. As Negro poet Francis Ellen Harper wrote:

> It shall flash through all the ages;
> It shall light the distant years;
> And eyes now dim with sorrow
> Shall be brighter through their tears.

The Emancipation Proclamation had an immediate effect upon the course of the war primarily because it authorized the United States Army to recruit Negroes for the fighting line. From the beginning the response of Negroes to recruiting agents was good. Eventually 180,000 Negroes were to serve in Union blue—and more than one-third of them, 68,178, were to die. They fought valorously on every front and at sea. Whatever doubts others might have about the war, Negroes knew why they were fighting.

It was not made easy. Negroes had to serve longer terms of enlistment than whites, they had almost no chance of becoming commissioned officers, their pay was lower, their food and medical care poorer, and their equipment inferior to that of white soldiers. And if a Negro soldier was captured by the Confederates, he would be treated as a rebel slave rather than as a prisoner of war. When, for example, the Union garrison of six hundred men (including about three hundred Negro soldiers) at Fort Pillow, Tennessee, was forced to surrender to six thousand Confederates under Major General Nathan Bedford Forrest on April 12, 1864, all the Negro troops (including the wounded) as well as a few Negro women and children in the surrendered fort, were massacred.

In spite of many disadvantages the Negro soldier fought well. He proved himself on five hundred battle fields from the Mississippi to Virginia, and earned the praise of all important Union commanders. Secretary of War Edwin Stanton reported to Lincoln on February 8, 1864, regarding Negro troops: ". . . they have proved themselves among the bravest of the brave, performing deeds of daring and shedding their blood with a heroism unsurpassed by soldiers of any other race."

The United States Navy had always enlisted free Negroes.

A Negro is lynched by New Yorkers during the Draft Riots of 1863.
(SCHOMBURG COLLECTION, NEW YORK PUBLIC LIBRARY)

They had fought with Perry on the Great Lakes, with Decatur at Tripoli, and in many a sea fight in between. Negroes formed fully one-quarter of the crews of Union warships. They received better treatment in the Navy than they did in the Army; they messed and berthed with whites and generally received equal pay for equal work. Four Negro sailors won the Navy Medal of Honor during the war, including Joachim Pease, loader of number one gun aboard the U.S.S. *Kearsarge*, who, though wounded, had the satisfaction of helping to send the dread Confederate raider *Alabama* to the bottom off the French coast.

But if the Negro was at last coming to grips with his enemies in the South, he found it harder to win his actual, as opposed to his theoretical, rights in the North. The long strain and anguish of the bloodiest war in American history, the centuries-old fear of the "alien" Negro, the complicated politics of "bossism" in the cities, and sometimes direct provocation by Confederate agents led to several bloody anti-Negro riots in Northern cities. In Detroit, on March 6, 1863, huge bands of drunken whites attacked the Negro community, beating, lynching, and burning men, women, and children. And in New York, in July, 1863, opposition organized by Southern agents to the new Federal

Draft Act took the form of city-wide riots. White workers felt that the new draft law discriminated against them and were hostile to the competing Negro labor force anyway. Taking out their frustrations in a blind fury of destruction, they burned and looted through the city streets, killing any unfortunate Negroes who fell into their hands. Only the arrival of Federal troops put an end to the riots—after hundreds of Negroes and whites had been murdered. It is noteworthy that, as in the South, it was the poorest and most exploited class of the white population in the North, whose own lives were warped by oppression, who were the agents of violence.

Negroes realized that the freedom granted them by the Emancipation Proclamation was, first of all, partial, and secondly, *unreal* without a basis of political power to back it up. They pressed Lincoln and Congress all through the last half of the war to pass a Constitutional amendment which would finally and forever abolish slavery throughout the entire United States, and they demanded the right to vote. Negro petitions to this effect flooded Washington after 1862. No one had to remind Lincoln of the gaps in his famous Proclamation; but, an acute politician, he proceeded cautiously and acted only when he was sure of widespread support. After the battle of Gettysburg, the President urged Congress to pass an amendment guaranteeing freedom, and in the presidential election campaign of 1864, at Lincoln's insistence, the Republican Party made such an amendment a part of the party platform. Finally, on January 31, 1865, after Lincoln had been re-elected by a comfortable electoral margin, Congress adopted the Thirteenth Amendment, which definitively abolished slavery throughout all the territory and possessions of the United States. Legislation regarding the Negro's right to vote, however, was not immediately adopted. Some assumed that as he was no longer a slave, he must be a citizen, with all the rights of a citizen; others preferred to leave the question in comfortable abeyance for the moment.

There was no longer any doubt about the outcome of the war. By the time Congress had passed the Thirteenth Amendment, Sherman's army had already cut a swath of destruction sixty miles wide "from Atlanta to the sea" on its march through Georgia, and Grant's veterans were tightening their iron grip on Lee's worn-out army in Virginia. When at long last Richmond finally fell to the Army of the Potomac on April 3, 1865, the first Union troops into the former Confederate capital were elements of the 29th Connecticut Colored Infantry Regiment.

A few days later, President Lincoln, standing on the steps of the Confederate capitol building, spoke to a large and deliriously happy crowd of Negroes and white soldiers:

"In reference to you, colored people, let me say God has made you free. Although you have been deprived of your God-given rights by your so-called masters, you are now free as I am, and if those that claim to be your superiors do not know that you are free, take the sword and bayonet and teach them that you are — for God created all men free, giving to each the same rights of life, liberty, and the pursuit of happiness."

Lincoln's advice to the Negroes to defend their newly won rights to the last extremity was good advice — as the stormy years ahead were to show.

7 The Light That Failed

*When I was going to the polls there was a man
standing in the door and says, 'Here comes you,
God damn your soul, I have got a coffin already
made for you.' I had two tickets in my pocket then;
a democratic ticket and a radical ticket; I pulled
out the democratic ticket and showed it to him, and
he says, 'You are all right, go on.'*

—JOHN CHILDERS, testimony before the Joint
Congressional Committee to Inquire into . . .
Affairs in the Late Insurrectionary States

ABRAHAM LINCOLN DIED ON APRIL 15, 1865, VICTIM OF A
conspiracy that, in slightly different form and intention, had
been approved by the leading members of the Confederate
government, who were also leaders of the slaveholding Southern aristocracy. The idea that Lincoln's death (or, as was originally planned, his kidnaping) could have a definitive effect on
deep-running and all but inevitable historical currents was
simply part of the superficial view of history held by a class
that could not foresee its own extinction when it launched a
hopeless war and was determined to avoid its fate by any means
whatsoever after it lost that war. Of course, the immediate
effect of the insensate act was to arouse a spirit of icy rage
throughout the North. As Herman Melville wrote:

> There is a sobbing of the strong,
>   And a pall upon the land;
> But the People in their weeping
>   Bare the iron hand;
> Beware the People weeping
>   When they bare the iron hand.

And if the "iron hand" was not felt immediately in the
South, the assassination of Lincoln created a public temper in

the North that would gladly support the harshest kind of treatment of the former Confederacy upon the slightest provocation.

It is probable that such Congressional radicals as Thaddeus Stevens and Charles Sumner wasted few tears on the fallen President; his policy of reconciliation toward the South was one they had bitterly opposed all along. During the war years, the Republican Party, now under the leadership of the radicals, had become almost exclusively the voice of industrialists and financiers—men who had a large investment in the industrial plant and railroads that had come into being through the war and in the capitalist Industrial Revolution that was unfolding throughout the North. These men foresaw great possibilities in the unrestricted exploitation of the national wealth if only they could retain absolute control of the government. But this control was now threatened by the readmission of the Southern states to Congress. For though slavery had been abolished, the economic interests of the Southern agriculturalists had not appeared to change; Southern politicians would still demand low tariffs for cheap manufactured goods and would oppose the exploitation of their wealth by Northern industrial monopolies. Hence any excuse or provocation that could be used by Republicans to keep Southern Democrats out of Congress would be welcome. The postwar Southern leadership, which had "forgotten nothing and learned nothing," did not fail to provide the provocation.

Lincoln's plan for the restoration of Confederate states to the Union, put into practice by Federal commanders as early as December, 1863, had provided that when ten percent of the citizens in any Southern state had taken an oath of loyalty to the Union, that state could establish a new government. And when the new state government had agreed to abolish slavery and comply with other Union laws, it would be recognized by the Federal government and its representatives welcomed back to Congress. Despite violent radical opposition to this generous plan, Lincoln's successor, President Andrew Johnson, attempted to carry it through.

Andrew Johnson, by no means the intemperate drunkard he was painted by Republican radicals, was a loyal Democrat from Tennessee. Looking upon himself as a leader of the poor white farming class, he hated the old Southern planter-aristocracy which had brought ruin to the South. On the other hand, he had no use at all for the newly powerful industrialists of the North. Both these groups, he felt, would maintain their power through the same old exploitation of the poor people, North or South. And he was against slavery because it had been the chief weapon of exploitation in Southern planter hands. But although he saw all this clearly enough, Johnson could not escape the psychological heritage of his own people, the poor white Southern farmers. He was frightened by the prospect of Negro political power. While he would grant the Negro certain civil rights, he was opposed to unlimited Negro suffrage. Rather than run the risk of establishing Negro-dominated governments in the Southern states, he was prepared to risk those governments coming once again under the domination of the old planter-aristocracy. He failed to see that only through an alliance between poor whites and a free Negro community could the exploitive power of the rich be broken in the South.

Radical opposition to the Lincoln-Johnson lenient readmission policy was violent, and strong enough completely to sabotage his program. Republican control of the country depended, as Senate radicals knew, upon Republican control of the Southern states. And that control could only be based on Negro suffrage. But at the same time, some radical leaders, such as Charles Sumner, did sincerely believe in equal rights for Negroes and were convinced that unless the Southern states were compelled to grant Negroes free schools, free homesteads, and a base of economic power, the Civil War would have been fought in vain. Sumner once wrote, "Only through him [the Negro] can you redress the balance of our political system and assure the safety of private citizens. . . . He is our best guarantee. Use him."

Negroes throughout the country were demanding the right to vote. On May 10, 1865, North Carolina Negroes submitted a petition to President Johnson which stated:

"We have always loved the old flag, and we have stood by it. . . . Some of us are soldiers and have had the privilege of fighting for our country in this war. . . . We want the privilege of voting."

Such petitions multiplied over the ensuing months.

A meeting of Norfolk, Virginia, Negroes on May 11, 1865, resolved that ". . . as far as lies in us, we will not patronize or hold business relations with those who deny us our equal rights." Which may have been the first attempt at using the boycott for political ends in the South.

Tobacco workers in the factories at Richmond and Manchester, Virginia, protested the new and more brutal exploitation which had been imposed upon them. On September 18, 1865, they declared, "They [the white apologists for exploitation of Negroes] say we will starve through laziness — that is not so. But it is true we will starve at our present wages." In the North Frederick Douglass warned, "Slavery is not abolished until the black man has the ballot. . . . But let the civil power of the South be restored, and the old prejudices and hostility to the Negro will revive."

The Southern planter-aristocrats were indeed resuming control of the state legislatures. Wherever they came back into power, they instituted new sets of "Black Codes"—similar to the old slave codes—for the regulation of the freedmen (as former Southern slaves were now called). The South Carolina code, for example, stipulated that in drawing up contracts "persons of color shall be known as *servants* and those with whom they contract shall be known as *masters.*" In Louisiana, every Negro was supposed to be in the service of some white person, who was held responsible for the Negro's conduct. In all states Negroes were forbidden firearms, in many states prohibited from testifying against white people in court, in most could be punished by fine, jail, or whipping for any "insulting act or gesture" toward whites, and almost everywhere they were forbidden to use the same public transportation facilities as whites.

The Black Codes were not haphazard. They were carefully calculated as a means of keeping the Negro in submission and degrading him—so that he would have neither the means nor the will to seek political power—and also as a means of maintaining the psychological tensions between the Negroes and the poorer classes of Southerners that enabled the old aristocracy to exploit them both.

But the radical Republicans, determined to use the Negro to maintain political hegemony over the South and genuinely concerned with securing his rights, had not waged a long and bloody war for such results. When the new Congress convened on December 4, 1865, it refused to seat the representatives of the new Southern state governments. Instead it denied the legality of the new Southern legislatures and established a Joint Committee on Reconstruction. Dominated by Thaddeus Stevens and Charles Sumner, the Reconstruction Committee began holding hearings and gathering evidence of the resurgence of the power of former slaveholders in the South and their attempt to replace slavery with near-slavery. The evidence was plentiful. And to underline it, anti-Negro riots took place in many Southern cities and towns. In Memphis on May 1st to May 3rd and in New Orleans on July 30th, gangs of whites roamed the streets murdering Negroes, burning down Negro homes, and looting Negro sections of the city. In both riots the city officials and local police either stood by applauding or helped the rioters; and there is evidence to show that both riots were carefully arranged by higher state authorities.

Congress reacted to continued Southern violence by passing

Drawing rations at one of the offices of the Freedmen's Bureau
(PICTURE COLLECTION, NEW YORK PUBLIC LIBRARY)

a Civil Rights Act in April, 1866. The act assured former slaves of all the rights of citizenship and provided for trial to be held in Federal courts in cases of anti-Negro discrimination. Later that same month the Reconstruction Committee proposed to Congress a new Constitutional amendment—the Fourteenth—which declared that all persons born in the United States were citizens and that no state could abridge the rights of United States citizens in any way. In addition the amendment provided that if proof could be offered that the ballot was withheld from any members of a state's adult male population, then that state's representation in Congress would be diminished proportionately. The amendment was adopted by Congress on June 13, 1866. But the Southern state governments refused (with the exception of Tennessee) to ratify it, thereby providing the radicals with exactly the provocation they required.

In November, 1866, at the next Congressional elections, radical Republicans secured an overwhelming majority in Congress. They could now override any attempted veto by the hapless President, Andrew Johnson. To start, on January 8, 1867, Congress conferred the right to vote on Negroes in the District of Columbia. This was followed by a measure which granted Negroes residing in United States territories the right to vote. And finally, on March 2, 1867, Congress enacted a Reconstruction Act. By this law, the Southern state governments were declared illegal. The South was divided into five military districts, each to be administered by a United States Army major general who was to prepare his "province" for readmission to the Union. This process involved the registration of all loyal voters in the province (Negro as well as white) who were to elect delegates to a convention. The convention was to prepare a new state constitution, which had to be approved both by the state's voters and by Congress. Then the state had to ratify the Fourteenth Amendment. Then, and only then, would Congress consider readmitting it to the Union.

The new political power of the Southern Negro (aided by more than a few Southern whites who *had* learned something from the war) was quickly demonstrated. The planter-controlled postwar state governments were swept from office in most of the South by the summer of 1867, and the state conventions and new state governments were dominated by Republicans and contained a large proportion of Negro representatives.

The political power of Southern Negroes was not simply established by Congressional decree. Careful organizational work had gone into it, through private and public organizations and clubs, one of the most influential being the Freedmen's Bureau. The Freedmen's Bureau had been established in 1865 as a service administered by the War Department to try to ameliorate the lot of freed slaves in the territories coming under Union military control. From the beginning, the Freedmen's Bureau established a good record in helping not only Negroes, but also thousands of impoverished Southern whites. It distributed over twenty-one million meals to the hungry, established forty hospitals, and also established more than four thousand free public schools throughout the South, at which nearly 250,000 former slaves learned to read and write. The Freedmen's Bureau also acted as a legal representative of former slaves to make sure they were not too ruthlessly exploited by their former masters. It negotiated contracts for Negro laborers and distributed confiscated lands (most of which were of the poorest quality) to Negroes. The Freedmen's Bureau became a special target of hate to Southern white leaders. They were bitterly opposed to educating Negroes, resentful of the bureau's interference on behalf of Negro labor, and above all, terrified of the bureau's basic assumption that Negroes were legally and civilly the equals of whites.

Southern leaders, in the immediate postwar months, had justified their attempt to resubdue the Negro by claiming that without control he was lazy, childish, and disposed to aimless violence. And no doubt there were Negroes to whom freedom meant freedom from work as well as tyranny. There were also some who, on the glad day of liberation, simply picked up their belongings and started walking—anywhere, so long as it was away from the old plantation. But most Negroes were willing and able to work to make their own way in the new South.

Reports made by Northern generals and correspondents in 1865 and 1866 were eloquent on this point. General Rufus Saxton reported to the War Department on the readiness of slaves for freedom: "[They] have shown that they can appreciate freedom as the highest boon; that they will be industrious and provident with the same incitement which stimulates the industry of other men in free societies."

The new Reconstruction state governments throughout the South, established by Negroes and white radicals, were never under Negro control. In none of the new legislatures did Negroes have a majority, in none of the states did a Negro become governor. But Negroes did exercise great political power, and they filled some notable offices, such as associate justices of state supreme courts, commissioners of education, secretaries of state, district attorneys, sheriffs, and mayors. And the Reconstruction governments accomplished some notable improvements in Southern life. They provided for more universal suffrage by removing property requirements for voting; abolished the medieval system of imprisoning people for debt; abolished such cruel and unusual punishments as whipping and branding; reduced the number of crimes for which a man could be executed (in the case of South Carolina, which was fairly typical, from twenty to two) and established statewide free public school systems (the first in Southern history). Although they did not redistribute the land, they did pass laws to protect the small farmer, and they attempted to institute a rational system of taxes. Nor were these benefits intended exclusively for Negroes. They were vital advantages also to the poor Southern whites. In effect, the Reconstruction state governments were attempting to bring about a peaceful socio-economic revolution in Southern society which would have benefited most Southern whites as well as Negroes. For this they earned the deepest hatred of the Southern ruling class.

The new Southern state governments quickly gained Congressional recognition and were allowed to send representatives to Congress. Mississippi sent two Negroes to the United States Senate and from eight Southern states came twenty Negro members of the House of Representatives. These men earned the praise of their Congressional associates.

The Republican policy of enfranchising the Southern Negro paid off for the party in the elections of 1868, when General Ulysses S. Grant won the presidency with the help of 450,000 Negro votes. So impressed were Republicans by this success that they hastened to safeguard it by putting through Congress yet another Constitutional amendment, the fifteenth, which forbade the states to deny the vote to any citizen because of his race or color. It was ratified on March 30, 1870. Hailing the new amendment, Frederick Douglass, who understood the uses of political power, declared, "We have a future; everything is possible to us."

But Southern conservatives planned otherwise. Recognizing the new state governments as the potential revolutionary forces they were, Southern "Bourbons" (as they came to be called) set about to undermine them. Their attack was waged basically on two fronts. First, by terror, murder, and corruption to frighten Negroes and radical whites from the use of political power and to violently rob them of whatever economic advantages they had won; second, to convince the North that: 1 — These events were not happening; 2 — They might be happening, but they were justified; 3 — They might not be justified, but they were expedient; 4 — Expediency would bring profit to the North as well as the South.

As part of their campaign of slander against the Reconstruction governments, Southern conservatives spread abroad the picture of drunken, illiterate, and power-mad Negroes and radical whites stealing from state treasuries and bringing ruin to the Southern economy. Of course there were corrupt Negro and white legislators, and there were ignorant ones. But the scale of their crimes was no greater than those committed in legislatures throughout the country and were small indeed compared to the corruption of the Northern big city political machines. Certainly sober, intelligent, and industrious Reconstruction legislators far outnumbered the few corrupt ones. And the legislative records of the Reconstruction governments stand for themselves as thoughtful, progressive, and favorably comparable to the records of pre-Civil-War Southern governments and postwar Northern legislatures. But these facts were to be submerged in the tidal wave of lies spread abroad by Southern Conservative apologists.

The primary militant arm of the Southern conservatives was the Ku Klux Klan, a secret society with ritual names, grips, and signs, all sorts of secret paraphernalia, and the somewhat ridiculous costumes of white robes and hoods, modeled after the robes and hoods of the medieval monastic orders of Europe. The Klan was originally established in 1865 in Pulaski, Tennessee, as a social, fun-making group, but it was noticed that the strange costumes had the effect of arousing fright among onlooking Negroes. The Klan idea quickly spread throughout the South until, by the spring of 1867, it had become a widespread organization. And the ridiculousness of its appearance was quickly outweighed by the terror of its brutality. Although the Klan attracted lawless elements and was composed for the most part of the poorer whites, it included many respectable Southern leaders in its ranks and was, for a while, headed by no less a personality than former Confederate General Nathan Bedford Forrest—the same gallant officer whose men had murdered their prisoners at Fort Pillow during the war.

The Klan used terroristic techniques against the Negroes and radical whites not dissimilar to those later employed by the Nazi Storm Troopers at another place. Its program included beating, burning, robbery, and murder. It selected as its victims those who might provide leadership in the Negro community, but also maintained a campaign of random murder to spread general terror. The Klan particularly delighted in torturing the defenseless, and on those occasions when it was faced with armed opposition, even on the part of a single resolute man, its members generally fled.

For example, in testimony before a Congressional committee in 1871, Will Johnson, a South Carolina Negro, described how he routed the Klan:

"When I awoke, as near as I can tell, it was between twelve and one o'clock. I heard some one call 'Sims.' I held still and listened . . . they [the Klansmen] blew a whistle. Another whistle off a piece answered, and then men seemed to surround the house and all parts of the yard. Then they hallooed 'Open the door.' I said nothing. I went to the head of the bed and got my pistol, and leaned forward on the table with the pistol just at the door. . . . They went to the wood-pile and got the axe, and struck the front door some licks, bursted it open. . . . They said 'Strike a light.' . . . two of them stepped in the front door. . . . As soon as they did that, I raised my pistol quickly, right up to one's back, and shot, and he fell and hallooed, and the other tried to pull him out. As he pulled him I shot again . . . and, when the whole party was out on the yard I stepped to the door and shot again." The Klansmen fled.

On the other hand, when it came to women and children, the Klan proved itself relatively fearless. Testifying before the same Congressional committee in 1871, Hannah Tutson, Negro, of Jacksonville, Florida, declared:

"When they came to my house that night the dog barked twice . . . five men bulged right against the door, and it fell right in the middle of the floor, and they fell down. George McRae was the first to get up . . . and he went to where I had left all the children . . . and I said 'Who's that?' . . . George McRae ran right to me and gathered me by the arm. As I saw him coming I took up the child—the baby—and held to him . . . then there were so many hold of me I cannot tell who they were. George

"The Experiences of a Northern Man Among the Ku Klux" (from a pamphlet published in 1872) were unpleasant, to say the least.

(PICTURE COLLECTION, NEW YORK PUBLIC LIBRARY)

McRae and Cabel Winn were the first to take hold of me. He said: 'Come in True-Klux.' I started to scream, and George McRae catched me right by the throat and choked me . . . and he catched the little child by the foot and slinged it out of my arms. . . . I cast my eye up to the elements and begged God to help me. George McRae struck me over the head with a pistol . . . they tie me to a tree and whipped me for a while."

"How old were your children?" [Examiner's inquiry.]

"One was about five years old, another betwixt nine and ten, and the other was not quite a year old, lacking two months."

"Did the baby get hurt?"

"Yes, sir; in one of its hips. When it began to walk, one of its hips was very bad, and every time you would stand it up it would scream."

Thousands of Negroes were murdered throughout the South by the Ku Klux Klan, and many more thousands beaten and driven from their land. President Grant tried to enforce law and order in the South with those elements of the army which were still stationed there. But the Grand Army of the Republic had long since been disbanded. The forces stationed in the South were few — and they were no longer the idealistic volunteers of 1861, but professional soldiers. The Klan was carrying on a real guerrilla war against Federal authority, and it had the over-whelming support of most Southern whites. Klansmen appeared and disappeared from place to place, emerging and then hiding within the general population of their various districts. And when on the rare occasions a Klansman was caught and brought to trial, he was certain of acquittal since witnesses were afraid to testify against him and the judge and jury were in deepest sympathy with Klan aims if not themselves Klansmen.

Fraud and violence succeeded, despite the protests and brave resistance of Southern Negroes. Conservatives recaptured the state legislatures beginning in 1870 with Virginia and North Carolina. By the spring of 1877, the Reconstruction govern-ments throughout the entire South had been swept away and the conservatives were firmly back in charge. And once in control they made certain that Negroes would not again exercise political power by passing restrictive legislation which effec-tively barred Negroes from voting. Other state legislation guar-anteeing citizens equal rights was also quickly repealed.

Southern conservatives were able to carry out their program for two primary reasons. First of all, they had succeeded in enlisting the aid of the poorer classes of Southern whites — by far the majority of the population. They had done this by play-ing carefully and expertly on the old fear and hatred of Negroes prevalent throughout Southern society. The loss of the Civil

War and the emergence of former slaves as free men had threatened most Southern whites on the deepest psychological level —they feared a loss of identity. Living just above or beneath the poverty line, many Southern whites had clung for centuries to contempt for the Negro as an essential part of their own self-definition. The Reconstruction governments offered them an opportunity, in alliance with the Negroes, of rising above poverty and ignorance by destroying the economic stranglehold that Southern conservatives had maintained on them. But few Southerners enjoyed the political literacy to understand this. The old aristocracy played on their fears—and hysteria proved a more potent incitement than reason.

The second reason for Southern conservative success was that Northerners were no longer ready to aid the Negro. Most Northerners were sick of fighting. Furthermore, the opening of the West and the Industrial Revolution now at flood tide throughout the North were absorbing most of the North's attention. Since the Negro had been emancipated and Congress had passed legislation guaranteeing his rights, Northern consciences were at rest concerning him. But a weightier factor than this was the realization among Northern industrialists and politicians that the vital Congressional legislation which was enabling them to exploit continental wealth was no longer in danger of repeal after 1876. Big business interests were now firmly in control—they no longer required the support of Negro Congressional votes. On the other hand, they had come to see in the South a large potential market. But in order to exploit that area, a peaceful climate was essential. Therefore they were content to adopt a "hands off" policy toward the South and allow the Southern conservatives to solve their own problems in their own way. Besides, Southern conservatives themselves showed increasing interest in industrialization. They were willing to invest in Northern companies and, more important, to control their section of the nation as a source of cheap raw materials and cheaper labor for the benefit of Northern industrialists—provided they could share in the exploitation and run their domains as they saw fit.

In the presidential election of 1876, the bargain between Southern conservatives and Northern businessmen was sealed. Rutherford B. Hayes, the Republican candidate, had won the election by the narrowest of margins over his Democratic opponent. So close was the electoral vote that a special

The Ku Klux Klan riding away from the scene of one of their lynchings
(HISTORICAL PICTURES SERVICE — CHICAGO)

electoral commission was appointed by Congress to decide just who had won. At stake were the electoral votes of three Southern states which had each sent in two sets of election returns, one Republican, the other Democratic. After much hard bargaining, the Southern votes went to Hayes. And in return for this, Hayes ordered the last Federal troops removed from the South. When they went the last props were kicked out from under the remaining Reconstruction governments and the South was delivered back into the hands of the men who had always ruled it. The party of Lincoln had announced its lack of any further interest in the fate of Negroes. The Negro, both as a cause and as an instrument, had secured for the ambitious businessmen of the Republican North their domination of American society; now they were willing to discard him.

The campaign of violence and fraud by which the Southern Bourbons had wrecked the Reconstruction governments and obliterated Negro political power was at least illegal, according to the new Congressional Civil Rights Act of 1875, not to mention the Fourteenth and Fifteenth amendments, or so Negroes thought. And with political power shorn from them, they sought redress from the judiciary. But during the early 1880's the Supreme Court, in a series of decisions, effectively gutted the Civil Rights Act of 1875. The principles adopted by the Court were basically designed to restore to the states the rights and privileges they had lost due to the expansion of Federal power during and just after the Civil War. It held that the Fourteenth and Fifteenth amendments were Federal restrictions only on the powers of the states or of their agents, not on the powers of individuals within those states. Thus it was still illegal for a state to deny votes to the Negro, but if a private citizen or a group of them (such as the Ku Klux Klan) within any state actively prevented the Negro from voting, then his or its criminal acts would come under state not Federal law. The Court also adopted the rule that if a state's laws did not on the surface appear to discriminate against Negroes, then the Federal courts had no right to investigate as to whether those laws were actually being applied equally. Again, that was a matter for private parties to press within the state's own courts. Thirdly, the Court held that the police power of a state, its right to regulate the lives of citizens for the public safety, was more important than the individual rights guaranteed by the Fourteenth and Fifteenth amendments. Finally, the Court held that "distinction" between the races (as opposed to "discrimination") was perfectly constitutional—thus in effect sanctioning segregation, which in itself was not held to be necessarily discriminatory.

So harsh were the Supreme Court edicts of the 1880's that eighteen Northern states adopted civil rights acts of their own to protect Negro citizens, but in the South the Negro was now all but defenseless.

8 Domestic Reaction;

Foreign Adventure

Take up the White Man's burden—
  Ye dare not stoop to less—
Nor call too loud on Freedom
  To cloak your weariness;
By all ye cry or whisper,
  By all ye leave or do,
The silent, sullen peoples
  Shall weigh your Gods and you.

—RUDYARD KIPLING

POLITICAL POWER AND JUDICIAL REDRESS HAD BOTH failed the Negro as weapons for equality largely because of a lack of economic power. But for a very few, Negroes North and South had gone into the Civil War and the Reconstruction period with no economic power at all—except the potential negative power of denying their labor to those who would exploit them. But even this negative power had been destroyed, partly by the resumption of control by the Southern Bourbons (and their colleagues, Northern industrialists and financiers), partly also by the harsh economic dogmas of nineteenth century capitalism.

In the South, almost seventy percent of the population, white as well as Negro, remained farmers. But while some poor white farmers owned their own land, Negroes almost universally were tenant-farmers—sharecroppers. Even when Negroes somehow accumulated sufficient wealth to buy land, Southern whites were reluctant to sell, for that would change the status of the Negro. Without land and without money, the Southern Negro farmer was reduced to near-slavery.

A sharecropper had but one thing to sell—his personal labor. The tools of his trade—work animals, seed, farm implements, and fertilizer—all had to be purchased on credit from the landlord. And with no cash to see him through the year until harvest time, the sharecropper also had to buy his food, pay for his cabin, and buy feed for his animals on credit from the landlord. Thus, at the end of the year, the sharecropper not only had to pay the landlord's basic share (generally about fifty percent) of the crop he had grown but also to pay all the debts he had incurred while growing it. The landlord generally charged a high price for anything he sold his sharecroppers, and on top of that he charged a high rate of interest for the credit he extended. Also, sharecroppers were generally illiterate, and the landlord kept the books. So on "settling-up day" the sharecropper almost always found himself so far in debt to the landlord that he had to pledge his labor for another year in order to work off what he owed.

While theoretically free to leave the land, the sharecropper was actually bound to it as strictly as any serf of old. And if he attempted to flee his debts the grim prospect of the chain gang awaited him. He would be caught, convicted of any one of dozens of offenses, sent to prison, and then, with other convicts all chained together by the ankles when they marched, rented out for labor to the highest bidder.

Southern Negroes who were not sharecroppers fared almost as badly. The small number of salaried Negro agricultural workers received, on the average, $60 *per year* in wages. And Negroes who lived in towns and cities faced increasing competition from white workers for jobs. Before the Civil War, almost five out of six artisans in Southern towns had been Negroes, but by 1895 the proportion was closer to one out of every hundred. Only the heaviest and most dismal work was open to the Negro laborer—and, as always, the domestic service occupations. But even in these jobs the pay seldom rose above $60 per year.

In the North, Negroes were growing accustomed to a permanent economic depression. No matter whether times were good or bad for other workers—for the Negro worker they were always bad. This was not due primarily to the policies of Northern industrialists, who would have been quite willing to exploit cheaper Negro labor, but to the hostility of the white labor force, which feared Negro competition and excluded Negroes from trade unions. The great migratory tides from Europe that washed over American shores during the last half of the nineteenth century had made labor plentiful in Northern cities. And many of the immigrants were willing to take the jobs in domestic service or heavy labor that had once been reserved for Negroes. Employers were able to play off white and Negro

Nat Love, the famous "Deadwood Dick" (from his book, The Life and Adventures of Nat Love)

workers against each other, the American trade union movement was barely getting started, and government protection
of labor was decades away. Like his white brother worker, the
Negro was in an economic strait jacket; but his was tighter.

During those years of labor unrest that accompanied the
growth of monopoly capitalism in the United States, the Western frontier acted as something of a "safety valve" for the
Negro as well as the white worker. During the early 1870's
Negro cowboys were no novelty on the Western plains. They
seemed to enjoy a better relationship with the Indians than
most whites, possibly because they understood what it meant
to be dispossessed in one's own country. Perhaps the best-
known Negro cowboy was Nat Love, who was part of the
legendary group of citizens (including Wild Bill Hickok and
Calamity Jane) who "tamed" the roaring town of Deadwood
in the Dakota Territory. Nat, through his marksmanship and
riding ability, won the title of "Deadwood Dick." But Negroes
had been part of the West even before the Civil War. They were
among the '49ers who panned for gold in California and were
to be found on every Western frontier so long as a frontier
existed.

The greatest mass migration of Negroes to the West occurred
in 1879. The murder of Reconstruction, a year of bad crops, an
outbreak of yellow fever, and the increasing violence and discrimination which they suffered caused Negroes from Louisiana to Tennessee to undertake a great exodus to Kansas. The
decision was not so sudden as it appeared when fifty thousand
Negroes throughout the South simply picked up their belongings and headed west. Several years of careful preparation and
agitation on the part of various Negro organizations had gone
into the migration. Prime mover in this effort was Benjamin
"Pap" Singleton, an illiterate Tennessee-born ex-slave who
traveled through the South beating the drum for "sunny Kansas" as a Western paradise. By August 1, 1879, nearly ten
thousand poor Negro "exodusters" (as they called themselves)
had arrived in Kansas, and thousands of others had reached
Iowa and Nebraska. By fall of that year an estimated fifty
thousand had arrived in the frontier settlements. But then, as
suddenly as it had arisen, the great wave of migration subsided.

The Negro exodus of 1879 was criticized by Frederick
Douglass as being a solution of Negro problems by flight rather
than by right. But the main reason for the dwindling of the
migration was to be found in the experiences of Negroes who
had discovered that "sunny Kansas" was something less than
the Western paradise it had been painted. The severe winter
of 1879–1880 on the Kansas prairies brought death to hun-

dreds of penniless Negro migrants and starvation to others. And anti-Negro discrimination followed the newcomers wherever they went. White settlers in the West (many from the South) regarded the Negro migrants as competitors for land and jobs and treated them accordingly. Some stuck it out, but many returned poorer and wiser. Nevertheless, the sudden migration had alarmed white employers in the South, as had the findings of a Senate committee appointed to investigate it. Concessions were made to Negro workers for a brief period of time; as soon as the migration ceased, the concessions were withdrawn.

What might have become an important means of fighting for livable working conditions, North as well as South, was the Negro trade union movement. Originally, it was hoped that trade unionism might grow as an interracial movement. When the National Labor Union (the first important coast-to-coast federation) was established in Baltimore in 1866, Negroes were urged to join and to found union locals of their own. But opposition to Negro labor on the part of the sorely pressed white workers was so intense that at the second meeting of the N.L.U. in Chicago in 1867, it was resolved that no action be taken on the subject of enlisting Negro workers. Rebuffed by white unions, in 1869, Negroes established in Washington the National Negro Labor Union and the National Labor Convention of Colored Men. Leadership in these two unions naturally gravitated to men, such as Frederick Douglass, who had been leaders in the fight for emancipation. But these men, who had devoted their lives to political action, tended to view unionism as another means to political ends. And like his white brother worker, the laboring Negro was more interested in immediate goals involving wages and hours than in long range political warfare. By 1874 the separate Negro labor movement was dead.

But by that time white union leaders (and some members of the rank and file) were beginning to learn that as long as Negroes remained outside the unions, employers could use them as strikebreakers; that Negro competition for jobs might be preferable to the continued use of available Negro labor as an economic weapon against the unions. When the Knights of Labor was founded in 1869, its leaders announced that there would be no discrimination practiced in their union; and during the following years they made so determined and successful a drive to enlist Negro workers that by 1887 approximately ninety thousand Negroes were members. But the Knights of Labor organization soon fell victim to the open warfare practiced against all labor unions during the '80's by government-backed industrialists. Its battle was carried on, however, by the American Federation of Labor, which was founded in 1881.

The A.F.L., like the Knights of Labor, originally declared that it would accept Negro members; and, in fact, in order to join the national federation, local unions had to swear not to discriminate against workers because of creed or color. But the A.F.L. was a federation of craft and skilled-labor unions; unskilled labor, the category into which most Negroes had been forced, was outside its organizational scope. Furthermore, in its desperate fight against business interests, the A.F.L. was more interested in winning support from local unions than in forcing doctrine upon them. Thus, although A.F.L. President Samuel Gompers bore no malice toward Negro workers, he was willing to sacrifice Negro labor (and A.F.L. principles) to expediency. By 1900, the A.F.L. was admitting unions such as the Boiler Makers, which barred Negroes from membership. And although the A.F.L. was willing to grant charters to all-Negro union locals, it refrained from employing Negro labor organizers. Negro membership remained small.

For a while, the struggle for Negro equality seemed to merge into the populist movement that arose during the '80's and '90's as a farmer-labor alliance to combat the unchecked and uncontrolled exploitation of the national wealth by large corporations. Growing out of the discontent and desperation of Western farmers who had seen the government bestow huge land grants on the transcontinental railroads, who had to pay those same railroads exorbitant and discriminatory freight rates, and whose homesteads were steadily being lost to Eastern banks, financiers, and insurance companies, the populist movement soon attracted the support of large masses of workers in the East and of Negroes and poor white farmers in the South. For the first and only time, poor white farmers in the South appeared willing to set aside their racial animosities and work with Negroes to secure a better life. An example of the very real threat such an alliance posed to the exploiting class of Southern Bourbons was the victory of the Readjuster Party (a coalition of Negroes and poor white farmers) in Virginia. The Readjusters controlled the state from 1879 to 1883. But although many Negroes were active in the populist movement throughout the country, it was not long before Northern industrialists and their junior partners in the South were able to split Negroes from the populist ranks.

Frightened by the possibility of a poor white-Negro alliance in the South, conservative leaders determined to establish legal and permanent means of depriving Negroes of the vote instead of relying on violence. Beginning with Mississippi in 1890, one after the other, the Southern states adopted laws which set up various restrictive conditions for voting. These included payment of a poll tax, the ability to read and expound on some obscure section of the state constitution, a good character test, and tricky registration procedures. Of course these laws were rigorously applied to Negro voters, seldom to whites. To further insure Negro disfranchisement, "white primary" laws were passed which stated that since the Democratic Party was a voluntary association of citizens—a club— it could limit voting in primary elections within the party.

Southern conservatives were encouraged in these anti-Negro policies by a Supreme Court decision of 1896. In the case of *Plessy* vs. *Ferguson* the Court ruled that the "separate but equal" accommodations laws throughout the South were constitutional, thus giving final legal sanction to segregation. The Court observed that laws in themselves were "powerless to eradicate racial instincts or to abolish distinctions based upon physical differences."

One of the most formidable weapons employed by conservatives, North as well as South, to "keep the Negro in his place" (that is, economically exploitable, politically isolated, and socially segregated) was simple slander. It was during the last decades of the nineteenth century that newspapers and magazines, reflecting the direct or indirect influence of their conservative owners, attempted with a fair degree of success to create a stereotyped and brutal image of the Negro in American minds. Generally, the Negro was fitted into one of seven categories: the Contented Slave, the Wretched Freedman, the Comic, the Brute, the Tragic Mulatto, the "Local Color" Negro, or the Exotic Primitive. Some examples:

The Comic Negro (from *Harper's Magazine*, 1878):
Dr. Crane: "Naow, as de modern poet says our swoards rust in deir cubbards, an' peas, sweet peas, covers de lan'. An' what has wrot all dis change? De pen. Do I take a swoard now to git me a peck ob sweet-taters, a pair ob chickens, a pair ob shoes? No, Saar. I jess take my pen an' write a order for 'em . . ."

A year earlier, *Harper's* had published a version of the Wretched Freedman in "A Kingdom for Macajah" by Virginia Frazer Boyle:

I wants ter git shet er dis hear freedom! I hain't nuffin but des er po' fool nigger, Ole Marse . . . You knows what's de bestes' fur me, Ole Marse, an' you knows I hain't fitten ter breave de bref er life! Kill me, Ole Marse, kill me; but 'fore you does hit take de cuss er freedom offen my soul!

The Local Color Negro—combined with the Contented (if wistful) Slave—appeared in *Scribner's Magazine* in 1877:

*I heahs a heap o' people talkin', ebrywhar I goes
'Bout Washingtun an' Franklum, an' sech genuses as dose:
I s'pose dey's mighty fine, but heah's de p'int I's bettin' on:
Dere wuzn't nar a one ob' 'em come up to Mahrs John.*

Northern magazines in the "genteel" tradition of *Harper's, Scribner's, The Atlantic, Century,* and *The North American Review* regularly referred to Negroes as "niggers," "darkies," "coons," "Mammies," and "bucks." Negroes were almost universally supposed to speak in a dialect (torturously reproduced by phonetic spellings) which had as little literary merit as it had validity in real life.

Much more dangerous in inciting anti-Negro violence was the consistent pattern of anti-Negro news reporting in which

Henry W. Grady
(HISTORICAL PICTURES
SERVICE—CHICAGO)

almost all Northern and Southern newspapers indulged. Negro victims of lynchings (of which there were well over one hundred every year from 1877 to 1900) were generally reported as guilty of whatever atrocious deed they had been accused no matter how improbable. Many newspapers actually urged on the lynch mobs. For example, the *Memphis Commercial Appeal* of October 6, 1896, carried the story of a lynching in a set of inclusive headlines:

HORROR REIGNS IN FAYETTE
A NEGRO RAVISHER RECEIVES THE USUAL
PUNISHMENT
BESTIALITY OF THE CRIME ALMOST
WITHOUT PARALLEL

The Fiend Chased All Day by Infuriated
Neighbors of the Afflicted Family, and Besieged
Last Night about Four Miles from Mason—
Support Accorded Him by a Gang of His Race . . .

While in 1883, the *Philadelphia Inquirer*, as was its custom, judged the victim of a lynching in its headlines:

RETRIBUTION
JACOB NELLING LYNCHED BY A MOB
RED-HANDED MURDERER OF ADA ATKINSON
PAYS THE PENALTY FOR HIS HORRIBLE CRIME

As late as 1900, *The New York Times* still dispensed with trial by jury in judging Negroes accused of crimes:

NEGRO MURDERS A CITIZEN
POSSES ARE LOOKING FOR HIM AND
HE WILL BE LYNCHED

While the common people of the country were liberally dosed with such nonsense, the Northern industrialists and businessmen who, through investments, owned much of Southern industry, had to take some care that violence did not get out of hand. Fearing that lynch law, the disfranchisement of Negro voters, and the violence and fraud committed against white and Negro populists in the South might provoke Congressional action which could endanger their holdings, Northern industrialists invited the Southern conservatives to prove to the nation that a new spirit of forward-looking progressivism beat in their breasts. On December 22, 1886, Henry W. Grady, one of the editors of the *Atlanta Constitution*, was invited to deliver an oration on "The New South" to the annual dinner of the New England Society.

Grady's "New South" speech, which he thereafter delivered from lecterns throughout the country, succeeded in convincing credulous audiences. With mighty rhetoric Grady invoked the picture of the "chivalric grace and strength" of the old South, insisted that the Civil War and its issues were dead, and described the growth of industry in the new South that "challenged your spinners in Massachusetts and your iron-makers in Pennsylvania." As for the Negro, he enjoyed the "fullest protection" of laws and the friendship of the Southern people: "Faith has been kept with him. . . . Faith will be kept with him in the future. . . . The new South represents a perfect Democracy, the oligarchs leading the popular movement."

The reception accorded this speech by the dinner guests (who included such titans as J. P. Morgan, Charles Lewis Tiffany, General William Sherman, and Charles Ransom Miller, editor of *The New York Times*) was tremendous. It was exactly what they wanted to hear, and they made sure that the rest of the country heard it too.

If populism was defeated in the South through slander, fraud, and violence, it was defeated in the North because a large proportion of the American people were now dependent on the giant industrial plant which by the 1890's had made the United States the world's largest manufacturing nation. They were willing to pay the price of unchecked exploitation of the country's natural and human resources to achieve this end. The giant trusts (such as United States Steel, the world's first billion-dollar corporation) with their price-fixing, their ruthless gouging of the natural resources of the land, their buying and selling of political representatives, their armies of Pinkerton agents (supported, when necessary, by the National Guard) who broke strikes casually and violently; these were part of the price. The ruin of small farmers in the West was part of the price, and so too was the suppression of the drive for Negro equality, North as well as South. Another vital factor in the downfall of the populist movement was the emergence of the spirit and national policy of imperialism.

Imperialism in itself, with its threat of war and disruption, was not attractive to American business and financial leaders, but the prospect of opening and exploiting new foreign markets definitely was. And the politicians who represented their interests in Washington saw in imperialism a means of diverting national interest from those pressing domestic problems which had given rise to the populists. The imperialist view of the world, which had already transformed all of Africa and much of Asia into European colonies, might be diametrically opposed to traditional American beliefs and values; but by beating the imperial drums, politicians of both parties hoped to drown out the populist clamor. Furthermore, many of the more energetic of the younger politicians, such as Theodore Roosevelt and Henry Cabot Lodge, foresaw the day when expanding American industry would require captive colonial markets and sources of raw materials. In almost exact inverse proportion to the decline of populism on the national scene, imperialist ambitions and propaganda rose. The emerging target of the imperialists was Spain—partly because that nation was the most militarily helpless of all possible opponents, and possessed rich colonies in the Far East, and partly because the inefficient Spanish rule of Cuba had transformed that island into a running sore of misery for which American public sympathy might easily be aroused.

If the defeat of populism meant the destruction of the Negro's post-Reconstruction hopes of justice and equality, the rise of imperialism posed a new threat in itself. If the United States was to embark on the conquest and rule of dark-skinned natives in far corners of the world, it meant that national attitudes toward dark-skinned people at home would have to harden into set patterns of indifference and contempt. It was against this complex political background that the struggle for Negro rights was enacted in the last decades of the nineteenth century.

In the face of political disfranchisement and economic exploitation, the undermining of the populist movement and the rise of imperialism, Negroes were unsure how to cope with their engulfing misery. Many of the voices of the older generation of Negro abolitionist leaders were now stilled (Frederick Douglass died in 1895), and new leaders who had matured during the decades of post-Reconstruction despair began to assert themselves. The most influential of these was Booker T. Washington.

Born in 1858, Booker T. Washington had devoted himself to the education of Negroes—one of the few fields (like the independent Negro churches) in which whites took little or no supervisory interest. The public school system which had been established in the South by the Reconstruction state governments had always been run on a segregated basis. Economy-minded Southern legislators in the post-Reconstruction period had given little enough money to the white public schools; to the Negro public schools they gave almost nothing. Negroes who wanted a decent education for their children were forced to turn to privately supported schools. Many, if not most of these, were established by the various Negro church groups; some found support among white philanthropists and foundations, most outstanding of which prior to 1900 was the American Missionary Society.

Since Negro problems centered around the economic handicaps under which they struggled, many Negro leaders and educators thought that the teaching of trade skills was of the first importance. Hence many of the privately supported Negro schools and institutes devoted themselves primarily to vocational training, to the detriment of a general education. Such was the policy of the Tuskegee Institute in Alabama, founded (in 1881) and run by Booker T. Washington. Tuskegee students were taught carpentry or mechanics or farming or other

Booker T. Washington in his office at Tuskegee Institute (1906). On the other side of the desk, reading, is his secretary, Emmett J. Scott.
(HISTORICAL PICTURES SERVICE —CHICAGO)

occupations from which they might earn a living.

Washington's view—that Negroes should, for the moment at least, abandon political agitation and seek to "get along" with whites, while concentrating on improving their economic lot—found a hearty acceptance among the whites. They welcomed the idea that Negroes should settle down and accept their status of second-class citizenship and at the same time train themselves in exploitable laboring skills. This role for the Negro in America fitted both the myth of the "New South" which Southern conservatives were attempting to foist on the country and also the aims of Northern businessmen concerned with industrial peace; it also offered no threat to the ambitions of the imperialist politicians.

Booker T. Washington emerged as a national spokesman for Negroes (and a spokesman whose influence was to dominate his era) when he delivered a speech at the Cotton States and International Exposition in Atlanta on September 18, 1895. Washington was introduced by the governor of Georgia, and he was applauded by many Southern leaders as he declared:

"As we have proved our loyalty to you in the past, in nursing your children, watching by the sick beds of your mothers and fathers, and often following them with tear-dimmed eyes to their graves, so in the future, in our humble way, we shall stand by you. . . .

"The wisest among my race understand that the agitation of questions of social equality is the extremest folly. . . . The opportunity to earn a dollar in a factory just now is worth infinitely more than the opportunity to spend a dollar in an opera house."

And so on, not omitting a humorous aside about the supposed propensities of Negroes for stealing chickens. The Atlanta Exposition speech was reprinted far and wide, and while many Negroes resented Washington's apparent readiness to accept an inferior role for the Negro, whites hailed the address as "The Atlanta Compromise" — that is, an end to Negro agitation for equality in return for a chance to gather economic scraps from the booming industrial table.

But there were other voices among the Negroes. John Hope, president of Atlanta University, declared on February 22, 1896, "If we are not striving for equality, in heaven's name for what are we living? I regard it as cowardly and dishonest for any of our colored men to tell white people or colored people that we are not struggling for equality."

And Negro poet Paul Laurence Dunbar, referring to vocational training, wrote (in August, 1898), "At this late date the Negro has no need to prove his manual efficiency. That was settled fifty years ago when he was the plantation blacksmith and carpenter and shoemaker."

But militant Negro voices did not resound among whites now deafened by the rising storm of imperialist propaganda, nor did they appeal to most Negroes, who were beginning to think of their position as all but hopeless. The way of accommodation and acceptance offered by Booker T. Washington seemed to many to be the only way, for the present at least. Andrew Carnegie donated $600,000 to Tuskegee Institute; Booker T. Washington was consulted on the appointment of Negroes to those few traditionally "Negro posts," such as minister to Liberia or Haiti, that the Federal government granted; and, as one Negro historian has put it, "All roads

Hot action at Las Guasimas, Cuba, in 1898
(HISTORICAL PICTURES SERVICE—CHICAGO)

seemed to lead to Booker T. Washington." In 1898 they also led to war.

There were, of course, some Negroes who understood what the real meaning of the Spanish-American War had to be. Charles G. Baylor, an attorney from Providence, Rhode Island, observed, "Shall the Liberty Cause in Cuba be thus betrayed and sacrificed without a determined resistance by liberty men and women everywhere? . . . I ask the question because the American Negro cannot become the ally of imperialism without enslaving his own race."

Nevertheless, the "splendid little war" (as U.S. Ambassador John Hay described it) took place, and Negroes participated. Four Negro regular army regiments fought in Cuba (and later in the Philippines), took part in the famous charge up San Juan Hill, and received unstinted praise from their white commanding officers.

But despite the pride Negroes could feel in the undoubted heroism of Negro troops, they could not remain blind to the fact that they were fighting in a questionable cause. When the Spanish-American War ended, and the much longer and bloodier undeclared war to subjugate the natives of the Philippine Islands commenced, Lewis Douglass, the son of Frederick Douglass, wrote (in October, 1899): "It is a sorry, though true, fact that whatever this government controls, injustice to dark races prevails. The people of Cuba, Porto Rico, Hawaii, and Manila know it well as do the wronged Indian and the outraged black man in the United States . . . its [American] expansion means extension of race hate, and cruelty, barbarous lynchings, and gross injustice to dark people."

Perhaps the dilemma of the Negro fighting an imperialist war was best expressed by William Simms, a Negro soldier in the Philippines, who wrote home: "I was struck by a question a little boy asked me, which ran about this way — 'Why does the American Negro come from America to fight us when we are much friend to him and have not done anything to him? Why don't you fight those people in America that burn Negroes, that made a beast of you, that took the child from the mother's side and sold it?'" Simms admitted he could not answer the question.

But other questions, which had been debated all through the post-Reconstruction decades, seemed now to have been settled. The United States would enter the new century united North and South over the grave of Negro hopes, and as an urbanized, centralized industrial world power over the hungry hearts and stomachs of her workers. The Negro had been offered a lowly but secure niche in the imposing edifice of American power. Many saw no hope of ever escaping it. Yet even during the darkest days, hope did not completely die. For at the turn of the century if the road ahead looked long and toilsome, it at least had the advantage that it could go in only one direction: up.

9 From White Supremacy
To "Black Thursday"

Rep. Martin Dies *(Dem., Texas): We have solved
the problem . . . and white supremacy is a fixture.*
Archibald Grimké *(witness): You cannot solve it
that way. You think you have solved it . . . but . . .
in fifty years everything is going to be changed . . .
these people are going to be your equal if God
made them your equal.*

—HEARING BEFORE THE HOUSE COMMITTEE
ON CIVIL SERVICE REFORM (1914)

BUT AT THE TURN OF THE CENTURY, WHITE SUPREMACY DID,
in fact, seem a permanent fixture of American life. In 1900 there
were about 8,800,000 Negroes in the United States, of whom
almost eight million lived in the South. Their acknowledged
spokesman was Booker T. Washington, and there seemed no
one else to whom Negroes could turn for leadership. With the
final disfranchisement of Negroes in the South, the defeat of
the populist movement throughout the country, and the new
spirit of aggressive imperialism, the path toward equality
seemed finally closed. And the continuing abysmal economic
condition of Negroes everywhere seemed to mock the hopes
of those who expected the Negroes to somehow lift themselves
by their own bootstraps.

Booker T. Washington, for example, founded the National
Negro Business League (a sort of Negro Chamber of Commerce) in 1900, with the object of helping the aspirations of an
emerging Negro middle class (and through them, it was hoped,
the masses of poor Negroes). But although the League had developed more than six hundred local and regional branches by
1915, Negro business endeavors did not succeed—except in
those fields in which they did not have to fight entrenched

white businesses, such as banking and insurance, neither of which attracted white competition for Negro clients.

Dr. Washington, with his policy of acceptance of the status quo (although behind the scenes he often worked quietly to fight restrictive laws) and the influence of his personal "quietism," was regarded by whites as an "ambassador" from Negro Americans. In October, 1901, he dined at the White House with President Theodore Roosevelt (to the great outrage of various Southern congressmen), and he continued to act as a sort of unofficial dispenser of the few political jobs open to Negroes. But there were many Negroes who disagreed with his policies. In 1906, the Reverend Adam Clayton Powell, Sr. (father of Congressman Adam Clayton Powell, Jr.) wrote to *The New York Times:* ". . . under Dr. Washington's policy the two races in the South are a thousand times further apart than they were fifteen years ago and the breach is widening every day."

Tragically symbolic of the failure of Booker T. Washington's policies was the fact that in 1911, four years before his death, the aged and respected Negro leader was badly beaten by one Henry Ulrich in New York City. Ulrich fell upon Dr. Washington simply because he saw him trying to enter an apartment building in which Ulrich's mistress happened to live. Despite the fact that Washington received a letter of condolence from President Taft himself, his charges of assault against Ulrich were dismissed by the New York Court of Special Sessions.

But of course none of the more than one hundred Negroes annually lynched in the United States received letters of condolence from so august a source (or any source at all). While lynching was a typically Southern phenomenon, it was by no means restricted to the states below Mason and Dixon's line. In 1912 a Negro named Wyatt was murdered in Belleville, Illinois, as reported by *The New York Times:*

"The mob hanged Wyatt to a telephone pole in the public square. Even while his body was jerking in the throes of death from the strangulation, members of the mob began building a fire at the bottom of the pole. The flames flared and licked at the feet of the victim, but this did not satisfy the mob and another and larger fire was started.

"When it had begun burning briskly, the negro, still half alive, was cut down, and after being covered with coal oil was cast into the fire. Moans of pain were heard from the half-dead victim of the mob and these served further to infuriate his torturers. They fell upon him with clubs and knives and cut and beat the burning body almost to pieces, and not until every sign of life had departed did they desist and permit the flames to devour the body."

In the face of hysteria of such depth, it was perhaps too much to hope that Dr. Washington's policies could form a channel of communication between white and Negro Americans. New voices in the Negro community, first raised at the turn of the century, were now being heard with growing insistence—and they did not counsel moderation or acceptance of the status quo. Preeminent among the new leaders was William Edward Burghardt DuBois. Born in 1868, DuBois received his education at Fisk University, the University of Berlin, and Harvard, where in 1895 he became the first Negro to receive a Ph.D. A man of great intellectual gifts, DuBois' doctoral dissertation, *The Suppression of the African Slave Trade*, became the first published work in the Harvard Historical Studies series. Booker T. Washington tried to enlist DuBois' help to further his own policies, but early in his career DuBois made it plain that he thought Washington was leading the Negro on a backward path. Enlisting the support of other college-trained Negroes, DuBois set about opening new paths toward equality (and wresting leadership of American Negroes from Dr. Washington's hands).

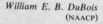

William E. B. DuBois
(NAACP)

In the summer of 1905, DuBois gathered together twenty-nine Negro leaders (mostly professionals such as doctors, teachers, and lawyers) at Niagara Falls, Canada, to launch what was to become known as the Niagara Movement. While they avoided any open criticism of Booker T. Washington's policies, the men at Niagara reaffirmed the necessity of a real struggle for Negro rights. Though the Niagara Movement developed about thirty branches throughout the country and held annual meetings at such historic places as Faneuil Hall in Boston and Harper's Ferry, it gained but little ground. It was desperately poor—because most money to support Negro advancement continued to go to Booker T. Washington—and by 1910 it had disbanded. But from its short life sprang a much more important organization—the National Association for the Advancement of Colored People or N.A.A.C.P.

On February 12, 1909, the hundredth anniversary of the birth of Abraham Lincoln, Oswald Garrison Villard (grandson of *"I will be heard"* William Lloyd Garrison) called for a national conference for "the renewal of the struggle for civil and political liberty." Signing the call were fifty-three distinguished Americans, including pioneer social worker Jane Addams, Rabbi Stephen S. Wise, the philosopher John Dewey, and Reverend John Haynes Holmes. Among the Negroes who signed Villard's appeal were DuBois, Reverend Francis J. Grimké, and Bishop Alexander Walters. A conference was held from May 31 to June 1, 1909, in New York City, and after much work by various permanent committees, a second conference took place in New York in May, 1910. At this second conference the N.A.A.C.P. was formally established. Its first president was famed Boston attorney Moorfield Storey (later president of the American Bar Association) and its director of publicity and research was W. E. B. DuBois. Villard, editor of the *New York Post*, became treasurer. Although its original membership list was modest, the N.A.A.C.P.'s rosters included many influential and prominent men. The organization raised a voice which could not be ignored. Its publication, the *Crisis*, under DuBois' editorship, climbed to a monthly circulation of nearly thirty-five thousand by 1914.

It was well that the N.A.A.C.P. was founded when it was, for the affairs of Negroes in America were moving into a time of crisis. The policies of imperialism and uncontrolled exploitation of the national wealth which had brought the nineteenth century to a close were moderated during the first decades of the twentieth century by a new spirit of reform. Under the general name of progressivism, critics of American life began raising a storm of protest regarding everything from the canning practices of Chicago meat packers to the price fixing and other tactics of the giant trusts. The administration of Theodore Roosevelt had been active in "trust-busting" under the Sherman Anti-Trust Act and had passed other national legislation to protect the poor. But although, like other Americans, Negroes benefited indirectly from such legislation, their own problems continued to be largely ignored. Lynchings continued at the rate of one hundred to two hundred a year, and race riots occurred with increasing frequency. In Atlanta in 1906 the police sided with white mobs and twelve people died. In Brownsville, Texas, that same year, a shooting affray between Negro soldiers and white citizens, provoked by the whites, led President Roosevelt to summarily deal out dishonorable discharges to the personnel of three companies of the Negro Twenty-fifth Infantry Regiment. Such outbursts showed that Negro-white tensions were mounting. Reflecting this, a shift in Negro political allegiance was now taking place that was to have profound repercussions in the future.

The Republican Party, which had, since the administration of President Chester Arthur, abandoned the Southern Negro to his fate, now under the leadership of President Taft, tried to recapture some of the political power it had once enjoyed in the solidly Democratic South. It sought to do this by establishing a "lily white" political machine there which would presumably appeal to white Southerners by out-demagoguing the Democrats on racial matters. Negroes, North as well as South, who had traditionally voted Republican (more in wistful memory than current hope) began to waver in their party allegiance.

While the Republican Party had become the spokesman for conservative elements of American life, the Northern Democrats had inherited something of the impulses and dreams of the populist movement. The Democratic Party in the North was rapidly becoming the party of exploited foreign immigrants, oppressed laborers, and small Western farmers. Many of the progressives who had hoped for solid advances under Theodore Roosevelt were now shifting their allegiance to a new Democratic political leader—Woodrow Wilson, intellectual president of Princeton University and spokesman for an entire program of reform which he dubbed the New Freedom. Despite the fact that he was the leader of the political party which had traditionally opposed all Negro hopes, especially in the South, Wilson's eloquent appeals for justice and for economic equality for all Americans, as well as his pledge to treat Negroes with absolute fairness, attracted the support of Negro intellectuals like W. E. B. DuBois for his presidential campaign in 1912. When Wilson was elected, many Negroes settled back to see what benefits the New Freedom would bring them.

Their disappointment was immediate and sharp. Whatever Wilson's personal views on racial equality may have been (they were conservative), his party was still dominated by the representatives of the Solid South. The President's cabinet heads began at once to reaffirm and to strengthen the color lines within their departments. Offices, especially in the Treasury and Post Office departments (in which many Negroes served), began to be partitioned off, as were lunchrooms and restrooms—one side for Negroes, the other for whites. Furthermore, the few decent jobs open in government to Negroes, such as the ministries to Haiti and Liberia, were now assigned to whites. Then, in May of 1914, the Civil Service began to require photographs of applicants, for the avowed if idiotic reason of "preventing impersonation." Wilson, a native son of Virginia, was aware of and to a certain extent approved these actions.

It was now that the newly formed N.A.A.C.P. first proved its merit. The organization sponsored mass meetings in cities throughout the country, sent letters with impressive signatures to leading newspapers and gathered petitions (the largest of which bore twenty thousand names) to present to the President. The campaign waged by the N.A.A.C.P. against discrimination in government employment bore fruit late in 1914 when the Treasury and other departments began to retract their anti-Negro rules and regulations. In 1915 a Negro was offered the Ministry to Liberia.

In 1915, too, deciding a suit brought by the N.A.A.C.P. the Supreme Court held that the various "Grandfather clauses" (which prohibited those whose grandfathers had been non-residents, i.e., slaves, from voting) in Southern state voting and registration laws were unconstitutional. Although this represented a slight inching forward of the Court's view of Negro rights and their enforcement, it was a decision made in a vacuum. The basic reason why Negroes in the South could not vote was not the laws—it was the threat of violence which lay behind the laws.

Under the circumstances, it might have been expected that Negroes would have viewed America's entry into World War I, the "war to end all wars," the war to "make the world safe for democracy," with more than a little irony. But the clamor of the drums in April, 1917, was accompanied by an upsurge of Negro patriotism. Like other Americans, Negroes rushed to "make the world safe for democracy." They might have asked, "Democracy for whom?" but except for a few lone voices they did not. The principles for which Wilson assured the nation it was fighting were perhaps even more precious to Negroes than to whites; and as they had hoped with each of America's wars, Negroes dreamed that a substantial contribution on their part toward victory overseas would somehow lead to an improvement in their status at home. Negroes flocked to enlist, and the War Department was deluged with offers of Negro troops. But the War Department was uncertain as to what policy it would pursue in regard to Negro soldiers. A month after war was declared the department stopped the enlistment of Negroes. As barbershop proprietor George Myers told customer Thomas R. Marshall (Vice-President of the United States), "it looks as if the Negro, like a burglar, would have to break into this war as he did the others."

For after decades of anti-Negro propaganda the War Department seemed to have forgotten the excellent record of Negro troops during the Civil War and even the heroism of the Negro regiments during the Spanish-American War. The old fears that Negro troops would not or could not fight made themselves felt once again in conservative military circles. However, the Selective Service Act of May, 1917, at least made certain that Negroes would not "miss" this war. Although volunteering was closed to him, the Negro found himself drafted — and over-drafted. For although the Draft Act was not in itself discriminatory, its administration through local boards, especially in the South, certainly was. Of all Negroes registered for the draft, 31.74 percent were called to arms, while only 26.84 percent of registered whites were actually enrolled. More than 335,000 Negroes were eventually taken into the armed forces.

Once in the Army, the Negro soldier was placed in strictly segregated units all the way — and if he was unfortunate enough to receive his training at an army post in the South, the local civilian population did not hesitate to discriminate against him and bait him in the old, time-honored ways. Such treatment led to a riot in Houston, Texas, in 1917, during which members of the Negro Twenty-fifth Infantry Regiment, goaded to desperation by white civilians, killed seventeen whites, shouting: "To hell with going to France, let's clean up this dirty town!" After the most summary of trials, thirteen Negro soldiers were hanged and forty sentenced to life imprisonment.

Yet, as always, Negro troops established a good record on the fighting front. In spite of the fact that most of their officers were white (a few Negroes were commissioned during the war), that more than two-thirds of the Negro troops in France were relegated to the Quartermaster Corps, where they did the back-breaking, humdrum, and essential heavy labor which kept the armies supplied at the front, the Negroes who managed to reach the trenches made an impressive record. American Expeditionary Force commander, General John Pershing, remarked of the all-Negro Ninety-second Division, "This division is one of the best in the A.E.F." And the all-Negro Ninety-third Division, whose units were brigaded with French troops and scattered throughout the battle line, made as excellent a record; its 370th Infantry Regiment won twenty-one U.S. Distinguished Service Crosses and sixty-eight French War Crosses. The 369th Infantry was awarded a unit Croix-de-Guerre for exceptional gallantry under fire. The 371st Infantry was given a special citation by French Marshal Henri Pétain, while the 372nd was cited by Vice-Admiral Jean Moreau (commanding the French division with which it was brigaded) as having shown "the finest qualities of bravery and daring exploits." The 369th not only boasted a unit Croix-de-Guerre, but also two privates, Henry Johnson and Needham Roberts, who, though badly wounded, routed an attacking party of two dozen Germans and won individual Croix-de-Guerre. And the 369th was accorded the honor of leading the march of the Allied Armies to the Rhine after the Armistice was signed.

Back home, Negroes followed W. E. B. DuBois' advice to forget their grievances and join in with whites to support the war effort. Negro groups throughout the country gave help to the families of soldiers, while the Mutual Savings Bank of Portsmouth, Virginia (an all-Negro institution), won first place among all the nation's banks in the Third Liberty Loan Drive, having oversubscribed its quota of Liberty Bonds nineteen times. Home-front Negroes worked hard for the war effort in order that, as Charles H. Wesley, Negro educational director of the Y.M.C.A. at Camp Meade, put it, "innate racial superiority as championed by the Germans and as practiced by other races and groups may die a deserving death." Certainly those hopes were shared by the men of the 369th Infantry, who marched in a victory parade down New York's Fifth Avenue, banners unfurled, drums pounding, to the cheers of hundreds of thousands of onlookers; and also by the men of the 370th Infantry, who returned to Chicago to find the entire city closed down in their honor and marched down Michigan Boulevard while bells tolled and whistles sounded. But, as any Negro veteran of the Grand Army of the Republic might have warned them, while war makes for triumphant parades, it does not breed tolerance or respect for liberty.

Postwar America underwent a violent attack of xenophobia. After the fighting stopped, the fears and hatreds aroused by the war found expression in a wave of hysterical persecution of foreigners and minority groups. The establishment of a Communist government in Russia during the closing years of the war led to a widespread and virulent case of "Red-scare jitters," during which anyone of liberal opinions might find himself mobbed, jailed, deported (if he was not a citizen), fired from his job, or slandered. And of course, the hysteria was quickly extended from those whites who advocated Negro equality to Negroes themselves.

Late in November, 1915, the Ku Klux Klan, which had disbanded during the 1870's (its work accomplished), was revived in Atlanta, Georgia, by one William J. Simmons. After the war, the new Klan expanded its membership rapidly, until it reached one hundred thousand in 1919. Ominously, the new Klan was strong in the North as well as the South — its activities extended across the nation. Furthermore the new Klan added to its targets — Catholics, Jews, Orientals, and other foreigners as well as Negroes were intimidated. A Klan victim might have a fiery cross burned on his lawn, or he might have his house blown up, or he might be beaten and murdered. Local police and sheriffs seemed powerless to afford protection against the new Klan — in many cases they were members.

But Negroes throughout the country were not now disposed to take persecution either by the Ku Klux Klan or by other hysterical whites without striking back. Negro veterans had not fought through the horror of the Western front to be intimidated by fellow Americans at home. During 1919 a wave of race riots erupted in cities scattered from Nebraska to Texas to Illinois. The most serious of these took place during late July in Chicago. It began when a little Negro boy decided to adventure into the waters of Lake Michigan aboard a homemade raft. The lad drifted on his raft into a section of the beach that had long been reserved for the exclusive use of whites. He was met by a hail of stones that knocked him into the water, and he drowned. The news quickly spread through the city and mobs formed. During the next two days gangs of Negroes and whites turned the streets of Chicago into a no man's land of rioting. Before the militia was called in to restore order, thirty-eight people had been killed and nearly six hundred wounded, while property damage ran into the millions.

The basic cause of the postwar wave of race riots (of which President Wilson observed, "the white race was the aggressor") was the sudden and heavy influx of Southern Negroes into Northern cities. The war had created a heavy demand for labor in new or expanded industries throughout the North; but at the same time it had closed the gates to European immigration. Desperate for workers, manufacturers had sent agents to recruit in the South. By 1920 nearly half a million more Negroes

New members being sworn into the Ku Klux Klan in Maryland in 1922

were jammed into the rat-infested and teeming Negro ghettos of the North than had lived there in 1910, and most of them were new arrivals. They competed for housing and services with poor white workers, and, after the war, for jobs. The wretched conditions under which both black and white laborers lived in Northern cities, combined with the tensions of new competition, were at the root of the race riots.

A postwar economic recession further aggravated race tensions. Government purchases from industry came to an end; four and one-half million troops were demobilized to flood the labor market, and the government did nothing to alleviate the decline. As workers were fired by the thousands from industries whose war work was done, Negroes were always the first to lose their jobs. And in the postwar competition for jobs, they were always the last to be hired. Only in the heaviest work, such as road building and longshore work, could Negroes hope to hold their jobs. The market for domestic servants was shrunken by the postwar introduction of domestic labor-saving devices such as washing machines. And, as always in a tight labor market, the Negro found himself dispossessed from those few jobs which had been traditionally available to him.

The possibility of intervention on the economic front by the Federal government was nil—the American people had overwhelmingly voted for a return to "normalcy" under the Republicans and their genial if corrupt presidential candidate, Warren G. Harding. Conservative policies in government had returned with a vengeance. Business influence in government was supreme. As Harding's successor, Calvin Coolidge, put it, "The business of this nation is business."

The quest for the dollar became a national crusade, prosperity was for those who could seize it, and the devil was welcome to the hindmost. The level of the national morality was well illustrated in 1925, when, with the government's permission, the Ku Klux Klan (which now boasted four million members) was allowed to parade in full white-sheeted regalia down Pennsylvania Avenue in Washington.

It was hardly surprising then that in their disillusionment and despair Negroes should turn to the black nationalism of the remarkable Marcus Garvey, the self-styled "Provisional President of Africa," whose appeal to the masses of urban Negroes for a "Back to Africa" movement was spectacular.

Born in 1887 on the British West Indian island of Jamaica, Garvey came to the United States in 1905, his object being to gain support for a black empire to be governed by black men. He established himself in Harlem and set about organizing the Universal Negro Improvement Association and its newspaper,

Marcus Garvey
(CULVER
PICTURES, INC.)

the *Negro World*. His success was immediate and amazing. He was an expert publicity man and filled Harlem and other Northern Negro ghettos with street parades and mass rallies. He bestowed titles such as "knight" and "duke" on some of his followers—titles which would be made good when the black empire came into being.

Marcus Garvey, for all his fanfare and posturings, had a message for Negroes which was justly appealing. He told Negroes of the glorious past of Africa, urged them to be proud of their race, and, in reciting the many accomplishments of Negroes in history, gave them a measure of self-respect. If his African Orthodox Church movement seemed faintly ridiculous to Negro intellectuals, the hint of black supremacy in his propaganda was understandable. It was a reaction to centuries of persecution. Pointing out that the United States was and always would be a "white man's country," Garvey insisted that Negroes must return to Africa to establish an independent nation there. To further his aims he created an armed "African Legion" among his followers and established business enterprises to raise money. But Garvey was by no means the financier he thought himself to be. Irregularities were found in his books and he was tried and convicted of fraud in 1925. Sentenced to five years in Atlanta Penitentiary, Garvey was pardoned by President Coolidge in 1927 and deported to Jamaica. He was to die there, penniless and alone, in 1940.

Another and older movement organized to help urban Negroes was the National Urban League, founded in New York in 1910 by white socialite Mrs. Ruth Standish Baldwin. The Urban League was established as an interracial organization of whites and Negroes and concentrated on practical assistance to ghetto-trapped Negroes. Starting with a modest budget of $8,500 in its first year, by 1925 the Urban League was spending $300,000 per year and had branches in fifty-one different cities and towns throughout the country. The League found homes and jobs for newly arrived Negro migrants from the South, petitioned employers to hire Negro workers, and set up educational and recreation programs to combat delinquency.

But neither the emergence of suddenly sky-rocketing (and as suddenly fading) emotional movements such as Marcus Garvey's nor the steady work of an Urban League or an N.A.A.C.P. could bring much relief to Negroes. The roaring "Gay Twenties" were not so thriving for Negroes — of the several million unemployed each year during America's biggest "boom," a large percentage was Negro.

When, on "Black Thursday," October 24, 1929, the stock market commenced its spectacular slide into disaster, Negroes were hardly affected. To many it simply seemed that the constant depression in which they had been living for nearly sixty-five years was now to be shared by whites. But in this, they were mistaken. For this depression was to be unlike any other both in depth and duration. It was to bring about changes in American life so profound as to alter thought patterns — and it was to lay the groundwork for most of the dramatic strides forward that Negroes have made ever since.

10 The Age of Roosevelt

Although she feeds me bread of bitterness,
And sinks into my throat her tiger's tooth,
Stealing my breath of life, I will confess
I love this cultured hell that tests my youth!

—CLAUDE MCKAY

She even thinks that up in Heaven
Her class lies late and snores,
While poor black cherubs rise at seven
To do celestial chores.

—COUNTEE CULLEN

THE FINANCIAL DISASTER OF OCTOBER, 1929, BROKE THE intricate chain of American banking and credit at its weakest link—the Negro banks. In July, 1930, Binga's bank in Chicago's South Side Negro ghetto closed its doors. On the street a large crowd shouted in panic for its life savings, now vanished. The same scene was quickly repeated in the Negro sections of cities throughout the country; it would become commonplace in white communities eighteen months later. Thus, while the entire nation plunged into the Great Depression, Negroes as a group were affected earlier and more harshly. The always-chronic underemployment of Negroes was rapidly transformed into mass unemployment on a far higher percentage scale than among whites. Of the twelve to fifteen million Americans without jobs in 1931, three million (one-quarter to one-fifth—although Negroes formed but ten percent of the population) were Negroes. The specters of starvation and homelessness, never far from the Negro, were now suddenly knocking violently at his door.

The first reaction to the realization that this Depression was something fearfully out of the ordinary took the form of panic.

Uncertain and dangerous mobs appeared in the streets of New York, Chicago, and other Northern cities. Some Negroes sought relief by organizing boycott campaigns against local merchants. While millions of Negroes were unemployed, white-owned stores in Negro ghettos continued to refuse to hire them. Committees were formed in various cities, especially Chicago and New York (where the fight was led by Adam Clayton Powell, Jr.), under the slogan "Spend your money where you can work!" The campaign was effective, and stores in Negro communities which had never hired Negroes before now made certain that Negro customers found Negro clerks and salesgirls waiting on them. Another stopgap means of trying to avert calamity was the spontaneous formation of "anti-eviction squads" in some cities. Usually composed of Negro students and the unemployed, these squads would prevent landlords from evicting Negro tenants by sitting on the furniture to prevent its removal or breaking back into a locked building in cases where the furniture had already been thrown into the street.

Such measures, however, could do little to attack the root causes of the pall of misery which now engulfed Negroes and whites throughout the nation. "The business of this nation is business," Coolidge had insisted. Now business was closed for the decade, and Coolidge's successor, Herbert Hoover, could offer little but brave words and a stiff-upper-lip philosophy to the growing millions of desperate poor. Only political action, it seemed, could effect a change. And although Negroes in the South remained completely without the vote, big city Negroes in the North now held a large share of the balance of power. How should they use it?

During the twenties, and now at the beginning of the thirties, the American Communist Party made a determined effort to enlist Negro support. It pointed out that neither of the two major political parties could be relied upon to fight for Negro interests. Furthermore the Communists made it a matter of strict party discipline that no party member could display the faintest trace of anti-Negro attitudes or feelings. Communists ate with Negroes, lived in the same apartment buildings with them, marched with them in demonstrations, and worked with them in organizations such as the Communist-organized American Negro Labor Congress. They also—through their International Labor Defense organization, which defended Negroes in court—fought many a battle against racist "justice."

But the Communist Party made few converts among Negroes. By 1928 there were about two hundred Negro members in the party. In that year, the Communist Party changed its tactics somewhat by coming out for the creation of an independent Negro republic in the United States. But this idea met with a cool reception. The fact was that Negroes, like other Americans, were deeply individualistic, not particularly class conscious, and deeply skeptical of total solutions or utopian schemes. Moreover, most rank-and-file Negroes followed the advice of their clergymen or of middle-class Negro leaders, the majority of whom had conscious reasons for opposing Communism.

The high-water mark of Communist influence among Negroes was reached when the party organized the defense in the Scottsboro Case. On March 25, 1931, nine Negro adolescents were accused of raping two white women on a freight train in Alabama. Tried in the little town of Scottsboro, Alabama, within two weeks eight of the boys were condemned to the electric chair. While such organizations as the N.A.A.C.P. volunteered help and legal counsel, the parents of the boys preferred to let the Communist International Labor Defense handle the case. For four years the I.L.D. fought the case through the courts, while Communist organizations in America and throughout the world maintained a tremendous propaganda campaign which succeeded in focusing international attention on racist "justice" in the United States. In 1935 the I.L.D. permitted other committees to aid in the work, and two years later they won acquittal for four of the boys and assured the eventual release of the others. But while Negroes were genuinely grateful to the Communists for such efforts, and genuinely admired their determined struggle for Negro rights, they did not flock to join the party.

Perhaps the primary reason that Negroes did not succumb to radical philosophies during the dark Depression years was the emergence of a new Democratic Party under Franklin D. Roosevelt. The earlier coalition of Midwestern farmers and big city workers which had brought Wilson to power was deepened and broadened by the terrible economic catastrophe of 1929–1930. The New Freedom had died with Wilson, but liberals within the Democratic Party had developed new plans and new appeals. Negroes, disappointed and embittered by Wilson's lack of interest in their problems, had largely returned to the Republican Party during the elections of the twenties. But big city Democratic Party bosses had taken careful note of the enlargement of the Negro vote due to immigration from the South. All during the twenties they made a determined bid to win that vote. Negroes were appointed to small political jobs, and Negroes received a share of the favors with which city bosses had long wooed other ethnic groups. A noticeable shift of political allegiance took place in Negro ghettos all over the North. It changed from a noticeable shift to a landslide after the Depression arrived. And in 1932 Negroes thought they detected a note of promise in the words of Democratic presidential candidate Franklin D. Roosevelt. They voted for him overwhelmingly, and hoped their ears had not deceived them.

Roosevelt's New Deal actually had no fixed policy toward Negroes. But the New Deal was a determined program to help the poor and the working classes — and Negroes bulked large in both groups. Neither Roosevelt nor any of his New Deal supporters or cabinet members would personally brook government discrimination against Negroes in the broad new programs which were now undertaken. The Public Works Administration, under Interior Secretary Harold Ickes, was required to employ a certain percentage of skilled Negro workers on all its projects. The Works Progress Administration, under Harry Hopkins, made sure that Negroes were well represented in all its undertakings and set up a Division of Negro Affairs under famed Negro educator Mary McLeod Bethune. The Civilian

A Negro sharecropper's "home" in South Carolina in 1938
(SCHOMBURG COLLECTION, NEW YORK PUBLIC LIBRARY)

Conservation Corps numbered sixteen thousand Negro youths among its members in 1935. And while such programs offered relief to the Negroes crowded into Northern city slums, Negro sharecroppers in the South were not overlooked. The Farm Security Administration was authorized to extend long-term, low-interest loans to poor Negro and white farmers throughout the country. In three years (1937–1940) the F.S.A. made loans to fifty thousand Negro tenant farmers. Of great importance to Negroes everywhere was the Social Security Act, passed in 1935. Besides welcoming its insurance and welfare provisions, as did tens of millions of desperate white Americans, Negroes viewed with special satisfaction its unwritten implication that the government had a responsibility to the less fortunate of its citizens.

Direct government assistance, while desperately needed and welcomed, was not in the long run to prove so effective in bringing permanent benefits to the Negro as was the Roosevelt Administration's attitude to the cause of organized labor. The passage of the Wagner Labor Relations Act of 1935 guaranteed government protection and backing for labor unions in their long and bloody fight for a share in the national wealth. It also assured the ending of organized labor's "lily white" unions policy.

Negro laborers, long effectively barred from the white labor movement, had had but indifferent success in attempting to organize their own unions. A notable exception was the Brotherhood of Sleeping Car Porters, organized by A. Philip Randolph. Randolph, born in 1889 at Crescent City, Florida, had received his education at New York's City College. Although a man of great intellectual attainments, he had had to work hard during his youth. He understood the problems of labor organizing and for ten years he devoted himself to the struggle of organizing the railroad porters. Beginning his drive in 1925, Randolph was not to be deterred by strikebreakers (who defeated a porters' strike in 1929) or the Depression itself. But it was not until 1935 (the year of the Wagner Act) that Randolph finally won recognition of his union from the railroad companies. Thereafter, as a member union of the A.F.L., the brotherhood fought to persuade the federation to drop its barriers against Negro workers.

In 1935, too, John L. Lewis, president of the United Mine Workers, departed from the ranks of the A.F.L. to form the Congress of Industrial Organizations. Taking its cue from the U.M.W. policy, the C.I.O. banned discrimination. It trained and employed Negro labor organizers and forced its member unions to support Negro members' drives for equal pay for equal

A corner of a room in a broken-down plantation house has been "remodeled" into a kitchen in 1938.

(SCHOMBURG COLLECTION, NEW YORK PUBLIC LIBRARY)

work and other long-overdue benefits. By 1940, the C.I.O. counted 210,000 Negro members—all of whom had a new consciousness of unionism and of solidarity with white workers.

The New Deal brought symbolic victories to Negroes, too. President Roosevelt made certain that eminent Negroes such as William H. Hastie and Robert C. Weaver were appointed to responsible government posts. He inclined a sympathetic and always personally friendly ear to advice tendered him by such men as N.A.A.C.P. leader Walter White and the indefatigable W. E. B. DuBois. Mrs. Eleanor Roosevelt also won great favor among Negroes for her sympathetic understanding of their problems. In 1939, when the Daughters of the American Revolution refused to allow Negro soprano Marian Anderson to sing in the D.A.R.'s Constitution Hall, Mrs. Roosevelt cancelled her membership in that organization—and made sure that Marian Anderson did sing in Washington, on the steps of the Lincoln Memorial, to a crowd of twenty-five thousand. The popularity of the Roosevelt family with Negroes was such that an estimated eighty percent of Negro voters cast their ballots for F.D.R. in 1936 and 1940.

Negro morale during the Depression, as in the past, was lifted by the individual and isolated successes achieved by outstanding Negroes in various fields. Probably of greatest importance, because of its widespread appeal, was the role of the Negro in sports. Here, as in every other field, the Negro had to fight hard to win recognition. The first area in which Negroes became prominent was horse racing. Stable boys, trainers, and jockeys in the old South, Negroes had a tradition of horsemanship which was reflected by the fact that in the first running of the Kentucky Derby in 1875, there were thirteen Negro jockeys mounted in a field of fourteen starters. Beginning with that year, Negro jockeys won the Derby no less than eleven times by the turn of the century—one, Isaac Murphy, won it three times.

That Negroes were playing baseball almost from the inception of the game is illustrated by the fact that the National Association of Baseball Players formally banned Negroes from membership in 1867. Nonetheless, by 1887 there were seven powerful Negro teams playing professionally. White teams refused to meet them, explaining frankly that if they lost they would lose their white fans. In 1901 John J. McGraw tried to smuggle Negro player Charles Grant into his Baltimore Orioles as an Indian—but was found out by the association. Not until 1947 would Jackie Robinson break the color line in baseball.

Boxing knew no color bar—precisely because it often involved a direct confrontation between white and black which inflamed (and lured) white audiences. Peter Jackson, the so-called "First Black Gentleman," won the Australian heavyweight championship and then fought James J. Corbett to a sixty-one-round draw in 1887. George Dixon and Joe Gans both held various world boxing titles before the turn of the century. But perhaps the most famous of all was Jack Johnson, who won the world's heavyweight crown in 1908. Johnson's victory so irritated white sports fans that they immediately launched a search for a white boxer (a "White Hope" as the newspapers put it) to defeat him. Jim Jeffries was goaded from retirement to meet Johnson at Reno, Nevada, on July 4, 1910. His fate was recorded by the *New York World* the next day: "That Mr. Johnson should so lightly and carelessly punch the head off of Mr. Jeffries must have come as a shock to every devoted believer in the supremacy of the Anglo-Saxon race." But Johnson was pursued by race prejudice throughout his career. His marriage to a white woman raised a particular furor.

On June 25, 1935, a young Negro boxer named Joseph Louis Barrow, the son of poor tenant farmers in Alabama, defeated Primo Carnera in just six rounds, thereby becoming a claimant to the world heavyweight title and an overnight hero to his people. Joe Louis polished off several of the other contenders for the title and then in 1936 came up against Max Schmeling, the German boxer who was the idol of the Nazi race propagandists. Louis lost to Schmeling by a knockout in the twelfth round. Hitler and his cohorts were transported with joy—and Joe Louis went back into training.

But 1936 was also the year of the Olympic Games held at Berlin. And there, to the anguish of the Nazis (Hitler, who presided, left his box seat in wrath and humiliation) such Negro athletic stars as Jesse Owens, Ralph Metcalfe, Johnny Woodruff, and Cornelius Johnson walked away with top honors, running, jumping, and vaulting the Nazis into the ground. Still, the Nazis could point to Max Schmeling. The "Black Uhlan," as he was called, had indulged in much boasting and race-superiority talk since he had beaten Louis; and he carried Hitler's personal wishes for success when he climbed into the ring at Yankee Stadium to meet the "Brown Bomber" again on June 22, 1938. According to Joe Louis himself, this fight was the only one he ever went into with hate in his heart. The Nazi superman walked into a fusillade of savage punches, had time to land exactly four blows of his own—and then was knocked out before the bell rang to end the first round! Negroes went wild with joy—and the majority of white Americans joined them. From that day forward, Joe Louis was a national rather than simply a Negro hero.

During the thirties, for the first time, Negroes won national recognition in fields other than sports. In poetry Claude McKay, Langston Hughes, and Countee Cullen achieved permanent fame—and belated praise was given to Paul Laurence Dunbar, Negro poet of the nineteenth century. Negro novelists such as Jessie Fauset, Jean Toomer, Rudolph Fisher, and Richard Wright drew from their own experiences and the vivid life of their people the inspiration for works of fiction which won national renown. And it was in the decades between the two world wars that Negro music and musicians changed the popular music of the entire world.

Growing out of the plantation spirituals and work songs, the sea chanties and chain-gang chants of the Southern Negro, popularized through post-Civil-War minstrel shows, came jazz and the blues. Starting (as an entertainment rather than functional music) in the Negro clubs in New Orleans, jazz was carried by Negro musicians such as trumpeter Louis Armstrong up the Mississippi to Saint Louis and Chicago, establishing different "schools" in different cities, until, by the end of World War I, it had caught the imagination of the entire country. Jazz became the musical idiom of America, and is considered today to be America's greatest contribution to the musical heritage of the world.

It was during the thirties too, that Negro historians, such as Carter G. Woodson (who had been trained at Harvard and the Sorbonne), began to reexamine Negro contributions to American life in the past. Out of obscurity were resurrected such names as those of Jan E. Matzeliger, Negro cobbler of Lynn, Massachusetts, who invented the lasting machine, which transformed the making of shoes from a handicraft into an industry; Granville T. Woods, New York electrician who introduced the "third rail" electric system for the propulsion of trains; Louis H. Latimer, who made the original drawings for Alexander Graham Bell's telephone and invented the carbon filament for electric lamps. In fact Woodson was able to remind Negroes that when the first official check had been made in preparation for America's participation in the Paris Exposition of 1900, it had been found that more than five hundred essential patents were held by Negroes. In rescuing such Negro history from oblivion, Woodson and his successors performed a vital service to Negroes, who could take pride in their achievements of the past.

Perhaps the most important effect of the Great Depression and the New Deal on the Negro's place in American society was one that was barely recognized at the time and still remains largely undefined today. The Depression undermined many of the old shibboleths of American society. The spokesmen for business and industry—the conservatives whose economic strictures, exploitive view of life, and restrictive opinions on all social problems, including race relations, had been taken by most Americans as gospel for so long—were now completely discredited. Their "business civilization" had collapsed and brought misery to millions and millions of people, and with it had collapsed, too, the respect which had formerly been accorded their opinions. In the popular mind economic conservatives were looked upon (and in some cases with justification) as traitors to their country. The old solutions, the old prejudices had been undermined; and Americans, white as well

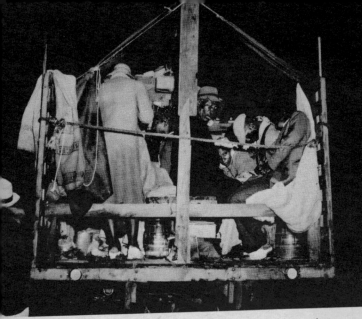

These agricultural workers paid $8.00 apiece to be driven by truck to a work camp at Bridgeton, New Jersey, in 1942. (CULVER PICTURES, INC.)

as black, had opened their minds to newer, more realistic and more progressive views. Under the benign if sometimes stormy leadership of Roosevelt's New Deal, the American climate of opinion changed. The Federal government was now looked to for help and guidance in areas which had formerly been the province of state governments; and the concept of states' rights, undermined in the economic sphere, was badly eroded too in the social sphere.

The acceptance of the idea that the Federal government had the right and the duty to regulate private enterprise on behalf of the people made it easier to accept the idea that the government also had the paramount right to intervene in any area in which the rights of individual citizens were being denied or threatened. Furthermore, the experience of the Depression was a salutary one for many white Americans in that it brought them firsthand and bitter knowledge of exactly how Negroes had been living for so many years. The shock of the Depression also provoked intensive research in economics and sociology, disciplines which gathered the basic knowledge upon which further advances would one day be made. Reexamination of American history led to the realization that the oppression of the Negro people and their exploitation had been fostered over the years as a means of exploiting for private profit *all* the American people.

Of course, at different times and places, the harsh life of the Depression years led to hysterical outbursts of fury. Downcast and hungry people who could not strike back at the forces which oppressed them found a handy scapegoat in the Negro. But lynchings actually diminished during the twenties and thirties. And the ideals of economic justice and social equality won a new victory in the minds of thoughtful and moderate men everywhere in the country—a victory which would bear fruits in the future.

But as the thirties drew to their close, it was apparent that Americans would not be left alone to solve their domestic problems. For the philosophy (if it may be distinguished with that name) of fascism and nazism, with its insistence on racial doctrine and embodied in the military might of Italy and Germany, was on the march; and after war broke out in Europe in September of 1939, it was apparent to many Americans that they would eventually be drawn into it.

Negroes were not new to the fight against fascism. They had been fighting a racist philosophy in the United States for centuries. More immediately, some had fought against the fascists during the Spanish Civil War with the International brigades. The all-American George Washington Battalion of the Fifteenth (International) Brigade, which had fought for the Spanish Republic, had been commanded by Negro Oliver Law, who had given his life at the battle of Brunete. But although Negroes recognized the implicit threat to their very existence in Hitler's race doctrines, many had been too disillusioned by the results of their efforts in World War I, with its aftermath of race riots and disappointments, to grow overly enthusiastic about making new sacrifices on behalf of other people's freedom.

The most immediate consequence in the United States of the war in Europe was the ending of the Depression. As the European democracies reeled beneath the blows of the *Wehrmacht*, President Roosevelt declared a state of emergency, and the nation's resources were thrown into a mighty effort of military preparedness and aid to Britain and, later, Russia. Industries that had been working at only part capacity now had more work than they could handle, while giant new factories were rushed into construction throughout the country. Prosperity was returning with a vengeance. But not for the Negroes.

The new war plants, operating with government contracts, were refusing to hire Negro workers. According to the 1940 census, there were almost five and one-half million Negroes in the American labor force; but of thirty thousand employees in ten war plants in the New York area, for example, only 140 were Negroes; in fifty-six war plants in Saint Louis only 168 Negroes found employment. In a survey conducted by the U.S. Employment Service, fifty percent of all war plants queried stated flatly that they would not hire Negroes. And all this at a time when the labor shortage created a serious crisis in American defense efforts! Negro leaders such as Walter White and A. Philip Randolph pleaded with authorities in Washington to allow Negroes to take part in defense industries. As Walter White put it:

"We pleaded with the President to break his silence and to speak out against discrimination which not only was doing an injustice to the Negro, but was definitely jeopardizing our national security . . . but for five months we were given the run-around."

In actuality, President Roosevelt was facing a real struggle to unite the American people for the fight against fascism. The spirit of neutrality and isolationism was strong in the land. Yet unless America could be brought united into the struggle, Hitler and his gang might win in Europe—with consequences for the United States which would be disastrous. To press for Negro equality on any front just now might prove divisive, might add to the main problem, which was, as Roosevelt saw it, simply one of national survival. But in this, the President underestimated the American people—something he rarely did at any time.

Fed up with the prolonged "run-around" they were getting in Washington, Walter White, A. Philip Randolph, and other leaders decided to stage a massive Negro march on the nation's capital. Fifty thousand Negroes were organized to march in protest right up to the White House. But at the very last moment the march was called off. For on June 25, 1941, under increasing pressure from Negro leaders, white liberals, the threat of the massive demonstration, and Mrs. Roosevelt, the President issued Executive Order Number 8802. The order declared:

". . . the policy of the United States [is] to encourage full participation in the national defense program by all citizens of the United States, regardless of race, creed, color, or national origins."

Furthermore, the order had teeth. It established a Fair Employment Practices Committee to investigate hiring policies and enforce the program. The way was open now for Negroes to enter the defense effort. And they did this in huge numbers. Many received specialized training for new jobs—training which would inevitably lead to better jobs after the war.

In 1940, before the Draft Law went into effect, there were but 13,200 Negroes in the Army and four thousand in the Navy. In both services they were rigidly segregated from whites. After the beginning of Selective Service, the War Department announced that as a general policy Negroes would be drafted in numbers corresponding to their proportion of the population—and the policy of segregation would be continued. Unlike World War I draft procedures, the new system was generally fair, and fairly administered. Negroes served as high officials in the Selective Service System, and eighteen hundred Negroes served on local draft boards.

After the Japanese attack on Pearl Harbor on December 7, 1941, a group of Negro leaders urged the War Department to create at least one nonsegregated volunteer division; but the suggestion was turned down. The only area in which the Army would give in on its policy of segregation was in the training of Negro officers. Since Negro officers were now urgently required to handle the increasing numbers of Negro soldiers and since separate training facilities would prove too costly and inefficient, Negro officer candidates were trained in the same schools and classes as whites. Negro officers graduated at a rate of about two hundred a month all during the war—and no instances of trouble were noted in the nonsegregated Officer Candidate School program.

Nearly one million Negroes served in the armed forces during the war. Of these about one hundred thousand saw duty with the Navy. At first the Navy maintained its old policy of "messmen only" in regard to Negroes (a policy which would have amazed John Paul Jones, Oliver Hazard Perry, Stephen Decatur, and David Farragut, all of whom prized their Negro gunners). But after considerable agitation, on April 7, 1942, the Navy Department inaugurated a policy of using Negro enlistees for general service. The next month the same policy was applied to the Coast Guard; and in June, 1942, for the first time in its history, the United States Marine Corps began to admit Negro volunteers.

The Air Corps (then a part of the Army) maintained a policy of strict segregation but did train Negro pilots. An all-Negro pursuit squadron, the 99th, was trained at Tuskegee. Assigned to the Twelfth Air Force in Tunisia, the "Red Tails" (as the 99th came to be known) ran up an exceptional total of "kills" over Africa, Sicily, and Italy. Later, other Negro pursuit squadrons were organized; and in whatever skies they fought, they established impressive records.

Most Negro troops in Europe were in the Quartermaster Corps, as they had been in World War I. And in the task of servicing the fighting fronts, Negro units performed prodigies of stevedoring, trucking, wire-laying, beach-clearing, and evacuation of the wounded. Some forty thousand Negroes were the majority of the men who formed the amazing "Red Ball Express," a truck supply route in Europe that ran from the ports and beaches right up to the front lines. Bumper to bumper, in any weather, under strafing and shelling, the Red Ball trucks went through night and day. Disabled trucks were pushed off the road (which was five times as long as the famed Burma Road), but the Red Ball Express kept moving—a feat that amazed the military commanders of all nations and a vital, if not *the* vital, key to Allied victories in Europe. On top of this, when the Red Ball men delivered their supplies, they often picked up rifles and fought. At Bastogne, Belgium, during the Battle of the Bulge, the Red Ball Express rolled into the beleaguered American pocket as German forces closed in behind them. After distributing their supplies, the truck drivers grabbed weapons and helped the 101st Airborne Division make its legendary stand against the last great German offensive of the war.

Negro combat units were to be found in every branch of the Army: coast artillery, field artillery, tank corps, signal corps, and infantry. The 761st Tank Battalion, an all-Negro outfit, was commended by four generals and the Secretary of War for its gallant fighting. The only Negro infantry division in Europe was the 92nd, which fought in the long, bloody, and dreary Italian campaign. There was a morale problem in the 92nd due to the fact that its white senior officers ran it like an old-time Southern plantation. Negro junior officers were seldom accorded the military courtesy due them, and most Negro soldiers in the division thought the divisional commander was sending them forward to needless slaughter. The 92nd also suffered from supply problems and the entire snarl of attempting to fight a modern war on a segregated basis. Nevertheless, the 92nd, which numbered about twelve hundred men, won 12,095 decorations and citations—a very creditable record.

Badly needing infantry replacements in Europe in the winter of 1945, the Army was forced to organize Negro platoons to serve in white regiments. The experiment was an immense success. White officers, questioned later about the performance of the mixed units, were unanimous in their praise.

With the usual touch of irony so common in the Negro's history, while Negro soldiers and sailors and airmen were piling up impressive records on the various fighting fronts of the world, Negroes in the United States were finding that this war, like all previous wars, was heightening racial tensions. Negro soldiers training at Army camps in the South were the special targets of race hatred. There were race riots at Fort Oswego, Camp Davis, Fort Huachuca, and Fort Bragg. Negro Army nurse Nora Green was badly beaten by a white bus driver in Montgomery, Alabama, following a dispute over where she should sit. At Little Rock, Arkansas, a platoon of Negroes of the 94th Engineer Battalion was chased off the road by a gang of armed whites led by state troopers. And lynchings continued.

Members of the 92nd Division in a fire fight with German troops near Massa, Italy, 1944 (WIDE WORLD PHOTOS)

While Nazi saboteurs and spies were given calm, fair, and prolonged trials, Negroes were dragged from jails in Mississippi and hung from bridges. In Washington, D.C., a crazed white man named Eugene Ekland, vowing to exterminate the Negro race, took out a shotgun and murdered five Negroes. He was sentenced to fifteen years' imprisonment — with time off for "good behavior."

Tensions in Northern cities erupted into race riots on several occasions. As in World War I, the demand for labor in Northern industry had brought about another wave of Negro migration from the South to the already overcrowded Negro ghettos of the North. About 330,000 Negroes moved North or to the Pacific Coast during the war. Riots occurred in New York, Los Angeles, and Detroit. The worst took place in Detroit, during the week of June 20, 1943. Twenty-five Negroes and nine whites were killed, scores were injured, and property damage ran to $2,000,000.

As in the past, competition for housing and better jobs and the influx of many poor white Southerners as well as Negroes accounted for these explosions. A new factor was the bitterness felt by some whites because of the tremendous economic advances made by Negroes during the war years. Between 1940 and 1944, for example, the number of Negroes employed in government service jumped from sixty thousand to three hundred thousand, the ratio of skilled to nonskilled Negro workers doubled, and the number of Negro women employed in industry quadrupled.

When victory in World War II came in 1945, Negro Americans could look back with pride on their contribution to the war effort—a contribution made despite continued opposition and discrimination. They mourned, as did most Americans, the passing of Franklin D. Roosevelt, who had died in April of 1945. But the impetus of the New Deal and the new modes of thought did not die with him; they were carried on by President Harry S. Truman's Fair Deal and given special urgency by America's new role in world affairs.

The central forum for that role was to be the United Nations Organization, established during the last days of the war as the latest of mankind's attempts to bring rationality and order into international relations. But unlike the earlier League of Nations, the U.N. did not limit its interests to purely international themes. Its charter, to which all member nations had to subscribe, announced certain domestic policies and attitudes which were of special interest to American Negroes. Walter White, Mary McLeod Bethune, and W. E. B. DuBois were present as officially invited observers at the U.N.'s founding convention in San Francisco in 1945. And each of them expressed cautious optimism over the fact that the United States, as a signatory member, might now actually begin to attempt to live up to the U.N.'s Declaration of Human Rights. This Declaration was actively pushed at the convention by (among others) Ralph Bunche, the State Department's Acting Chief of the Division of Dependent Territories. But most Americans, whether in the

State Department or not, chose to interpret the Declaration as a weapon in the fight for the liberation of African peoples (and Asians) from colonial domination rather than as a goal for domestic achievement. Thus, although Ralph Bunche was to become chief of the U.N.'s Trusteeship Division in 1946, to bring peace to the troubled Arab-Israeli area in 1948, and to win the Nobel Peace Prize in 1950—to become, in other words, one of the world's leading statesmen—he was to be considered a second-class citizen at home because he was a Negro.

On the domestic scene after the war, Negroes once again found that as war industries cut back production, they were the first to be fired. But fortunately, the Great Depression had taught America some important lessons in economics. This time the Federal government intervened with public assistance programs to cushion the blow; and in any event after a brief slump in 1946, American industry moved into boom times as it strove to meet the high demand for consumer products following five years of austerity and to supply a devastated world beyond America's borders. Negro participation in prosperity was assured by the Fair Employment Practices Committee. For although the original F.E.P.C. went out of existence in 1946, it was renewed in various forms by presidential decree thereafter.

Nor had the lessons of World War II been lost on the military. The Defense Department, after studying a series of reports, and at the insistence of President Truman, finally brought segregation in the armed forces to an end between 1950 and 1955. Desegregation of the military was also due in part to the outbreak of the Korean War. Battling against communist forces for the avowed purpose of preserving a democratic form of society among Asians, the United States could no longer afford world-wide criticism of an official policy of discrimination against its own colored population.

And American sensitivity to world opinion explained much of the progress that Negroes were to make after World War II. As African and Asiatic nations won freedom from their former white imperialist masters, they also won a majority of the votes in the United Nations General Assembly. And as America entered a new cold war against world-wide communism, the support of uncommitted nations and of the world's majority of colored peoples became a key to survival. Communist spokesmen were quick to criticize anti-Negro discrimination in the United States; and such criticism was their most effective weapon against America in the vital propaganda war to win the allegiance of Africans and Asians. A lynching in Georgia, a race riot in some Northern city, a protest march—these events were now trumpeted to the world by America's enemies and critics. And when they pointed out such evidences of anti-democratic injustice, most thoughtful Americans could only admit that they were right. Making democracy work in the United States became more than an urgent domestic problem — it became a necessary step toward national survival in the atomic age.

11 We Shall Overcome

*If there is no struggle, there is no progress. Those
who profess to favor freedom, and yet deprecate
agitation are men who want crops without plowing
up the ground. They want the ocean without the
awful roar of its many waters.*

— FREDERICK DOUGLASS (1855)

*Today, I want to say to the people of America and
the nations of the world: We are not about to turn
around. We are on the* move *now. Yes, we are on
the move and no wave of racism can stop us.*

— MARTIN LUTHER KING, JR. (1965)

EARLY IN 1951, OLIVER BROWN OF TOPEKA, KANSAS, DE-
cided he had had enough. For years now he had lived within
five blocks of a public school, but every school day his eight-
year-old daughter, Linda Carol, had to trek across a railroad
freight yard to catch a bus which would carry her twenty-one
blocks to a segregated all-Negro school. He got together with
twelve other Negro parents, and with lawyers supplied by the
N.A.A.C.P. they brought suit against the city to end segregation of its public schools. These Kansans were not alone. Other
suits were being filed in Virginia, Delaware, South Carolina,
and Washington, D.C. For in those days nearly eleven million
children—two out of every five in the United States—were
attending legally segregated schools.

The lower courts, in which the suits were brought and
through which they were appealed, were forced to follow the
Supreme Court's decision of 1896 in *Plessy* vs. *Ferguson* that
segregation was constitutional, provided the separate facilities
were equal. Therefore the 1951 suits were aimed at the Supreme Court itself—inviting the Court to change its mind on
the ground that separate schools could not be defined as equal
simply because they *were* separate. A child going to a segre-

gated all-Negro school was well aware of *why* he was going there, and the feelings of inferiority and resentment this aroused interfered basically and vitally with education.

Franklin Roosevelt, when faced with a conservative majority on the Supreme Court that threatened to undermine his New Deal, had tried to pass new laws which would enable him to appoint additional members to the Court. He had lost that fight, but won the battle; the Court had become more liberal in its interpretations. And as old members died and new ones were appointed by Roosevelt and later Truman, the Court developed a more progressive complexion. In 1944, in *Smith* vs. *Allright*, the Court had decreed that political parties could not exclude voters of any race from participating in primaries; in 1946 it ruled (in *Morgan* vs. *Virginia*) that segregation on interstate carriers was illegal; in 1948, in *Shelley* vs. *Kraemer*, the Court decided that private agreements to bar citizens from purchasing property because of race or color could not be enforced in the courts. And in a series of test cases (brought by the N.A.A.C.P.) from 1938 to 1950 the Supreme Court had tried to make the states meet the "equality" test of *Plessy* vs. *Ferguson* by providing truly equal facilities for Negro students. For example, in 1938 the Court forced Missouri to admit a Negro law student to the University of Missouri Law School because there was no equivalent facility, and in 1948 and 1950 made similar rulings against Oklahoma and Texas—all on the basis that separate schools were not equal in educational facilities.

The N.A.A.C.P., which had brought these suits, had hoped that when the Southern states were faced with the expense of providing truly equal schools for Negroes, they would begin to integrate their school systems instead. On the contrary, the Southern states began to appropriate more money for all-Negro schools. The antisegregation suits of 1951 were the result.

These suits reached the Supreme Court in 1953, all of them in the name of *Brown* vs. *Board of Education*. Almost a year later, on May 17, 1954, completely reversing *Plessy* vs. *Ferguson*, the Supreme Court's nine justices (three of them Southerners) *unanimously* declared that segregation in public schools on the basis of race was unconstitutional. The Court's decree held that separate schools were inherently unequal and deprived the segregated child of his equal protection under the law as set forth in the Fourteenth Amendment. The Court set no deadline for an end to segregation in the schools—it simply said that desegregation would have to proceed "with all deliberate speed."

The reaction to this momentous decision was varied. In

those Northern states and border states where segregation did exist, it was brought to an end relatively painlessly and speedily (Topeka, Kansas, had desegregated its schools even before the Supreme Court's verdict). But in the states of the Deep South a sense of crisis prevailed. The Court's decision was a direct attack against the entire social structure of the South. Poor whites, who had been subjected to anti-Negro propaganda for centuries, were hysterical in their response; the politically powerful and industrially powerful among the South's rich were deeply alarmed. If Negro and white children went to school together, it would be much more difficult to get them to hate each other in their adult years. They might even band together. In that case political and economic power might be wrested from the conservative rich. So while the violence of the poor whites' reaction to the Court's decision was spontaneous, that violence was also carefully and discreetly fostered by the leaders of the Southern economy and their political spokesmen.

The immediate consequence in the Deep South of the Court's decision was the formation of White Citizens' Councils. First organized in Indianola, Mississippi, less than two months after the Court's decree, the councils rapidly spread through every Southern state. Their activities were exemplified by what happened in a Mississippi town when fifty-three Negroes petitioned for integrated schools. The council took out a full-page ad in the local paper, listing the name and address of each and every Negro who had signed the petition. The Negroes were fired from their jobs, refused service in local stores, and in some cases, forced to leave town. The White Citizens' Councils were made up of businessmen and professional men who were too clever to indulge personally in violence. But the councils supported the activities of the Ku Klux Klan, which mobilized poor whites to commit outrages on Negroes and whites who supported the cause of integration.

A major turning point in the fight for integration came at Little Rock, Arkansas, in September, 1957. Ever since the Supreme Court decision, the Little Rock school officials had worked with moderate community leaders to plan for peaceful integration of Little Rock Central High School. Hoping that by admitting a token group of nine Negro students to the school, they could escape complete integration, the Little Rock authorities had laid careful plans to avoid violence. But the day before school opened, Arkansas Governor Orville Faubus stepped uninvited into the situation. Like many Southern politicians, he owed his position to the support of large corporations and the votes of masses of poor whites. He had sworn to oppose integration to the last ditch as part of his rabble-rousing political campaigns. Just what this meant for Little Rock was soon demonstrated.

When fifteen-year-old Elizabeth Eckford, first of the Negro students to arrive at Central High, rounded the corner and started down the street toward the school building, she found a crowd of four hundred angry white ruffians waiting for her. And lined up outside the entrance to the school was a row of armed and uniformed Arkansas National Guardsmen, stationed there on Governor Faubus' orders to keep the Negro students out. Elizabeth walked through the crowd, ignoring a barrage of shouts, catcalls, and obscenities. But when she reached the line of guardsmen, they would not admit her. Then the crowd began inching forward. Someone shouted "Lynch her!" Elizabeth looked around, scared, trying to find a friendly face. One old woman seemed to have a kind face, but as Elizabeth appealed to her the woman spat on her. Finally one of the guardsmen escorted Elizabeth to a bus stop bench. There she was joined by a single white woman, who put her arm around her and called to the mob, "She's just a girl! She's scared! Aren't you ashamed?"

The National Guardsmen stayed outside Central High for three weeks. By that time the Federal courts had ordered Faubus to withdraw his men. They left and the Negro students entered. But for less than a day. A mob again gathered, and this time it rioted outside the school, beating and kicking passing Negroes, throwing bricks, and threatening to lynch the Negro students. The Negroes were sent home for their own safety.

President Dwight D. Eisenhower, whose own views on integration were somewhat conservative, was charged as President with seeing that the laws of the nation were enforced. He had been patient. But the former commander of the Allied Armies in Europe was not about to tolerate insult and rebellion on the part of a Faubus or of Arkansas mobs. He ordered the 82nd Airborne Division into Little Rock and shortly thereafter Federal troops were patrolling Southern streets—for the first time since Reconstruction. Under protection of the paratroopers Elizabeth and the other Negro students went to school. Later, still seeking ways to get around the law, Little Rock closed its entire school system, from 1957 through 1958, but opened it again in 1959. By 1962 there were still only seventy-eight Negro students attending formerly all-white schools.

The Little Rock rioting taught Americans some painful lessons. The incident was broadcast to the entire world and badly damaged American prestige abroad. Furthermore the business leaders of Little Rock and, for that matter, of all Arkansas had found that stirring up poor white mobs to hysteria could be

Arkansas National Guardsmen "protect" Little Rock Central High against the possible arrival of Negro students. (WIDE WORLD PHOTOS)

terribly costly. The state of Arkansas had been held up to ridicule and contempt throughout the nation and the world — and under such conditions it was difficult to attract industrial investments. But Arkansans, rich as well as poor, badly needed industrial development. Violent opposition to integration, it was seen, could actually hurt Southern conservative leaders in that most vital of all areas, their purses.

The disgraceful affair at Little Rock alerted some moderate Southerners to the potential dangers ahead. In Atlanta, white women formed an organization called H.O.P.E. (Help Our Public Education) in 1958, which devoted itself to educating people to acceptance of and enlisting their support for a program of peaceful integration. The organization's efforts were moderately successful in Atlanta, where, within three years, peaceful integration of buses, public libraries, taxis, and even golf courses had been carried out. But by 1961, H.O.P.E. (after an intensive campaign) could bring about only "token" integration (on the basis of nine Negro students) of Atlanta's public schools. And Atlanta, which boasted that it was a city "too busy to hate," was in the hands of moderate politicians. Other cities were not.

In the fall of 1962, twenty-nine-year-old Negro Air Force veteran James H. Meredith tried to enroll in the University of Mississippi. Despite a court order that he be enrolled, Mississippi Governor Ross Barnett refused to allow Meredith on the campus. On September 30th, President John F. Kennedy sent 320 Federal marshals to the University to enforce the Court order. They put Meredith into a dormitory on campus. But all that night waves of rioting students, egged on by outside rowdies, stormed through the campus, attacking the Federal marshals with bottles, rocks, acid, and guns. Fearing that the marshals might be overwhelmed, Kennedy dispatched Federal troops to Oxford, Mississippi, where the University campus was located. Once again the nation and the world witnessed the spectacle of Federal troops landing from huge transport planes and helicopters to scatter hysterical rioters at bayonet point. Eleven months later James Meredith became the first Negro to graduate from the University of Mississippi.

Today, almost fifteen years after the Supreme Court's ruling against segregation, only about one Negro child out of forty in the South is attending school with white children. But in most areas, integration is proceeding peacefully, if painfully slowly. The damage done to the image of America abroad and the image of the South in the United States, by violence directed against children and open resistance to the law, has been incalculable. Southern conservative business leaders have found that large corporations will not expose their personnel to the kind of life awaiting them in communities which disobey the law, nor will banks invest in the municipal and state bond issues of areas in which violence prevails. But aside from economic pressures, until Americans as a people become decisively committed to democratic principles in practice as well as theory, violence will remain a part of the American scene.

If Oliver Brown's exasperation at seeing his daughter off on a two-mile trek to school each day had momentous results, equally far-reaching were the consequences of Mrs. Rosa Parks's sore feet.

Rosa Parks was a Negro seamstress in a downtown Montgomery, Alabama, department store. She rode the bus every day to and from work. One evening in December, 1955, Mrs. Parks boarded her bus as usual and found there were no seats in the rear. Negroes were required to sit in the rear of Montgomery buses or in a sort of "neutral" zone in the middle of the bus — provided no white people required the "neutral" seats. Mrs. Parks sat in the "neutral" zone, but only for a short time. Boarding white passengers demanded that she give up her seat. But Mrs. Parks had worked hard all day, and her feet hurt. She refused to budge. The driver stopped the bus and had Mrs. Parks arrested. As she was being taken off to jail, the news of what had happened spread quickly through the Negro section of Montgomery.

E. D. Nixon, former state N.A.A.C.P. president, bailed Mrs. Parks out of jail and then got busy telephoning Negro leaders in the city. One of the men he called was the twenty-seven-year-old minister of Dexter Avenue Baptist Church, the Reverend Dr. Martin Luther King, Jr. Dr. King had grown up in Atlanta, Georgia, gone to college there, and studied for the ministry in Pennsylvania. He had lived in Montgomery for only one year but was already acknowledged as a leader of its Negro community. Nixon and King got together forty of Montgomery's most influential Negroes and decided to organize a boycott of the city's buses. Until Negroes were accorded decent treatment on the buses, they would simply not ride them — and since fifteen thousand Negroes rode Montgomery's buses every day, this had to hurt the city's revenues.

The boycott was to last one year. During that time some Negroes lost their jobs in Montgomery, some were threatened by the police, some were beaten, Martin Luther King's home was bombed, as was E. D. Nixon's, and eighty-nine of the boycott leaders, including Nixon and King, were arrested on charges of plotting to ruin the bus company's business (King eventually paid a $500 fine). But all during the year, Martin Luther King kept hammering at a single theme to Montgomery's Negroes — there must be no violence. Negroes must not strike back when they were insulted or beaten, but must simply stand up for their rights and take whatever violence was meted out to them.

Martin Luther King had arrived at his concept of nonviolent resistance through reading, especially the work of the great Indian philosopher-leader Mohandas Gandhi, and through the Christian religion. Christianity preached love for all men, including one's enemies. Gandhi had shown how nonviolent resistance to unjust laws or customs could win permanent and decisive results. The application of nonviolence required great discipline and great faith, but in Montgomery it worked. After twelve and one-half months of the boycott, the Supreme Court ordered Montgomery's buses desegregated. At six o'clock on the morning of December 21, 1956, a bus stopped at the corner where Nixon, King, and other Negro leaders waited. As King stepped aboard and paid his fare, the white bus driver said:

"I believe you're Reverend King, aren't you?"

"Yes, I am," King replied.

"We're glad to have you this morning," the driver said as the integrated bus sped on its customary way.

Martin Luther King and his policy of nonviolence leaped into national and world prominence during the Montgomery boycott. King was invited everywhere throughout the country to lecture on nonviolence and tell the Montgomery story. Negro clergymen, heartened by King's success, began to join the front ranks of the civil rights movement. In 1956 they founded the Southern Christian Leadership Conference, and elected Martin Luther King its president. Soon the organization had dozens of affiliates and scores of workers throughout the South. And Martin Luther King became the most popular of the new Negro leaders. People remembered that he had been jailed twelve times, that his home had been bombed, that he himself had been stabbed and constantly threatened — and that he continued to respond nonviolently. Moreover, he was eloquent. In 1960, he told an audience, "I am not concerned with the New Jerusalem, I'm concerned with the New Atlanta, the New Montgomery, the New South."

The victory in Montgomery emboldened other Negroes in the South to take direct action against segregation. Especially heartened by Martin Luther King's example, and the logic of his policy of nonviolent resistance, were Negro college students. On February 1, 1960, McNeil Joseph, a seventeen-year-old freshman at the all-Negro North Carolina Agricultural and Technical College at Greensboro, North Carolina, led three fellow students to the segregated lunch counter at a local Woolworth store. Following ancient custom, the Negro students were refused service. But instead of leaving docilely, they remained in their seats, until the store manager was forced to close down the lunch counter forty-five minutes later. The next day the students returned to "sit-in" at the counter again. In the meantime, a local Negro dentist, learning of what was going on, had put through a call to Congress of Racial Equality headquarters in New York. Within hours a band of trained C.O.R.E. field workers was on its way to Greensboro.

Neither the technique of the "sit-in" nor the C.O.R.E. organization were new to the Negro community. Sit-ins and ride-ins had been used to fight segregation since Reconstruction days. For instance, a ride-in on the horse-drawn streetcars of Louisville, Kentucky, in 1871 had ended in Negroes winning free seating rights. C.O.R.E. had been founded in Chicago in 1942 under the leadership of James Farmer, race relations secretary of the pacifist Fellowship of Reconciliation. Farmer, devoted like Martin Luther King to the philosophy of Mohandas Gandhi, organized C.O.R.E. as an urban interracial movement in Northern cities. The organization, which preached and practiced nonviolent resistance, began to spread to the

South during the late fifties; and by the spring of 1963 C.O.R.E. was to have a national membership of more than seventy thousand and branches in towns and cities across the country.

When the C.O.R.E. field workers from New York arrived in Greensboro, they started to train the Negro students in the techniques of nonviolence: how to keep from answering back when they were insulted; how to protect themselves against beatings and kickings without striking back; above all, how to control their tempers under any and all kinds of provocation.

As students in other cities learned of the Greensboro sit-in, the technique spread in a swift and dramatic chain reaction. Within two weeks of the Greensboro sit-in, students were sitting-in in fifteen cities; within a month thirty-three cities were involved; within two months sixty-eight cities witnessed sit-ins. And the campaign kept growing until seventy thousand people had taken part in it. All of them faced insults, most faced some sort of violence, many suffered severe beatings, and four thousand went to jail. But they never answered insult with insult, argued with the police, or struck back at their assailants.

In April, 1960, the student sit-in movement had grown to such proportions that it was decided to form a new organization to coordinate it. Under the guidance of Martin Luther King, the Student Nonviolent Coordinating Committee (S.N.C.C. or

Martin Luther King, Jr.   (MAURY ENGLANDER)

"Snick" for short) was established, with headquarters in Atlanta and James Foreman as executive secretary.

The sit-ins, which took place at lunch counters, movies, parks, anywhere that segregation was practiced, once again brought the South to the point of a hard decision. Either it was to present a picture to the world of well-behaved, well-dressed young people being beaten and dragged off to jail simply for sitting at public accommodations, or it would have to desegregate. In addition, many of the businesses affected were branches of nation-wide chains, such as Woolworth's; and the loss of business these chains faced in the North more than counterbalanced any urge they may have felt to abide by Southern customs. Business after business in cities and towns throughout the South quickly and quietly desegregated public facilities.

A much more difficult and, as it proved, inflammable endeavor than the sit-ins was the attempt to win enforcement of the Supreme Court's 1961 ruling that segregation was illegal not only on buses and trains but also in stations and waiting rooms. Under the leadership of C.O.R.E., a campaign of "freedom rides," in which Negro and white volunteers undertook to travel through the South by bus to test desegregation of public transportation facilities, was instituted in 1961. The first "freedom riders" left Washington, D.C., on May 4 aboard two buses bound for New Orleans. Trouble started in Alabama. Mobs burned one of the buses outside Anniston, and when the remaining bus reached Birmingham, the riders were mobbed and beaten. Unable to persuade the bus companies to risk another bus, the undaunted riders finished their trip by plane. They were followed by other "freedom riders," always white and Negro mixed groups, throughout the summer of 1961, until more than one thousand of them had risked the jailings and beatings of hate-filled mobs to win compliance with the Supreme Court's decrees.

But certainly the most revolutionary and bitterly fought struggle of all the new waves of Negro rights movements was the fight to win the right to register and vote in the states of the Deep South. While desegregation of buses and lunch counters and parks and churches and terminals may have irritated Southerners, the attempt to win political power for the Negro frightened Southern leaders as had nothing since Reconstruction. This was a direct assault on the entire politico-economic power structure of the South, and as such it called forth waves of violence and reprisal not unlike the post-Civil-War campaigns of the Ku Klux Klan.

During the spring of 1963, Negroes organized marches in several small Southern towns to protest their exclusion from

he polls. But it was not until April of that year, when Martin
Luther King led a task force of Negro leaders and organizers
to Birmingham, Alabama, that the movement reached important
proportions. When King organized protest marches into downtown Birmingham, the city police, led by tough Commissioner
T. Eugene "Bull" Connor, broke up the marches and arrested
many of the Negro participants. "Bull" Connor promised to
fill every jail in Birmingham if the Negroes continued to march.
But on a sunny morning in May, Martin Luther King sent a
new army to downtown Birmingham—one composed entirely
of children, grade and high school students whose average age
was fourteen. Adults watched them march off that morning,
singing "We Shall Overcome," the civil rights anthem.

"Bull" Connor's police tried to stop the children, but many
slipped through police lines and ran into downtown Birmingham.
Connor's men arrested more than seven hundred children that
day (some of them of kindergarten age). The sight of helmeted,
armed police manhandling children into police wagons aroused
a storm of indignation and contempt throughout the country,
all directed at Birmingham, a city trying very hard to attract
new industries.

The day after the "children's crusade" another march of
adults and young students took place. This time the exasperated
Connor ordered his men to open up on the marchers with high-
powered fire hoses—followed by growling police dogs. The
violence continued over the following days, to mounting con-
sternation not only among Northerners but also among the
civic and business leaders of Birmingham itself. Finally, the
Federal government intervened by sending negotiators to the
city to effect a truce between Negroes and the city's white
administration. A compromise was reached whereby the city
leaders agreed to end segregation and open the polls to Negroes
in return for an end to Negro protest marches. Peace returned
to Birmingham, until three days later, when dynamite bombs
blasted the home of Martin Luther King's brother, the Reverend A. D. King, and a motel where Martin Luther King had
been staying. So enraged were Birmingham Negroes by the
bombings (which purely by chance injured no one) that they
forgot nonviolence that night and rioted. But the truce was re-
established at dawn.

The protest marches and civil rights demonstrations spread
so far and so fast after Birmingham that the summer of 1963 witnessed the birth of two journalistic phrases: *the Negro Revolution*, and *the long, hot summer*. Neither description was quite
accurate. The "long, hot summer" was simply another summer
in a long, hot battle that had been going on for centuries. And

188 THE NEGRO REVOLUTION

the "Negro Revolution" was not a revolution at all—it was simply an attempt to win the rights and privileges of American citizenship due them on the part of a segment of the American people, and that fight had been going on for a long time too. The struggle was going on now with certain differences, of course. First of all, through the medium of television, people all over the country and the world were now immediate witnesses to what was happening. Anti-Negro violence now had to display itself in the open and it aroused a storm of protest from liberal Americans such as had not been heard since the days of abolitionism. Second, the technique of nonviolence was a terribly effective weapon. It left the "Bull" Connors of America with nothing to really strike out at; and it made compromise and accommodation possible on the part of moderate white Southerners. Third, the South, like the rest of the country, was changing and had changed dramatically since World War II. Southern economic and social interests were now more national than sectional. More and more Southerners realized that they simply could no longer afford discrimination and violence. And many Southerners were becoming convinced of the justice of the Negro cause.

Tragically, violence continued to flare. N.A.A.C.P. leader Medgar Evers was murdered in Jackson, Mississippi; in Birmingham, a bomb demolished a Negro church, killing four little girls; civil rights workers James Chaney, Andy Goodman, and Mickey Schwerner were to be killed outside Philadelphia, Mississippi; Mrs. Violet Liuzzo, mother of five and a volunteer civil rights worker from Detroit, was to be murdered between Selma and Montgomery, Alabama. There were other deaths and innumerable beatings, but violence was becoming less and less effective as a response to the civil rights movement.

Another aspect of the summer of 1963 was the enlistment of whites in the struggle for Negro equality. Negroes had never been alone in their fight—throughout American history they had been helped, and powerfully helped, by many whites. But the summer of 1963 saw such an outpouring of white activity within the civil rights movement that it was transformed into something of an all-American crusade. As such it was to have immediate and important political results.

Congress had passed no notable civil rights legislation since the Civil Rights Act of 1875 (which had been struck down by the Supreme Court a few years later). The excuse offered had always been that laws protecting the rights of all Americans already existed, they only needed to be enforced. This was true. But law is the codification of human beliefs and attitudes and customs; and the repetition—through Congressional action—of

Harlem remembers — and protests.
(DIANA J. DAVIES FROM INSIGHT)

what those beliefs and customs ought to be in American societ
was vital to the progress of American Negroes.

In 1957 Congress had passed a Civil Rights Act aimed a
preventing discrimination against Negroes at the polls. The ac
was largely ineffective in the South, where it was most needed
However, in the North, Negroes were voting in larger an
larger numbers. It was their support of John F. Kennedy i
1960 that provided him with his slim margin of victory ove
Richard M. Nixon. By 1962 Negroes comprised over seven
teen percent of the voting population in the twenty-five larges
Northern cities. Their wishes could no longer be safely ignored
And the demonstrations of the summer of 1963 (there wer
more than sixteen hundred marches, mass meetings, and pro
tests all over the country that summer) showed that the Negr
civil rights movement enjoyed tremendous support among vot
ing whites also.

In June, 1963, President Kennedy had sent a new and ver
comprehensive Civil Rights bill to Congress. It was in suppor
of that bill that the great March on Washington took place o
August 28, 1963. More than two hundred thousand Americans
white and black, converged on the nation's capital that day t
demand immediate freedom, justice, and equality for the Negr
Many of the men who had devoted their lives to the Negro'
cause were there: A. Philip Randolph; Roy Wilkins, successo
to Walter White as head of the N.A.A.C.P.; Urban League
President Whitney Young; and, of course, Martin Luthe
King. Present also was Mrs. Rosa Parks, whose sore feet hac
touched off a national crusade. Representatives of labor unions
stood beside college students, housewives marched alongside
veterans' organizations—a mighty and impressive cross sec
tion of America gathered at the steps of the Lincoln Memoria
to hear speeches and to affirm, by its presence, that the time
had come to give meaning to the promise of American democracy.

Three months later, John F. Kennedy, who had encouraged
the Negro civil rights movement, was assassinated. His successor as President, Lyndon B. Johnson, was a Southerner.
But whatever apprehensions Negroes may have felt on that
score were almost immediately relieved when Johnson bent
his formidable energy and powerful influence with Congress to
secure passage of the Kennedy Civil Rights Act.

On July 3, 1964, President Johnson signed the Civil Rights
Act of 1964, stating at that time, "It [the new law] does say
that those who are equal before God shall now also be equal
in the polling booths, in the classrooms, in the factories, and in

*n 1963 they marched on Washington, D.C., demanding freedom and equality
ow.*

(DECLAN HAUN FROM BLACK STAR)

the hotels and restaurants and movie theaters, and other place
that provide service to the public."

While enactment of the Civil Rights law of 1964 was a
notable symbolic victory for the civil rights movement, it did
not have immediate practical results. (The murders of Mrs
Liuzzo and of Chaney, Goodman, and Schwerner took place
after enactment of the Civil Rights bill.) But it was now possible
for Negroes to sue people who discriminated against them in
public facilities. White Americans who denied Negroes their
constitutional rights could now be sent to jail. And in the face
of the new law, some Southern cities and towns put an end to
some of their segregationist policies. The entrenched habits,
customs, and interests of the South were not to be overturned by
a law in a single day or a single year or perhaps even a single
decade. But a start had been made, and if progress continued
to be paid for in bruises and blood, it nevertheless took place.

While the South had been the special target of Negro civil
rights efforts until 1964, with the passage of the new Civil
Rights Act the attention of Negro and white activists turned
increasingly to the North. Despite the difference in custom
and law, segregation was almost as much a part of Negro life
in Northern cities as it was in the South. Economically deprived and exploited Negroes were jammed into indescribably
filthy slums in all the great Northern cities. As a result, they
found that their children were forced to attend all-Negro
schools (of generally inferior quality) and that full participation
in the life of the Northern city was effectively denied to them by
poverty. Furthermore, Northern liberal opinion, which backed
wholeheartedly Negro efforts to win equality in the South, was
by no means so united when faced by Negro efforts to win
equality in the North. Northern discrimination against the
Negro, Northern prejudices, were masked behind a liberal
structure of law and much lip service to democratic ideals. But
hysterical fear and hatred of the Negroes could manifest itself
just as violently in Chicago or Brooklyn as in Birmingham.
While Negroes enjoyed political power in the North, that power
had done little to win for them a decent life.

Indicative of the despair and frustration of slum-living
Northern Negroes was the rise of the Black Muslim movement.
Organized by Elijah Poole, a Negro who was born in Georgia,
the Nation of Islam held that Allah had commissioned its
founder (known as Elijah Muhammad) to lead the Negro out of
servitude. Establishing headquarters in Chicago during the
1930's, Elijah Muhammad's movement spread to more than
thirty states and claimed more than fifty thousand members by
1963. The Black Muslim movement taught that Negroes and

Malcolm X addresses a street rally in Harlem.   (WIDE WORLD PHOTOS)

whites could never live together in peace, and it resurrected the old idea of setting up a separate Negro state or nation in the United States or Africa. Black Muslins trained for what they believed to be inevitable conflict with whites—nonviolence was not for them. For years their most popular spokesman was Malcolm Little, who in accordance with Black Muslim practice had dropped his last name (because it had probably been given to his ancestors by slave owners and was therefore not his true name) and called himself Malcolm X. In 1964, after a dispute with Elijah Muhammad, Malcolm X led some Black Muslims into a new movement called the Organization of Afro-American Unity. He urged his followers to arm themselves and to meet violence with violence. But early in 1965, Malcolm X met a violent end. He was shot down by three men, two of whom were Black Muslims, while addressing a meeting of his followers.

Although the Black Muslim movement never attracted more than a fraction of the Negro people, its activities and policies were indicative of growing anger among Northern big city Negroes. In the summers of 1964, 1965, 1966, and 1967, these frustrations boiled over into riots. New York, Philadelphia, Los Angeles, Jersey City, Detroit, Chicago—all witnessed fighting, looting, burning, and mob disorders. Negroes charged white police with brutality and white civic leaders charged Negroes with irresponsibility. Joint Negro-white commissions were hastily organized in many cities to try to ameliorate some of the worst aspects of life in the Negro ghettos — but their efforts seemed too little and too late. Every spring new predictions of violence were made, and every summer they came true.

In actuality, the problems of Northern Negroes — unemployment, poor housing, poor schooling, the constriction of life by poverty — merged with national problems which transcended race. While Martin Luther King now led marches in Chicago and other Northern cities to protest the exclusion of Negroes from all-white neighborhoods, the harsh fact was that even without discrimination in housing, Negroes suffered from a poverty which kept them isolated and exploited. While new laws could serve as a framework to end discrimination in such areas as housing, only a massive assault on such supraracial problems as the decay of American cities, Federal support for education, increased social security, and the training of poor people (white as well as black) for jobs in an increasingly specialized and technical economy could bring real relief. The extent to which Negro problems merged more fully with the problems faced by all Americans was in itself a measure of how far Negroes had come on the road to equality.

But in the North as well as the South that road stretched a long way ahead. Anti-Negro prejudice remained a crippling psychological disease among white Americans and a reproach to Americans before the world; and while some Negroes continued to follow Martin Luther King's way of nonviolence, others were turning, increasingly, to more militant leaders and more violent policies. Among white Americans the realization was growing that the problem of racism went to the very heart of American life. If, within the framework of the structure of American society, fear and hatred could not be erased, then that structure would have to be changed. Many white Americans would oppose change, some, violently. But many more were sick of their burden of fear and hatred; they had borne it too long. For these people, as well as for Negroes, the words of Martin Luther King, spoken when he was awarded the Nobel Peace Prize in 1964, have a special meaning: "To the degree that I harm my brother, no matter what he is doing to me, to that extent, I harm myself."

Epilogue

The Fire Next Time

God gave Noah the rainbow sign;
No more water—the fire next time.

—NEGRO SPIRITUAL

I've never known a white person I could trust.

—STOKELY CARMICHAEL

BY THE FALL OF 1968, SOME CONCLUSIONS COULD BE DRAWN from the wave of protest and struggle which had started in the early 1950's; and certain new trends in a continuing battle could be identified.

The civil rights movement had won notable victories. It had solidly aligned the Federal government on the side of Negro equality for the first time since early Reconstruction days; it had won almost all the legal weapons it could use to battle segregation; it had forced the integration of many public aspects of Southern life; and it had alerted the entire nation to some dangerous and basic problems woven into the fabric of American society. It had also suffered some defeats.

The most important area in which the fight for equality had made little progress was in the integration of housing in Northern cities. Considered by civil rights leaders to be at the very core of *de facto* segregation of Negroes in the North, segregated housing policies became the focal point of protest activity by the Southern Christian Leadership Conference, C.O.R.E., the Urban League, and S.N.C.C. during the summers of 1965 and 1966. The problem was plain enough. If Negroes were not allowed to live in the same areas as whites in Northern cities, then their children could not attend mixed schools, and the walls of personal suspicion and dislike would continue to be rebuilt with each generation.

Segregation in Northern housing was an unwritten code among real estate operators, building contractors, and civic leaders. White Northerners felt that if Negroes moved into their neighborhoods then the value of their own property would drop. And this fear was blatantly encouraged by real estate operators, who enjoyed huge profits from providing slum housing for Negroes and then overcharging them for it. By making protest marches into all-white neighborhoods, Martin Luther King and other Negro leaders hoped to dramatize the problem and force Congressional action on a bill outlawing discrimination in housing.

During the summer of 1966 the nation's television screens displayed hysterical mobs of Northern whites stoning and rioting against Negro marchers in white neighborhoods in Chicago. Except for a slightly more discreet attitude on the part of local police officials, the spectacle differed but little from scenes of violence in Birmingham and other Southern cities. Northern politicians, sensitive as ever to the shifting vagaries of public opinion, were not certain that an "open housing" bill would win favor with their constituents. And in spite of President Johnson's support for the measure, it was defeated in Congress. This defeat was then taken by some observers to signal the end of one phase of the civil rights movement. To them it appeared that nonviolence, public protest, the restriction of the struggle to specific targets at specific times had won all the victories that such policies could win for this generation of Americans. These observations seemed partly true and partly false.

It was certainly true that the more progress the civil rights movement made, the stiffer opposition to it became. Segregated housing in the North, like absolute white political power in the Deep South, appeared to mark lines beyond which whites would not retreat without severe struggle. But it was equally apparent that Negroes would not stop fighting now. What new forms would the struggle take?

In the late summer of 1966, one of the leaders of the Student Nonviolent Coordinating Committee leaped into public prominence with a new slogan, "Black Power." The young man was Stokely Carmichael, born in Port-of-Spain, Trinidad, on June 21, 1941. Carmichael and his family had moved to Harlem in 1952 and become naturalized American citizens. There he learned what life in a Negro ghetto could mean. By 1964 he had graduated with a degree in philosophy from Howard University, taken part in sit-ins and freedom rides, spent forty-nine days in the Mississippi State Penitentiary for his efforts, and been jailed twenty-seven times.

During the winter of 1965–1966, Carmichael and several

other S.N.C.C. leaders worked out a "position paper" outlining suggested new policies for the organization. Pointing out that white participation in S.N.C.C. field efforts in the Deep South was actually a handicap (since many rural Deep South Negroes remained frightened and suspicious of *all* whites, no matter what their credentials) and that white participation in policy-making meetings in the North was, at best, unnecessary, the paper called for the withdrawal of white volunteers from S.N.C.C. and also urged that Negroes in the United States be defined as "exploited colonials." Like colonials in Africa before the withdrawal of European imperialist powers, they had to develop a nationalistic self-view of themselves, insist on their ethnic heritage, and cultivate their differences from white Americans rather than try to submerge them.

The paper further urged that in order to develop a solid base for the harsher struggles ahead, Negro Americans must organize cooperative industries, stores, real estate agencies — build up an economic power base that would be independent of, parallel to, and as strong as the economic power of white society. Although the phrase "Black Power" did not occur in

Stokely Carmichael   (MAURY ENGLANDER)

this "position paper," all this was what the slogan meant, what it tried to sum up, when Carmichael uttered it. The S.N.C.C. membership was by no means unanimous in its acceptance of this view, but it was sufficiently impressed by it to accept the report.

White activists began to drop out of S.N.C.C. ranks, and during the winter of 1966–1967, S.N.C.C. leaders began to take Carmichael's "hard line" in addressing audiences throughout the country. Their efforts (especially those of the eloquent Carmichael) occasionally sparked riots, as in Atlanta in 1966 and in several Southern university towns during the spring of 1967. These new views also threatened to split the civil rights movement, as they were found unacceptable by the older and more conservative leadership of such organizations as the N.A.A.C.P. and C.O.R.E. Perhaps because of continuing resistance to the more extreme of his opinions, Stokely Carmichael resigned from S.N.C.C. in May, 1967, possibly to devote himself to building up his own organization.

The road of "Black Power" was not completely new. It will be recalled that more than once in the past, Negroes, despairing of winning equality within the framework of white society, had urged the establishment of Negro bases of economic power. The emotional impulse behind Black Power would not have surprised Marcus Garvey or Malcolm X, for example. On the other hand, while it was true that the political and economic position of Negroes in America bore certain resemblances to the position of exploited colonials during the age of imperialism, there were tremendous and probably decisive differences. The language, culture, ethics, and aspirations of American Negroes were—American. They were not, in fact, living under "foreign" domination; and they were intensely proud of their historic contributions to and involvement in their native country. They justly claimed a deep stake in the American heritage, and it was one which they would not easily relinquish.

However, there was always the possibility that white society —by continuing to close social doors to Negroes, by continuing to effectively disfranchise the great majority of Negro voters in the Deep South, and by increasing the undoubted economic exploitation of Negroes—might create the desperation which would finally and completely alienate Negroes from their own country. It was this possibility that most deeply disturbed such Negro leaders as Martin Luther King and that led to new directions in the civil rights movement after 1966. The majority of Negroes continued to look to Negro moderates such as King and the N.A.A.C.P. and C.O.R.E. for leadership. But there was a new sense of urgency and pressure. Unless the moderate program could bring decisive gains soon, Negroes might well adopt more extreme programs.

In April of 1967, Martin Luther King, to the surprise of many and the disturbance of some, lent the tremendous weight of his prestige to the protest against America's undeclared war in Vietnam. On April 15, 1967, Dr. King led a procession of more than two hundred thousand Americans, both white and black, through the streets of New York to the United Nations to protest America's role in the Vietnam conflict. He was met at the entrance of the United Nations by another Negro Nobel Peace Prize winner, Dr. Ralph Bunche. Dr. Bunche, who supported American policies in Vietnam, said simply to King, "The march from Selma was longer, Martin." By which Ralph Bunche meant to remind King that while he had marched through Alabama with King for civil rights, he could not march with him for peace in Vietnam. And Bunche's attitude reflected an incipient split in the thinking of civil rights leaders throughout the country.

While this is not the place to discuss the pros and cons of American policy in Southeast Asia, Americans should not have been surprised by Martin Luther King's stand. In opposing what he considered to be an imperialistic adventure and a war of colonial oppression, King was acting in the great tradition of Negro leaders throughout American history. Frederick Douglass, it will be recalled, had denounced the American war against Mexico; his son had ridiculed and protested the American war against Spain. And to a man of Dr. King's historical scholarship, the dangers to the struggle for Negro rights of continued American participation in the Vietnam conflict seemed clear.

First of all, no matter what the proclaimed intentions of the American government might be, American soldiers were fighting against a colored people as they had in the Philippines from 1898 to 1901; and that could only aggravate anti-Negro feeling domestically. Secondly, Negro troops who provided more than eleven percent of the American combat forces in Vietnam and suffered eighteen percent of the casualties might well ask themselves the same question that Private William Simms found unanswerable during the Philippine campaign. In the third place, militarism had always been the arch-enemy of tolerance and progress. After each of America's wars, there had been a reaction of more or less severe hysteria against all progressive movements, including the struggle for Negro equality. And finally (as Dr. King reminded his critics), he *had* received a Nobel Prize for peace, he *was* a citizen of the world as well as an American Negro, and he felt himself responsible to work for peace everywhere. From the viewpoint of history, it would seem that Dr. King had no need to apologize at all for his new position.

When the summer of 1967 erupted like previous summers into riots in a dozen Northern cities, like the glow of heat lightning and the rumble of muffled thunder on history's horizon, a foretaste of what might lie over the horizon was shown in Detroit. There, during the week of July 23, thousands of Negroes, driven to desperation by ghetto life, police brutality, and the cumulative oppression of decades of white persecution, rioted throughout the downtown district. They overturned cars, stoned and shot at police, looted stores, and set fires that gutted square miles of the city. The only response that either the state of Michigan or the Federal government could imagine was force. When police reported that they could no longer control the rioters, state and Federal troops were rushed in. They came with tanks, self-propelled guns, heavy and light machine guns, trucks, jeeps, gas masks, and gas — the full panoply of war.

Dr. Benjamin Spock, Martin Luther King, and Monsignor Charles Rice lead New Yorkers in a march to protest the Vietnam war.

(MAURY ENGLANDER)

The United Peoples of African Descent join the peace march.

(ANNA KAUFMAN)

Thirty-eight people, mostly Negroes, were killed, hundreds more seriously injured.

To an older generation of Americans, anxiously watching their television screens, the scenes in Detroit were frighteningly reminiscent of newsreels of Allied armies fighting their way through German cities during World War II. It was clear to the thoughtful that what had happened in Detroit was nothing less than an act of war.

But it was an act of war of the nation upon itself. Congressional legislators used the Detroit riots as an excuse to bottle up new open-housing legislation in Congress. Congress, it was said, should not bow to the threat of force. Besides, there seemed some reason now to think that "white backlash" opinion would support more conservative policies. Even the most liberal whites, it was felt, must be repelled by the orgies of violence that had erupted in Detroit.

The Detroit riots, in fact, only underscored new questions for the civil rights movement. Among the most important of these was the question of continued white participation in the drive for Negro equality. As early as 1963, Martin Luther King (while serving a five-day sentence in Birmingham jail for leading a demonstration) had written, "I have almost reached the regrettable conclusion that the Negro's great stumbling block in his stride toward freedom is not the White Citizens' Councilor or the Ku Klux Klanner, but the white moderate, who is more devoted to 'order' than to justice; who prefers a negative peace which is the absence of tension to a positive peace which is the presence of justice . . . ."

Another question illuminated by the fires in Detroit was whether any further progress could be made through Dr. King's nonviolent means. Although practically all the nation's Negroes listened respectfully to King's advocacy of nonviolence, Northern urban Negroes who did not share the religious convictions of their rural brothers or of Dr. King himself seemed more and more inclined to seek violent solutions — solutions which, if they solved almost nothing, at least enabled them to vent their despair and resentment. As 1967 drew to a close it seemed uncertain whether Martin Luther King and other moderate Negro leaders could keep control of their own followers.

Just as he had seen the Vietnam conflict as close to the core of the national wellsprings of racial tension and hatred, so Martin Luther King recognized the disgraceful poverty into which one quarter of the American people (white as well as black) had fallen as a central obstacle to further civil rights progress. Poverty was the condition in which hatred and violence flourished. When, for example, a proposal was made to Congress during the winter of 1968 that a modest amount of money be allocated to combat the plague of rats that infested all big-city slums, the legislators found something terribly amusing in the idea — peals of Congressional laughter greeted the proposal.

It was to dramatize the plight of the nation's poor that Dr. King and his Southern Christian Leadership Conference determined to lead a march of thousands of poor people, white and black, to the nation's capital in the spring of 1968. There they would erect a shanty-town and wait for Congress to do something about the national scandal of abject poverty amid unprecedented prosperity.

But first there was the continuing daily battle to attend to. Trouble broke out again in Memphis, Tennessee, when the city's garbagemen (mostly Negroes) went on strike for higher wages in January, 1968. They were treated with brutality by Memphis police while attempting to picket city hall (which did, after all, house their employer). Negro militants in Memphis threatened reprisals, and Martin Luther King rushed to the city to prevent violence and to see whether a nonviolent campaign of protest marches could achieve an economic as well as a civil rights objective. But when King led his followers in a nonviolent march on city hall at the end of March, a handful of Negro youths suddenly began to break shop windows along the route and to stone policemen. The police responded with pistols—one Negro was shot to death.

Dr. King, alarmed at the outbreak of violence, determined to lead another march into downtown Memphis to demonstrate that his followers, despite the outburst of a few, still followed his nonviolent concepts and to dramatize the garbagemen's plight. But this was one march that Martin Luther King would never make. For on the night of April 4, as he took the air on the balcony of a motel in the Negro district of Memphis, he was shot to death by a white gunman.

There were a few hours of stunned and anguished disbelief across America. President Johnson appealed for calm. There were pleas from Dr. King's followers that the fallen leader's policy of meeting violence with love be maintained as a fitting monument to his memory. But even before Martin Luther King's body was buried in Atlanta, a mounting wave of violence broke over the nation. From New York to Los Angeles, from Seattle to Tampa, Negroes struck out in grief and outrage. They struck out at the only visible monuments of white supremacy which were within their reach—the nation's big-city slums. Symbolic of the terrible agony which descended upon America was the destruction of several blocks of downtown Washington, D.C. For days Negroes rioted, fought with police, burned and looted through the wreckage-littered, smoking streets of the nation's capital. The battle scenes of Detroit were repeated and magnified here within yards of Congress and the executive mansion. Heavily armed troops took up battle stations around the White House (for the first time since Jubal Early led Confederate cavalry on a daring raid more than a century before), and their presence seemed to underscore Stokely Carmichael's statement about Martin Luther King's assassination: "Last night white America declared war on black America."

Order was finally restored. And then belatedly and hurriedly Congress passed the Open Housing Act, which removed discriminatory bars from about 65 percent of the nation's housing. But across the land there was widespread apprehension that nothing Congress did or did not do would matter much now— because a final gulf had been created between whites and blacks. Yet this fear did not take into account the one hopeful sign on the American horizon—the attitude of the nation's young people.

If the Negro's struggle to achieve full participation in American life seems to have finally come up against the stone wall of armed force, it has also received new, immensely powerful though as yet incompletely defined support from a new generation of Americans. To be a prisoner of prejudice, to harbor contempt or suspicion of any race, are qualities considered definitely "square," old-fashioned, and despicable by the rising generation of white students in America. As part of their protest against many aspects of American society, white students on campuses throughout the nation have pointed scornful fingers at the attitudes of older Americans toward Negroes and other minority groups. This was evidence, they held, of the older generation's hypocrisy, fear, and insufficiency. Among youth, the social pressures were all against prejudice—and these young people would one day guide American society. But there was little time left to wait for a new generation of Americans to take charge.

What was being demanded of Americans, white and Negro, was not only some basic changes in the structure of American society and of its laws (the unwritten economic and unspoken social laws as well as the legal code), but also, more urgently, some basic changes in themselves. The path of nonviolent protest had probably come to an end. Beyond it lay the road of peaceful civil disobedience, and beyond, that of violent civil disobedience, and beyond, that of guerrilla warfare. In other words, the very fabric of American life soon might be rent to tatters. In the dreadful riots of 1968 might be glimpsed a very mild foresight of the dark road ahead. The future might well be lit only by the fires of violence and greeted by the desperate cry of "Burn, baby, burn!"

An old Negro spiritual (from which author James Baldwin derived the title of one of his books) describes how God punished the human race for its sins by sending a flood to wipe it out, leaving only Noah and his family behind. But in the age of the H-bomb and burning ghettos, God may not require a flood . . .

No more water—the fire next time.

Bibliography

(A suggested reading list will be found on page 209)

ABDY, E. S., *A Journal of Residence and Tour of the United States of America, 1835.* (n.p.), 1837.

ADAMS, ALICE A., *The Neglected Period of Anti-Slavery Days in America.* New York, 1908.

ALEXIS, STEPHEN, *Black Liberator.* New York, 1949.

AMERICAN ANTI-SLAVERY SOCIETY, *Annual Reports.* New York, 1834–1841, 1855–1861.

APTHEKER, HERBERT, *A Documentary History of the Negro People in the United States.* New York, 1951.

——*American Negro Slave Revolts.* New York, 1943.

BALLAGH, JAMES C., *A History of Slavery in Virginia.* Baltimore, 1902.

BANCROFT, FREDERICK, *Slave Trading in the Old South.* Baltimore, 1931.

BARDOLPH, RICHARD, *The Negro Vanguard.* New York, 1959.

BENTLEY, GEORGE R., *A History of the Freedmen's Bureau.* Philadelphia, 1955.

BRADFORD, SARA E. H., *Harriet, the Moses of Her People.* New York, 1886.

BRODERICK, FRANCIS L., *W. E. B. DuBois: Negro Leader in a Time of Crisis.* Stanford, 1959.

BROWN, STERLING A., ARTHUR P. DAVIS, and ULYSSES LEE, eds., *The Negro Caravan.* New York, 1941.

BUCKMASTER, HENRIETTA, *Let My People Go.* New York, 1941.

BUTCHER, MARGARET J., *The Negro in American Culture.* New York, 1956.

Cockrum, William, *History of the Underground Railroad*. New York, 1915.

Conrad, Earl, *Harriet Tubman*. New York, 1943.

Cook, James G., *The Segregationists*. New York, 1963.

Cornish, Dudley T., *The Sable Arm: Negro Troops in the Union Army, 1861–1865*. New York, 1956.

Cronon, David E., *Black Moses: The Story of Marcus Garvey*. Madison, 1955.

Davidson, Basil, *The Lost Cities of Africa*. Boston, 1959.

Delafosse, Maurice, *The Negroes of Africa*. Washington, 1931.

Douglass, Frederick, *Life and Times of Frederick Douglass*. New York, 1962.

Drake, St. Clair, and Horace R. Cayton, *Black Metropolis*, 2 vols. New York, 1962.

Drake, Thomas E., *Quakers and Slavery in America*. New Haven, 1950.

DuBois, W. E. B., *Black Folk Then and Now*. New York, 1939.

——*Black Reconstruction*. New York, 1935.

——*The World and Africa*. New York, 1965.

Dumond, Dwight L., *Antislavery: The Crusade for Freedom in America*. Ann Arbor, 1961.

Eaton, John, *Grant, Lincoln and the Freedmen*. New York, 1907.

Elkins, Stanley M., *Slavery, a Problem in American Intellectual and Cultural Life*. Chicago, 1959.

Filler, Louis, *The Crusade Against Slavery, 1830–1860*. New York, 1960.

Franklin, John H., *The Emancipation Proclamation*. New York, 1963.

——*From Slavery to Freedom*. New York, 1961.

——*Reconstruction After the Civil War*. Chicago, 1962.

Frazier, E. Franklin, *Black Bourgeoisie*. New York, 1962.

——*The Negro in the United States*. New York, 1957.

Garfinkel, Herbert, *When Negroes March*. Glencoe, 1959.

Gloster, Hugh M., *Negro Voices in American Fiction*. Chapel Hill, 1948.

Greenberg, Jack, *Race Relations and American Law*. New York, 1959.

Greene, Lorenzo J., *The Negro in Colonial New England, 1620–1776*. New York, 1942.

Greene, Lorenzo, and Carter G. Woodson, *The Negro Wage Earner*. Washington, 1930.

Harris, Abram L., *The Negro as Capitalist*. Philadelphia, 1936.

Herskovits, Melville J., *The Myth of the Negro Past*. New York, 1941.

Higginson, Thomas W., *Army Life in a Black Regiment*. New York, 1962.

Hirshon, Stanley P., *Farewell to the Bloody Shirt: Northern Republicans and the Southern Negro, 1877–1893*. Bloomington, 1962.

Holmes, D. O. W., *The Evolution of the Negro College*. New York, 1934.

JACKSON, LUTHER P., *Free Negro Labor and Property Holding in Virginia, 1830–1860*. New York, 1942.

JENKINS, WILLIAM E., *Pro-Slavery Thought in the Old South*. Chapel Hill, 1935.

JOHNSON, JAMES W., *Along This Way*. New York, 1933.

KENNEDY, LOUISE V., *The Negro Peasant Turns Cityward*. New York, 1930.

KING, MARTIN LUTHER, JR., *Stride Toward Freedom*. New York, 1958.

LINCOLN, C. ERIC, *The Black Muslims in America*. Boston, 1961.

LITWAK, LEON F., *North of Slavery*. Chicago, 1961.

LOGAN, RAYFORD W., *The Negro in American Life and Thought: The Nadir, 1877–1901*. New York, 1954.

—— ed., *What the Negro Wants*. Chapel Hill, 1944.

LOMAX, LOUIS E., *The Negro Revolt*. New York, 1962.

MANNIX, DANIEL P., and MALCOLM COWLEY, *Black Cargoes: A History of the Atlantic Slave Trade, 1518–1865*. New York, 1962.

MEIER, AUGUST, *Negro Thought in America, 1880–1915*. Ann Arbor, 1963.

MOON, HENRY L., *Balance of Power: The Negro Vote*. New York, 1925.

MYRDAL, GUNNAR, *The American Dilemma*. New York, 1944.

NEVINS, ALLAN, *Ordeal of the Union*, 2 vols. New York, 1947.

NICHOLS, LEE, *Breakthrough on the Color Front*. New York, 1954.

NORTHRUP, HERBERT R., *Organized Labor and the Negro*. New York, 1944.

OLMSTED, FREDERICK L., *The Cotton Kingdom*, ed., Arthur M. Schlesinger. New York, 1953.

PHILLIPS, ULRICH B., *American Negro Slavery*. New York, 1918.

POWELL, ADAM CLAYTON, SR., *Against the Tide*. New York, 1938.

QUARLES, BENJAMIN, *Frederick Douglass*. Washington, 1948.

—— *Lincoln and the Negro*. New York, 1962.

—— *The Negro in the American Revolution*. Chapel Hill, 1961.

—— *The Negro in the Civil War*. Boston, 1953.

RECORD, WILSON, *The Negro and the Communist Party*. Chapel Hill, 1951.

REID, IRA DE A., *The Negro Immigrant*. New York, 1939.

ROSS, MALCOLM, *All Manner of Men*. New York, 1948.

SCOTT, EMMETT J., *Official History of the American Negro in the World War*. Chicago, 1919.

SILBERMAN, CHARLES, *Crisis in Black and White*. New York, 1964.

SILVERA, JOHN D., *The Negro in World War II*. (n.p.), 1946.

STAMPP, KENNETH M., *The Peculiar Institution*. New York, 1956.

TERRELL, MARY C., *A Colored Woman in a White World*. Washington, 1940.

WASHINGTON, BOOKER T., *Up from Slavery*. New York, 1901.

WEAVER, ROBERT C., *Negro Labor: A National Problem*. New York, 1946.

WHITE, WALTER, *A Rising Wind*. New York, 1945.

WILLIAMS, ERIC, *Capitalism and Slavery*. Chapel Hill, 1944.

WOODSON, CARTER G., and CHARLES H. WESLEY, *The Negro in Our History*. Washington, 1962.
WOODWARD, C. VANN, *Origins of the New South, 1877–1913*. Baton Rouge, 1951.
YOUNG, A. S., *Negro Firsts in Sports*. Chicago, 1963.

Suggested Reading

APTHEKER, HERBERT, *A Documentary History of the Negro People in the United States.* New York, 1951. A brilliant work of scholarship; a massive sampling of the documents, including eyewitness and firsthand accounts of important events in Negro history up to 1910.

BALDWIN, JAMES, *The Fire Next Time.* New York, 1963. An incisive and moving examination of the effects of discrimination on the quality of American life by a leading Negro author.

DAVIDSON, BASIL, *The Lost Cities of Africa.* Boston, 1959. An exciting and comprehensive summation of what is now known regarding ancient Negro civilizations in Africa.

DOUGLASS, FREDERICK, *Life and Times of Frederick Douglass.* New York, 1962. This autobiography of the great Negro abolitionist is edited by historian Rayford Logan.

GRIFFIN, JOHN HOWARD, *Black Like Me.* Boston, 1960. A moving and observant account of white author John Howard Griffin's experiences traveling through the Deep South disguised as a Negro.

KING, MARTIN LUTHER, *Stride Toward Freedom.* New York, 1958. The story of nonviolent resistance at Montgomery, Alabama, by the leader of the movement.

MANNIX, DANIEL P., and MALCOLM COWLEY, *Black Cargoes: A History of the Atlantic Slave Trade, 1518–1865.* New York, 1962. A well-documented and eminently readable account of an exciting, if dark, page of human history.

MYRDAL, GUNNAR, *The American Dilemma.* New York, 1943. Since its publication this observation of race relations in the United States by a Swedish sociologist has become something of a modern classic.

INDEX

Italic numbers refer to illustrations.

abolitionism, 43, 46–48, 54, 56–57, 66, 70–73, 75, 81, 82, 84, 90, 91–94, 96–98, 100, 188; during Civil War, 101, 105–106, 107–108

Adams, Henry, 105

Adams, John, 54, 73

Addams, Jane, 148

Africa, 11–30, 33–36; return to, 92–93, 156–158, 193

African Society, 70

agriculture, U.S., and slavery, 46, 60–62, 63, 66–67, 74–75; *see also* plantation system

Alabama, 67, 140, 161, 173, 182–184, 186–188, 192, 199

Allen, Richard, 91, 93

America, Central, 30, 106

America, North, 32, 38; colonial, 43–46, 47, 51–54; economy, 45, 50; slave trade, 48–51

America, South, 30, 32

American Federation of Labor, 134, 163

American Missionary Society, 140

American Negro Labor Congress, 160

Anderson, Marian, 164–165

Arabia, 12, 14, 20, 25, 30

archaeology, and African civilization, 12, 22

architecture, African, 11–12, *12*, 13, 19, *23*, 22, 26

Arkansas, 173, 179–180

Armstrong, Louis, 167

Army, U.S., 101, 109, 180–181; soldiers in: Civil War, 101, 102–103, 107, 109–110, 111, World War I, 150–152, World War II, 171–173, Korean War, 175, Vietnam War, 199; and Reconstruction, 117–118, 124, 126

art, African, 12, *16–17*, 19, 22, *24–25*

Arthur, Chester, 149

Articles of Confederation, 57; *see also* Constitution

Atlantic Slaving Squadron, 104

Attucks, Crispus, *52*, 53, *56*

Axum, 14–15, 25–26, 30

Ayllon, Lucas Vásquez de, 43

"Back to Africa" movement, 156

Baldwin, James, 204

Baldwin, Ruth Standish, 158

banks, Negro, 145, 152, 159

Banneker, Benjamin, 75, 90–91

Baptist churches, Negro, 93

Barnett, Ross, 182

Baylor, Charles G., 143

Benezet, Anthony, 48

Benin, 21, 22–24, *24–25*, 29, 30, 35

Berkeley, George, Bishop of Cloyne, 46

Bethune, Mary McLeod, 162, 174

Bibb, Henry, 79

Biblical justification: of abolitionism, 48; of slavery, 45–46

Birney, James G., 73

Black Codes, 116; *see also* slave codes

Black Muslims, 192–193

black nationalism, 156, 192–193

Black Power, 196–198

black supremacy, 157

Boston Massacre, *52*, 53, *56*

"Bourbons," Southern, 120, 129, 134; recapture state governments, 123–126

boycotts, Negro: economic, 160; for integration, 182–183; political, 115

Brazil, 38, 44; Brazilians in Africa, 64

Brown, Henry, *80*, 81

Brown, John, 75, 98–100, *99*

Brown, Oliver, 177, 182

Brown, William Welles, 81, 85

Brown vs. *Board of Education*, 178

Bunche, Ralph, 175, 199

Burns, Anthony, 84, 86

business: Negro, 88–89, 145–147, 156–157, 196–198; segregated, boycotts and sit-ins *vs.*, 160, 184–186

214 THE NEGRO REVOLUTION

Calhoun, John C., 67

California, 82, 89, 174, 193

Canada, 69, 79, 82, 148

capitalism, U.S., 138–139; and labor, 133–134; and politics, 114, 124–126, 129, 130, 134, 137

Carmichael, Stokely, 196–198, *197*; quoted, 195

chain gangs, 130

Changler, Zachariah, 107

Chaney, James, 188, *189*, 192

Charles I, of Spain, 33

Charles II, of England, 34–35

Childers, John, quoted, 113

Christianity, 31, 183; in Africa, 14, 15, 22–25, 42; in America, 32, 43, 48, 67; quoted to control slaves, 68–69; hope of slaves, 68–69, 75; segregation in churches, 92–93, 94–95

churches, Negro, 92–93, 139; abolitionist movement, 75, 93; civil rights movement, 184; due to segregation, 93; educating, 93–94, 140

civilization, African, 12–13, 18–19, 21–22, 26, 157; archaeology and, 12; *cf.* medieval European civilization, 19; slave trade destroys, 23, 26–27; whites disavow, 12–13

Civil Rights Act: of 1866, 116–117; of 1875, 126, 188; of 1957, 189; of 1964, 189–192

civil rights movement, 184–192, 195–196, 198–204

Civil Service, U.S., 150, 162–163, 174

Civil War, 82, 99, 105, 107–108, 111–112, 123–124; border states, 101, 107–108; causes, 75, 98, 101–102; ends slave trade, 102–103; Negro soldiers, 100, 102, 108–110, 111, 151

Clay, Henry, 74

colonization by U.S. Negroes: Central America, 106–107; Liberia, 92, 106; Negro opposition, 92, 106–107

Colored Citizens of the State of Michigan, quoted, 87

Columbus, Christopher, 32–33

Communism, 152–153, 175; U.S. Communist Party, 160–161

Confederacy, 107, 111–114; bans slave trade, 102

Congo, 15, 21, 23

Congress, U.S., 70, 90–92, 98, 105–106, 113, 121, 124–126, 137; abolishes slavery, 107–108, 111; bans foreign slave trade, 64, 95–96; fugitive slave laws, 82–84; 96; Negro members, 119; open housing bill defeated, 196; pro-Negro laws, 116–117, 119–120, 188–192; slaves counted in determining representation, 57–58, 73

Congress of Industiral Organizations (C.I.O.), 163

Congress of Racial Equality (C.O.R.E.), 184–186, 195, 198

Connecticut, 46, 57, 60, 82

Connor, T. Eugene "Bull," 187–188

Constitution, U.S.: 13th Amendment, 111; 14th Amendment, 117–118, 126, 178; 15th Amendment, 119–120, 126; proslavery concessions, 57–58, 82

Constitutional Convention, 57, 60, 91

Continental Army, 53, 55

Continental Congress, 52, 55, 57

Coolidge, Calvin, 156, 158, 160

Copeland, John A., 99

cotton, 61–62; ideal "slave" crop, 62; *see also* plantation system

cowboys, Negro, 131–132, *131*

Craft, Ellen and William, 80

Cuba, 139, *143*, 143

Cullen, Countee, 166; quoted, 159

Davis, Jefferson, 107

Declaration of Independence, 73; antislavery clause omitted, 54

Declaration of Human Rights, 174

Delaware, 46, 177

Democratic Party: North, 20th century, 149–150, 161–163; South, post-Civil War, 114, 135; white primaries, 135

Dewey, John, 148

Dies, Martin, quoted, 145

discrimination: banned in C.I.O., 163; banned in government, 161; banned in war industries, 169–170; criticized by Communists, 175; Northern, 192–194; *see also* F.E.P.C., segregation

Dixon, George, 165

Djenné, 18, 21

Douglass, Frederick, 75, 94, *95*, 96, 101, 108, 115, 120, 132–133, 139, 143, 199; life as slave, 66; quoted, 177

Douglass, Lewis, 143, 199

Draft Riots of 1863, 110–111, *110*
Dred Scott case, 80; confirms Southern prejudice, 70–71
DuBois, William Edward Burghardt, 146–148, *147*, 149, 152, 164, 174
Dunbar, Paul Laurence, 142, 166
Dunmore, John Murray, Earl of, 55

Eckford, Elizabeth, 180
economic status of Negroes: pre-Civil War, 88–89; post-Civil War: North, 131, 145–146, 153, 158, South, 129–131, 141–142, 145–146; during Great Depression: North, 159–160, 162–165, *168*, 169–170, South, *162*, 163, *164*; post-Depression: North, 174–175, 196–199, South, 196–199
economy, U.S.: industrial *vs.* agricultural, 74–75, 114; Southern and slavery, 60–62, 64–65, 66, 114; and Western expansion, 74–75; *see also* Great Depression
education, Negro in U.S.: pre-Civil War, 48, 90, 92–93; post-Civil War, 115, 118–119, 139–140, 158; schools: integrated, 179–182, 195, segregated, 139–140, 177–180, 193
Egypt, 12, 14, 15, 19, 21, 30–31, *31*
Eisenhower, Dwight D., 180
Elizabeth I, of England, 34
Ellsworth, Oliver, 60
emancipation: English free slaves, 55; Negro struggle for, 70–71, 75, 89–94, 98, 99–100, 102, 105–106, 107–109, 111; in North before Civil War, 57
Emancipation Proclamation, 53, 108–109, 111
Emerson, Ralph Waldo, 73, 84, 96
England, 51, 60–61, 169; and abolitionism, 94–95, 105; anti-slave trade, 103–104; English in Africa, 20, 29, 33, 48–49; in America, 43; *see also* Navy, British Royal; Revolutionary War; Royal African Company
Episcopalians, 92–93
equality, Negro fight for, 142, 147–148, 153–156, 158, 169–171, 177–194, 199–201; *see also* civil rights movement
Ethiopia, 14, *16–17*, 21, 25–26, 30
Evers, Medgar, 188
explorers, white in Africa, 11–12, 20, 21–22, 26; *see also* missionaries, traders, slave trade

Fairbanks, Calvin, 82
Fair Employment Practices Committee (F.E.P.C.), 170, 175
Farmer, James, 184
farmers, Negro, 89, 118–119, 129–130, 138, *162*, 163, *164*, *168*; *see also* populist movement, sharecroppers
fascism, 169–170; *see also* Nazis
Faubus, Orville, 179–180
Fauset, Jessie, 166
Ferdinand V, of Spain, 32
Finney, Charles G., 73
Fisher, Rudolph, 166
Florida: Spanish, 44; U.S., 61, 121
Foreman, James, 186
Forrest, Nathan Bedford, 109, 121
France, 151; French in Africa, 33; in America, 76
Franklin, Benjamin, 54, 73
Free African Society, 91, 93
Freedmen's Bureau, *116*, 118
freedom, purchased by slaves, 88–89; petitions for, 90–91, 111; *see also* emancipation
freedom riders, 186, 196
fugitive slave laws, 82–84, 90–91, 96

Gandhi, Mohandas, 183, 184
Gans, Joe, 165
Garrison, William Lloyd, 73, 75, 88, 94–95, 148,
Garvey, Marcus, 157–158, 198
George III of England, 54
Georgia, 51–52, 55–56, 80, 111, 149, 153, 181, 198
Germany, 169; Germans in Africa, 33
Ghana, 15–19, 21, 30, 33
ghettos, Negro, 156, 157–160, 162, 174, 192–194, 196, 201
Gompers, Samuel, 134
Goodman, Andrew, 188, 192
Grady, Henry W., 137, *136*
grandfather clauses, 150
Grant, Charles, 165
Grant, Ulysses S., 107, 111, 119, 123
Great Depression, 158–160, 161, 162, 163, 167–168, 175
Greeley, Horace, 105
Green, Nora, 173
Grimké, Angelina, and Sarah, 73
Grimké, Archibald, quoted, 145
Grimké, Francis, 148
Guinea Coast, 33, 37, 41, 48

Haiti, 31–32, 51, 106, 142, 150
Hall, Prince, 91
Hamilton, Alexander, 57–58
Hannibal Guards, 102
Harding, Warren Gamaliel, 156
Harlem, 157, *189, 193,* 196, *201*
Harper, Francis Ellen, quoted, 109
Hastie, William H., 164
Hawkins, John, 34, *34*
Hayes, Rutherford B., 126
Help Our Public Education
    (H.O.P.E.), 181
Hispaniola, 32–34
history, Negro, 157, 166–167, 197
Hitler, Adolf, 166, 169–170
Holmes, John Haynes, 148
Hoover, Herbert, 160
Hope, John, 142
housing, segregated, 178, 194, 195–
    196
Hughes, Langston, 166

Illinois, 70, 89, 102, 146, 152, 153,
    159–160, 192–193, 196
imperialism, U.S., 138–139, 141–145,
    198–200; endangers Negro freedom,
    93–94, 143, 148, 199–200
indentured servants: Negro, 43, 46;
    cf. slaves, 45; white, 45–47
indentured servant ships, 45
Indiana, 89
Indians, American, 45, 53, 131; slaves,
    32–33; empires, 30, 44
Indies, West, 32–33, 38, 40, 45–47,
    48–51
Industrial Revolution, 31; financed by
    slave trade, 51, 60
integration: interracial efforts, 180–
    181, 185–186, 187–192, *191;* Negro
    efforts, 177–179, 181–187, *189,*
    195–196
International Labor Defense, 160–161
inventors, Negro, 167
Iowa, 89, 132
Isabella I of Spain, 32
Islam, 15, 18, 21, 24, 26; *see also*
    Black Muslims

Jackson, Peter, 165
Jay, John, 54
jazz, 167
Jefferson, Thomas, 54, 57–58, 61, 64,
    73, 90–91; quoted 43
Johnson, Andrew, 114–115, 117
Johnson, Henry, 152

Johnson, Jack, 165–166
Johnson, Lyndon B., 190, 196
Johnson, Will, 120
Jones, Absolom, 91, 93
Jones, George, 84–86
Jones, Jehu, 89
Jones, John Paul, 171
Joseph, McNeil, 184

Kansas, 98, 132, 177, 179
Kennedy, John F., 182, 189–190
Kentucky, 64, 79, 102, 184
Khartoum, 11, 14
King, A. D., 187
King, Martin Luther, Jr., 183–187,
    185, 189, 194, 196, *200,* 198–203
    quoted, 177
Korean War, 175
Krumen tribe, 37, 42
Ku Klux Klan, 120, *154–155,* 153,
    156, 179, 186; murders, *cf.* 123;
    Nazis, 121; terrorizes and tortures,
    122, 120–123, *125*
Kush, 11, 13–15, 21, 25, 30

labor, Negro, 115, 118, 130–131, 169–
    170; *see also* labor unions, populist
    movement
labor unions: exclude Negroes, 130,
    133–134; include Negroes, 162–
    164, 189; Negro unions, 133, 163–
    164
Lafon, Thomy, 89
Las Casas, Bartolomé de, 33
Latimer, Louis H., 167
Law, Oliver, 169
League of Nations, 174
Lee, Robert E., 98–99, 107, 111
legal status of Negroes, 46–48, 70,
    107–108, 111
legends, African, 11–12, 15, 20–21,
    24–25; about America, 37–38; and
    Greek epics, 11–12
legislation: anti-Negro, 123, 124–127;
    antislavery, 57, 82–84, 107–108,
    111; proslavery, 46, 63, 69–71, 82–
    84
Legree, Simon, 59, 96
Lewis, John L., 163
Liberia, 92, 103, 106, 142, 150
Lincoln, Abraham, 94, 96, 100–102,
    104, 105–106, 108, 109, 111–115,
    148; Emancipation Proclamation,
    108–109, 111

literature: African, 19; antislavery, 75, *97*, 96; Negro, 108, 166; *see also* newspapers and magazines
Little, Malcolm, *see* Malcolm X
Liuzzo, Violet, 188, 192
living conditions of Negroes post-Civil War: North, 153–157, 162, 174, 192–194, *195*, 196, 200; South, *162*, 163, *164*
Louis, Joe, 166
Louisiana, 31, 62, 65, 87, 116, 132
Love, Nat "Deadwood Dick," 131, *131*
Lovejoy, Elijah Parish, 96
Lowell, James Russell, 94
lynchings, *110*, *125*, 144, 146–147, 173, 175; newspapers urge, 135–137; number committed, 137, 146, 149, 169

Madison, James, 57
Maine, 75, 89
Malcolm X, 193, *193*, 198
Mali, Empire of, 18–21, 22, 26, 30
man, origin in Africa, 13; Negro, origin, 14
marches, protest, 170, 175, 186–187, *189*, 194, 203; March on Washington, 189–192; *191*; 1967 Peace March, *200*, 198–199, *201*
Maryland, 57, 63, 64, 82, 84, 87, 98, 102
Masonic Order, Negro, 91, 102
Massachusetts, 45, 46, 48–53, 57, 81, 84, 86, 89–90, 102, 108
Mather, Cotton, 48
Matzeliger, Jan E., 167
McKay, Claude, 166; quoted, 159
Melville, Herman, quoted, 113
Meredith, James H., 182
Meroë, 12, *13*, 14, 15; *see also* Kush
Metcalfe, Ralph, 166
Methodists, 76, 92–93
Mexican War of 1848, 94, 199
Mexico, 30, 33, 78, 94
Michigan, 102, 107, 110, 174, 193
Middle Passage, 38, 40, 45
militias, state, 53, 55, 69, 75, 78, 98; Negroes in, 55
missionaries in Africa: Christian, 12, 22, 26; Islamic, 21
Mississippi, 64, 65, 109, 135, 167, 173, 179, 181–182, 188, 196
Missouri, 70, 74–75, 102, 170, 178
Monroe, James 92

Montgomery bus boycott, 182–183
Morgan vs. *Virginia*, 178
Morocco, 15–17, 19
Muhammad, Elijah, 192
mulattoes, 53, 88
Murphy, Isaac, 165
music, Negro; *see* jazz, spirituals
mutual aid societies, Negro, 70, 86, 91–92, 118

National Association for the Advancement of Colored People (N.A.A.-C.P.), 148, 150, 158, 161, 164, 177–178, 183, 188, 198
National Guard, 138, 180, *181*
National Labor Convention of Colored Men, 133
National Negro Business League, 145
National Negro Labor Union, 133
Navy, British Royal, 37; anti-slave ships, 30, 96, 102–103
Navy, U.S., 103; Negro sailors in, 109–110, 171
Nazis, 121, 166, 169, 173
Nebraska, 132, 153
Negro Conventions of 1831–1853, 92
Negroes: origin in Africa, 14; first in America, 32–33, 43–44
Negroes, free, during Civil War: abolitionists, 102, 105–106, 108–109, 111; soldiers, 101, 103, 107, 109–110, 111
Negroes, free, pre-Civil War: economic status, 88–89; legal status, 47–48, 70–71, 87–88, 89; in North, 55, 75, 84–86, 88–89; number in North, 89; number in South, 87; origin of class, 57, 88; purchasing freedom, 87–89; in South, 56, 62, 63, 64–65, 82, 87–89
Netherlands: Dutch in Africa, 29, 33; in America, 43, 47
New Deal, 162, 164, 167, 174
New England, 47, 48–51, 53, 64, 74; *see also* individual states
New Freedom, 150, 161
New Hampshire, 57, 89
New Jersey, 193
New Mexico, 82
newspapers and magazines; 85, 146, 187; abolitionist, 73, 74–75, 88, 93–94, 96, 105–106; anti-Negro propaganda, 67, 98, 135–137; Negro, 89–90, 94, 148, 156

New York, 45–46, 47–50, *49*, 64, 85–
    86, 89, 96, 102–103, 105–106, 110,
    110, 146, 148, 152, 158, 159–160,
    170, 174, 184–185, 192–193, *200*,
    199, *201*
Niagara Movement, 148
Nieuw Amsterdam, 50, 90
Nigeria, 20
Nixon, E. D., 183
Nixon, Richard M., 189
Nobel Peace Prizes: Ralph Bunche,
    174, 175; Martin Luther King, Jr.,
    194, 198, 199
nonviolent resistance, 183–185, 187–
    188, 193, 194, 202; techniques, 184
North Africa, 15–16
North Carolina, 46, 51, 55–57, 115,
    123, 184–185
Northrup, Solomon, 62; life as slave,
    62–63, 64–66
Northwest Ordinance, 57

Odd Fellows, Negro, 91
Ohio, 82, 85, 89, 107
Oklahoma, 178
Olympic Games of 1936, 166
Oregon, 89
Organization of Afro-American Unity,
    193
Owens, Jesse, 166

Parker, Thoedore, 84
Parks, Rosa, 182, 189
Paul, Nathaniel, 94
Paul, Thomas, 93
Peace March, April 1967, *200*, 199,
    201
Pease, Joachim, 110
Pennsylvania, 46, 48, 51, 57, 80, 84,
    91–93, 96, 102, 106, 193
petitions, Negro: antidiscrimination,
    150; for education, 90, 180; for
    freedom, 90–91, 111; for voting,
    115
Philippines, 143–144, 199
Phillips, Wendell, 84
Pieterson, Anthony, 90
Pinkerton agents, 138
pirates seize slave ships, 29, 34, 43
Pires, Duarte, 22
Pitcairn, John, 53
plantation system, 41, 45–46, 48–51,
    54, 66, 74; idealization of life, 59–
    60, *61*; real life, 59–65

Plessy vs. *Ferguson*, 135, 177–178
political power, Southern: controlled
    by oligarchy, 66–68, 74–75, 113–
    116, 123–129, 197; Reconstruction,
    117, 119–120, 123–124
political status of Negroes: political
    power feared by Southern whites,
    115, 186; political power in North,
    148–150, 160–161, 162–163, 187–
    188, 189, 199; in Reconstruction
    governments, 117, 119–120, 123–
    124; in South post-Reconstruction,
    123–127, 137
poll tax, 135
Poole, Elijah; *see* Muhammad, Elijah
Poor, Salem, 53
populist movement, 133, 138–139, 145,
    149
Portugal, 32, 33; Portuguese in Africa,
    21–22, 32, 33, 64; in America, 44
Potter, George, and Rosella, 88
Powell, Adam Clayton, Jr., 146, 160
Powell, Adam Clayton, Sr., 146
prejudice, white: vs. African civiliza-
    tion, 12–13, 26–27; anti-Negro pre-
    Civil War, 47, 76, 78–79, 88–89,
    110–112; post-Civil War, 114, 118–
    120, 123–124, 130, 132–133, 135–
    137, 161, 166, 169, 174, 184–188,
    199; encouraged in South, 67–68,
    116; vs. integrated schools, 178–
    182; vs. Negro soldiers, 53, 55–56,
    102–103; Northern, 192–194
Presbyterian, 92
Prester, John, 25
Prioleau, Peter, 77
Prosser, Gabriel, 76–77
Purvis, Robert, 92

Quakers, 76; abolitionists, 48, 57
Quartermaster Corps, Negroes in,
    151, 171

race riots, 96, 110–111, *110*, 116, 149,
    151, 153–156, 169, 173, 175, 180–
    182, 185–187, 193, 196, 198, 201
radical Republicans: during Civil War,
    107; post-Civil War, 114–115, 116–
    117
Randolph, A. Philip, 163, 170, 189
Read, John, 84–85

Readjuster Party, 134; see also populist movement

Reconstruction, 129, 132, 181, 184, 186, 195; Joint Congressional Committee, 116–118; state governments, 117, 119–120, 123–124, 139

recreation facilities, integrated, 180–181, 190–192

Red Ball Express, 172

religion, pagan, 14, 15, 18, 21, 22–26; see also Christianity, Islam

Republican Party, 98, 100–101, 111, 114, 116–118, 119, 161; forsakes Southern Negroes, 126–127, 149

Revolutionary War, 52, 53–56, 56, 90; causes, 51–52; English free American slaves, 55; Negro soldiers for England, 55; for U.S., 52–56

Rhode Island, 50, 55–57

Roberts, Needham, 152

Robinson, Jackie, 165

Roman Catholics, 92

Roman Empire, 12, 14, 26, 30–31, 68

Roosevelt, Eleanor, 164, 170

Roosevelt, Franklin Delano, 161, 162, 165, 168, 169–170, 174, 178

Roosevelt, Theodore, 139, 146, 149

Royal African Company, 30, 35, 37, 46, 51

Rush, Benjamin, 91

Sahara Desert, 13–14, 15–16, 18, 19, 21

Salem, Peter, 53

Saxton, Rufus, 119

scapegoats, Negroes as, 47, 67–68, 169; see also prejudice

Schwerner, Michael, 188, 192

Scott, Dred, 70–71, 70

Scott, Emmett J., 140–141

Scottsboro Case, 161

"second-class citizenship," 141, 144

segregation, 177–178; banned in schools, 178; banned in U.S. Army, 175–176; in Federal government, 149; Northern, 192–194; sanctioned by Supreme Court, 127, 135; in U.S. Army, 151, 171–173; see also discrimination

separatists, 193; see also Black Muslims

Sewall, Samuel, 48

sharecroppers, Negro, 129–130, 162, 163, 164; life cf. slaves' life, 129–130

Sheba, Queen of, 14, 16–17, 25

Shelley vs. Kraemer, 178

Sherman, William Tecumseh, 111, 138

Simmons, William J., 153

Simms, William, 144, 199

Singleton, Benjamin "Pap," 132

sit-ins, 184–186, 196

slave codes, 47, 63, 69–70; applied to free Negroes, 87–88; see also Black Codes

slaveowning society: idealization, 59–60, 70–71, 113, 138; reality, 60–64, 66–68, 71

slave patrols, 69, 76

slave rebellions: in Africa, 35; in America, 32–33, 35, 44, 51; betrayed by slaves, 64, 77; on slave ships, 29, 35–36; in U.S., 64, 70, 73, 75–79, 79, 87; white fear of, 51, 69–70, 76, 78

slavery in America: cf. African slavery, 37; Biblical and scientific "justification," 46, 60, 67–68; economic basis, 32, 43, 47, 57–58, 60–62, 74; industrialization ends need for, 31; introduced, 32–33, 43; legal abolition, 56–57, 107–109, 111; legal establishment, 46, 63, 69–70; North-South division on, 75, 91, 96–102, 105–106, 108, 111; opposition, see abolitionism, slave rebellions, Underground Railroad; prevents free competition, 66–67, 74; see also slave codes, fugitive slave laws

slavery in ancient world, 30–32, 31; economic basis, 31

slavery in Europe, 31

slaves: employment, 46, 62, 63; field, 46, 61, 62–63; house, 46, 63–64; number in America, 47–48, 76, 87; use of slaves frees Southern men for Confederate army, 107; see also indentured servants

slaves, runaway, 53, 55, 69, 76, 78–84, 80, 81; and Constitution, 57; during Civil War, 107

slaves, sources of: criminals in Africa, 36; ancient world, 30–31; kidnaping in Africa, 36, 50; America, 62, 84–86; prisoners of war in Africa, 36; ancient world, 30–31

slaves, treatment of: branded in Africa, 36; "breaking," 66; dependent on number in population, 46–47, 51;

mortality rates, 41; "seasoning," 41; on slave ships, 38–40, *39, 41*; in U.S., 64, 69–70, 78–79

slave sales: in Africa, 36; bought with trade goods, 33, 36; "down river," 64–65; prices, *65, 67*; "scramble," 40; in U.S., 40, 43, *44, 49*, 64–65

slave ships, 33; conditions aboard, 29, 38–40, *39*; slaves' diet, 38–39; disease, 40; jettisoning slaves, 40, *41*; mortality rates, 40; slaves' suicide, 37, 39; transportation to ships, 36; U.S. owned, 29, 95; *see also* indentured servants ships

slave trade, domestic, 57–58, 64–66; "breaking in," 41, 66; destroys families, 65–66; selling "down river," 65–66

slave trade, foreign, 46, 48–50, 56–58; in Africa 21, 26–30, 33–35; and American economy, 48–50, 64; American ships, 48, 50, 64, 95, 103–104; Confederacy bans, 103; destroys African civilization, 22, 26–27; effect on traders, 30, 35–36; "factors," 36–37, 40; hazards, 29–30, 36; laws *vs.*, 51–52, 57, 64, 95–96; number of slaves shipped, 30, 103–104; opposition, 51–52, 57; profits, 30, 34, 51, 60, 95; Revolutionary War cause, 52; smuggling, 64, 96; traders arrested, 50, 95, 103–104; hanged, 104; and U.S. Constitution, 57; *see also* Royal African Company

Smith vs. *Allright*, 178

Social Security Act, 163

Society for the Promotion of the Abolition of Slavery, 54

soldiers, Negro: colonial wars, 52, 103; Revolutionary War, 53–54, 55–56, 88; Civil War, 99, 101, 102, 107, 109–110, 111, 115, 151; Spanish-American War, *143*, 143–144, 151, 199; World War I, 150–152; Spanish Civil War, 169; World War II, 170–174, *173*; Korean War, 175; Vietnam War, 199; whites oppose, 53, 55–56, 102–103

Solomon of Judea, 15, *16–17*, 25

Songhai Empire, 20–21, 22, 30

South, U.S.: pre-Civil War, 45–46, 48, 54–56, 63–65, 66–68, 69, 70–71, 74–75, 78–79, 82, 87–88; Civil War

and Reconstruction, 101–102, 113–120, 123–127; post Reconstruction, 129–133, 134–135, 159–160; post-World War II, 178–179, 181–183, 185, 188, 190–192; "New South," 138, 141; *see also* Confederacy, individual states

South Carolina, 47, 48, 55, 61, 77, 89, 116, 121, 177

Southern Christian Leadership Conference (S.C.L.C.), 183–184, 195

Spain, 16, 32–34, 139; Spaniards in Africa, 19–20, 29; in America, 32–34, 44

Spanish-American War, 143–144, 199; Negro soldiers, *143*, 143–144, 151

Spanish Civil War, 169

spirituals, Negro, 68–69, 108–109, 166–167, 195

sports, Negroes in, 165–166

states' rights, 124–127, 168

stereotyping Negroes, 135–136

Stevens, Thaddeus, 114, 116

Still, William, 81

Storey, Moorfield, 148

Stowe, Harriet Beecher, 96

Student Nonviolent Coordinating Committee (S.N.C.C.), 185–186, 195–198

Sudan, 12, 14, 18, 21

Sumner, Charles, 114, 115, 116

Supreme Court decisions: *Brown* vs. *Board of Education*, 178; Dred Scott case, 70–71, 98; grandfather clauses, 150; interstate transportation, 186; Montgomery buses, 183; *Morgan* vs. *Virginia*, 177; *Plessy* vs. *Ferguson*, 135, 177–178; *Shelley* vs. *Kraemer*, 178; *Smith* vs. *Allright*, 178; states' rights, 124–127

Taft, William Howard, 146, 149

Tanganyika, 26

Tappan, Arthur and Lewis, 73

technology, African, 12, 14, 15, 26

Tennessee, 109, 116–117, 132

Texas, 61, 63–64, 149, 151, 153, 178

Timbuktu, 14, 18–20, *23*, 21

Toomer, Jean, 166

trade, African, 12, 15, 17–18, 19–20, 21, 25

traders, white, in Africa, 12, 21–22, 27

transportation, 181, 184; freedom riders, 186; Montgomery bus boycott, 183–184; segregation banned interstate, 178

Transvaal, 13, 26

tribes, African, 11, 27, 30, 35

Truman, Harry S, 174, 175, 178

Tubman, Harriet, 82, *83*

Turner, Nat, 77, *79*

Tuskegee Institute, *140*, 140, 142, 171

Tutson, Hannah, 121–122

Uganda, 13

Uncle Tom's Cabin (Stowe), *97*, 96

Underground Railroad, 81–82, 87–92

United Nations, 174–176, 198

United States, 57, 64

Universal Negro Improvement Association, 156–157

Urban League, National, 158, 195

Utah, 82

Vermont, 89

Vesey, Denmark, 77, 87

Vietnam War, 199

vigilance committees, Negro, 86, 92

Villard, Oswald Garrison, 148

Virginia, 43, *44*, 46–47, 51, 55–57, 64–65, 76, 81, 85, 88, 98–99, 109, 111, 115, 123, 134, 177

vocational training, Negro, 140, 142

voter registration drives, 186–192

voting, Negro: denied post-Reconstruction, 123, 133–134, 160; denied pre-Civil War, 70, 87, 89–90; 15th Amendment, 119–120, 126; Northern post-World War I, 161–162, 163; petitions for, 115; poll taxes, 135; post-emancipation, 111, 113, 115, 117, 119

Wade, Benjamin, 107

Walker, David, quoted 73

Walters, Alexander, 148

wars, African, 14–15, 20, *31*; religious, 15–18, 26

Washington, D.C., 90, 156, 169–170, 173, 177, 186, 189, *191*

Washington, Booker T., 139–148

Washington, George, 53–54, 55, 73

Weaver, Robert C., 164

Webster, Daniel, 53, 74

Weld, Theodore, 73

Wesley, Charles H., 152

West, U.S., 131–133, 138; slave vs. free states, 74

White, Walter, 164, 169–170, 174, 189

White Citizens' Councils, 179

White House, Negroes first visit, 106, 146

white primaries, 135; banned, 177

white, poor Southern: anti-Negro prejudice, 67–68, 118–120, 123–124, 178; anti-Negro riots, 116; dominated by oligarchy, 66–68, 114, 124, 179; in Ku Klux Klan, 121

white supremacy, 67–68, 89, 152, 166

Whittier, John Greenleaf, 73

Wilkins, Roy, 189

Wilkinson, John, 85

Wilson, Woodrow, 149–150, 153, 161

Wise, Stephen S., 148

Woodruff, Johnny, 166

Woods, Granville T., 167

Woodson, Carter G., 167

World War I, 151, 171; Negro soldiers, 151–152

World War II, 169–174; Negro defense plant workers, 169–170; Negro soldiers, 171–173, *173*

Wright, Richard, 166

Young, Whitney, 189

More SIGNET and MENTOR Books of Special Interest

SIGNET Books of Special Interest

☐ **DOWN THESE MEAN STREETS by Piri Thomas.** A powerful auto-biography, unanimously praised by the critics, this is the story of one man's journey from childhood to maturity in the violent world of Spanish Harlem. (#Q3471—85c)

☐ **THE NEGRO REVOLT by Louis E. Lomax.** A Negro writer's blunt, brilliant report on the current racial unrest in America. (#Q3149—95c)

☐ **WHEN THE WORD IS GIVEN by Louis E. Lomax.** An eye-opening account of the Black Muslims in America, and of their late leader, Malcolm X. By the author of *The Negro Revolt*. (#P2429—60c)

☐ **THE BLACK PANTHERS by Gene Marine.** Exclusive probing interviews with such leaders as Huey Newton, Eldridge Cleaver and Bobby Searle have resulted in a definitive study of the Black Panthers—their origin, their organization and their policies. (#Q3834—95c)

☐ **INVISIBLE MAN by Ralph Ellison.** A novel of extraordinary power about a man's desperate search for his identity. Winner of the National Book Award. (#Y3814—$1.25)
